"Every high school physical education teacher, athletic director, counselor, and coach should make this book required reading for high school athletes."

— *Stedman Graham, president, Graham and Associates*

"Superb advice that is at once inspiring and practical."

— *Frank Lenti, head football coach, Mount Carmel High School*

"Even though Chris snubbed my alma mater (Northwestern) for Vanderbilt, this book proves that his mind is sharp and full of insight. My daughter is less than one year old, and yet I'm already eager to examine every chapter with a highlighter in hand. There's a wealth of terrific information and anecdotes that help make this the bible for parents who want to give their kids every chance to earn a free ride in college."

— *Teddy Greenstein, sports writer, Chicago Tribune*

"Chris Krause just gets it. When it comes to the recruiting process no one does a better job of breaking it down for parents and student-athletes. As parents, we have no greater treasure than our children and no greater responsibility than making sure our children have every opportunity available. Chris has lived this process and now has the dedication and expertise to help others avoid some of the pitfalls and truly take advantage of the myriad of opportunities that are out there in college athletics."

— *Tom Donahoe, former NFL executive*

"*Athletes Wanted* is an ultimate resource and starting point to help parents and student athletes better understand the tangibles and intangibles associated with college recruiting. Whether you are a blue-chipper or a sleeper, this book is a must read."

— *Izell Reese, former NFL player*

"*Athletes Wanted* is a straightforward message about how many talented athletes are overlooked and the proactive steps they need to take for recognition and exposure. Krause does an excellent job of explaining how the recruiting process works. He lays out a game plan for student-athletes and parents in search of the best college match."
> — Bill Conley, former assistant coach and recruiting coordinator for the Ohio State Buckeyes

"A great resource to help the student-athlete and parents in taking action to match the right college institution with the student-athlete."
> — Alberto Verteramo, high school coach

"Choosing a college or university is one of the most dramatic and difficult decisions a young person will have to make in his or her life. Athletes Wanted takes away a large part of the stress in this decision and provides the guidance and stability in making the right choice."
> — Aleks Mihailovic, president of Soccer Made in America, United States Adult Soccer Association Men's National Team Coach

"An honest and eye-opening resource for parents and student-athletes navigating the college recruiting process."
> — Mary O'Malley, director of admission at La Lumiere School

"Chris Krause uses life examples to open eyes and promote understanding of some of the underlying principles that sports serve in youth development."
> — Sonja Porter, University of Alabama coach

"A how-to guide that illustrates all of the different paths available to student-athletes as they try to play at the next level."
> — Jim Catanzaro, Lake Forest College coach

"*Athletes Wanted* is a must-read book by all parents and student athletes who aspire to play a sport in college."
— *Rich Hofman, high school coach*

"This book should be read and regularly referenced by every aspiring athlete and his parents."
— *Dion Wheeler, author of **Sports Scholarship Insider's Guide***

"Chris Krause has taken years of personal experience and knowledge and created a perfect how-to manual that is educational and entertaining. It is an excellent resource for anyone who wants to grasp the bigger picture and value of playing."
— *Nancy Campbell, college coach*

"Chris Krause has the ability to inform and inspire. That is a powerful combination."
— *Charlie Adams, sports anchor and educational speaker*

"*Athletes Wanted* provides a roadmap for all families to follow so they never have any regrets in this once-in-a-lifetime recruiting experience."
— *George Bauer, former high school coach*

"A great book and a great topic."
— *Kevin Downey, high school coach*

"*Athletes Wanted* is a tremendous eye-opener on how many opportunities are truly out there for our children that go untapped."
— *Barbara Moran, business owner and parent*

"Sports can promote academic excellence and challenge our children to do their very best on a daily basis."
— *Michael Grenda, principal North Chicago Community School District #187*

The Complete Guidebook for Maximizing
Collegiate Recruiting and Life Potential

ATHLETES
WANTED

CHRIS KRAUSE

Collegiate Athletic Educational Foundation
CHICAGO, ILL

Published by
Collegiate Athletic Educational Foundation
1415 North Dayton Street
Fourth Floor
Chicago, IL 60642

Visit our website at www.athleteswanted.org
for more resources for student athletes and their parents.

Publisher's Cataloging-in-Publication
(*Provided by Quality Books, Inc.*)

    Krause, Chris.
      Athletes wanted : the complete guidebook for
    maximizing collegiate recruiting and life potential /
    Chris Krause.
      p. cm.
      Includes index.
      LCCN 2008944115
      ISBN-13: 978-0-9821557-0-7
      ISBN-10: 0-9821557-0-0

      1. College athletes--Recruiting--United States.
    2. Sports--Scholarships, fellowships, etc.--United States.
    I. Title.

GV350.5.K74 2009   796.071'173
                QBI09-600031

Printed in the United States of America
Edited by Jocelyn Baker (www.jocelynbakereditor.com)
Book Design by Dotti Albertine (www.albertinebookdesign.com)

>>>

*This book is dedicated
to the athletes and scholars, boys and girls,
and men and women who were not given
the opportunity to participate in sports,
including my grandfather, who was confined
by the Great Depression, and my mother,
who was not allowed to participate
because of the limited opportunities for women.*

*Their struggles are not forgotten.
Let this book inspire parents and student-athletes
from any neighborhood—regardless of race, gender,
or socioeconomic standing—to build character,
earn scholarships, and win the game of life.*

ACKNOWLEDGMENTS

COUNTLESS PEOPLE CONTRIBUTED to the development of this book: The entire NCSA staff shared stories, experiences, and wisdom. In particular, Mark Bagdon, Ryan Ball, Carmen Bucci, Joseph Curtis, Brian Davidson, Adam Dew, Adam Diorio, Andrea Emmons, Ty Garland, Rick McDole, Dennis O'Brien, Amanda Rawson, Bob Shriner, Lisa Strasman, Adrienne Treado, Bridget Venturi-Veenema, Matt Webb, and Joyce Wellhoefer contributed their expertise and time reviewing the manuscript, as did my editor, Jocelyn Baker, who relentlessly edited and focused my thoughts.

A very special thanks to Mary Pat Chmiel, my executive assistant and a juggler-extraordinaire, for keeping me on track, staying calm, and picking up all the pieces.

Parents, coaches, athletes, and former clients generously donated their time and insight, including: Michel Balasis, Don Beebe, Kevin Carroll, Bob Chmiel, Tom Donahoe, Chris Ducar, Arne Duncan, Bo Eason, Heather Geck, Jim Goranson, Rob Ianello, Howie Jacobson, Frank Lenti, Ross Lerner, John Letts, Augie Maurelli, Andy Petranek, Billy Porter, Izell Reese, Cindy Smith, Crystal Smith, Michael Stonebreaker, Jay Straight, Randy Taylor, and Larry Wert.

This book would not have been possible without the coaches who mentored me in high school and college. Among the best the world has to offer, these coaches taught me to use my experience as an athlete to achieve great professional success. Namely, I would like to thank George McIntire and Brad Bates, both college coaches, and high school coaches Mike Coleman, Bob Brothman, and the late Amos Jones. I am just one of the many students whose lives were forever changed by a ball, a goal, and their nurturing guidance.

Finally, I want to acknowledge my parents and grandparents for encouraging me to compete in sports while maintaining a focus on academics; most importantly, my wife, Kameron, for giving me the confidence to share this story; my son, Christopher; and my daughter, Kaila, whom I hope to inspire in the same fashion as those who inspired me.

CONTENTS

FOREWORD by Tom Lemming

IF A STUDENT PLAYS FOOTBALL, he knows that facemasking is illegal. If he plays hockey, he knows that he will be penalized for high sticking. And if she plays soccer, she knows that she will be red-carded for receiving two yellow cards.

Athletes know the rules of the game. They know that they must play by these rules to be successful.

What student-athletes might not know is that they are simultaneously playing another game: the game of collegiate recruiting. And unlike other games, the rules of the recruiting process are not clear. Unfortunately, too many kids are left behind. Despite their skill level, academic success, motivation, and quality of character, too many qualified student-athletes are not recruited into college programs, and many more are recruited by the wrong schools.

Why?

They simply do not know the rules of the game.

Chris Krause, founder of the Collegiate Athletic Educational Foundation (CAEF), has dedicated his career to educating students and their families about the collegiate recruiting process and to empowering student-athletes to compete in college and maximize their collegiate recruiting potential. His mission has redefined collegiate recruiting through a system that explains the process, teaches families how to realistically assess their child's level of talent, and provides a roadmap for taking full advantage of the educational and life benefits that can be earned through sports.

Chris also founded the National Collegiate Scouting Association (NCSA) with a passion for turning dreams into realities and leveraging athletics to create amazing opportunities for education and life. Since its inception, NCSA has become the leader in matching college coaches with qualified high school student-athletes. The NCSA identifies talented athletes, verifies recruiting data, and provides enhanced highlight and skills streaming video to college coaches from more than eighteen hundred colleges and universities in twenty-five sports. Currently, more than ten thousand NCSA student-athletes are playing sports at a collegiate level, and more than ten thousand college coaches use recruiting information from NCSA's verified scouting reports every month. The information gathered from these student-athletes, coaches, and their relationships with one another has become the cornerstone of the educational content featured at high school Recruiting Simplified talks, as well as at the nation's top camps, clubs, and combines for prospective college athletes.

Within the pages of this book, Chris reveals and expands on this information, providing a complete guidebook to winning academic scholarships and life opportunities through sports.

Chris Krause knows from personal experience the value of successfully blending athletics with academics. As a kid, he spent summers on the swim team, autumns playing football, winters on the court, and springs playing Little League baseball. He watched neighbors win state championship games and scholarships for Division I college teams. Chris wanted this, and more. In the fourth grade, he set his sights on playing sports at the highest level possible.

Boarding his first airplane in 1984, Chris had no idea that the recruiting trip to Nashville would result in something better than a professional athletic career: a full scholarship to Vanderbilt University, totaling more than $100,000 in education, board, books, and fees (the 2009 equivalent of more than $200,000). Chris chose Vanderbilt University over Northwestern, Iowa State, and the Air Force Academy because Vanderbilt offered him a full scholarship and an opportunity to play in the football-crazy Southeastern Conference. But while Chris had a big heart and a lot of ambition, he realized early that he would probably not go on to play professional football as he watched several stars of his team get drafted to the NFL only to be cut early in the season.

Nonetheless, Chris knew that football was a vital part of his collegiate path. He also knew that it was the means to an end: a meaningful college degree through athletics. His football scholarship meant that Chris could receive an education from one of the top twenty-five academic universities in the nation.

Sports took Chris from a blue-collar town to one of the world's most prestigious universities, but this is not where Chris's story ends. Chris owes much of his life to sports and the intangible traits that separate an athlete from the crowd. Because of baseball, track, swimming, basketball, and football, all sports he competed in as a child, he carries with him the brand of the student-athlete: work ethic, character, dedication to goal-setting, fair play, accountability, achievement, leadership, prioritization, time management, and teamwork. His experiences as an athlete guided him to find and build the nation's largest collegiate scouting organization and start a non-profit educational foundation that helps high school coaches and student-athletes understand the recruiting process and empower student-athletes to continue in college, especially those from at-risk and underserved communities that lack recruiting educational resources. Chris has traveled the globe through his athletic affiliations. Sports have taken him around the world and to once-in-a-lifetime experiences that reflect the awesome power of the wanted athlete. His sports network has enabled him to attend post-game NBA championship celebrations, sit in an owner's box at the Super Bowl, and receive a backstage, all-access pass with the Rolling Stones. Sports have enabled him to participate in flight training on the USS Ronald Reagan in the Pacific Ocean and to tour the Middle

East watching one of his student-athletes from the Robert Taylor Homes of Chicago live out his dream of playing professional basketball.

Perhaps more importantly, he graduated from college not a penny in debt. Because his parents saved the money they set aside for Chris's college education, his parents were able to help fund his sister's education.

Chris was not an exceptional student, nor was he an exceptional athlete. Yet he has had exceptional experiences. He owes much of them to sports. His background as a student-athlete transferred into so much more than just a college education. Sports have been his personal backstage, all-access pass to foreign countries, once-in-a-lifetime experiences, and powerful networks of people and opportunities.

Chris was fortunate to learn the rules of recruiting so that he could play the game successfully. Many of his high school classmates, who were better students and athletes, were not so lucky, abandoning their dreams of athletic scholarships when college coaches failed to take notice.

Each year, I log fifty-five thousand miles traveling to almost all fifty states in search of the nation's top two thousand football players. For every one player I look at, thousands of others covet a spot on my All-American team. Some of them will never make the list simply because I have not heard of them. Others are good, but not good enough to be considered the best of the best. Unless they do their own recruiting, homework, and promotion, these other football players will likely never be offered a college scholarship.

And this just considers football players. What about the athletes who play soccer, baseball, volleyball, basketball, tennis, golf, hockey, or lacrosse? What about the swimmers and the runners? Who will find them?

Over eighteen hundred colleges and universities offer athletic programs. With fewer than 1 percent of high school athletes receiving full Division I athletic scholarships, one thing is certain: Student-athletes and their parents must be proactive and involved in the recruiting process if they hope to earn a spot on a college team. The good news is that 80 percent of all college athletic opportunities are outside of Division I programs. This book explains how to seize these opportunities and substantially increase a student-athlete's chances of continuing an athletic career in college.

This is the ultimate resource for athletes and their families. Part instruction, part inspiration, *Athletes Wanted* provides hope for maximizing athletic scholarship and life potential. Players cannot rely on luck—the chances are simply too slim with too much competition and too much at stake. An athlete must devote as much hard work and effort to the game of recruiting as he does to his sport. *Athletes Wanted* teaches parents, athletes, and high school and club coaches where to look for opportunities, how to initiate conversations with college coaches, and what everyone's role is in the recruiting process.

No doubt, this is a monumental task. To win the game of recruiting, student-athletes must know the ins and outs of college recruiting—no easy task, especially considering the process is constantly evolving. Within the pages of this book and corresponding website and interactive blog (www. athleteswanted.org), you will find invaluable up-to-date information, advice, and strategies for playing and winning the game of collegiate recruiting so that you are prepared and stay prepared for the journey ahead.

Remember: This game of recruiting is more than a game. It is a once-in-a-lifetime opportunity. You cannot go back and redo this process. By reading this book and following these proven steps, you will never have to look back and wonder *what if?*

—Tom Lemming, author of *Prep Football Report*

PREFACE

THE MIGHTY DALLAS COWBOYS might as well be squishing ants under their thumbs. Down by thirty-five points late in the fourth quarter, the Buffalo Bills stand no chance of winning. Super Bowl XXVII is all but over. The Bills know it. The fans know it. And Dallas Cowboy Leon Lett knows it.

The fumble he recovers is just a feather in the Cowboys' cap, and as Lett starts to make the fifty-five-yard run to the endzone, the fans know the Cowboys will score one more touchdown.

Twelve yards. Eleven yards. Ten yards.

The Buffalo Bills have already been defeated. The game is such a blowout that even Cowboys' fans are indifferent to yet another touchdown. And Leon Lett begins celebrating. Ignoring everything he knows, he holds the ball in front of him, his sprint transitioning into a strut.

Nine yards. Eight yards. Seven yards.

Tuck. That. Ball. During the course of his athletic career, how many times had Lett heard those words? How many times had he screamed those very words while watching a game on TV, or while cursing one of his team-mate's fumbles?

But the game is over for Lett. He has already won. Tuck that ball? Why bother?

Six yards. Five yards.

Suddenly, the cheers begin to swell. No doubt Lett, who would later admit that he was watching himself on the JumboTron, thinks the ascending excitement is because he is just yards away from another touchdown.

Lett does not see Don Beebe. Scrawny by football standards, Beebe comes out of nowhere, in more ways than one.

After his NCAA eligibility expired years earlier, Beebe transferred from Western Illinois University to Nebraska's Chadron State College, enrollment three thousand, with dreams of an NFL career fading. But in typical Don Beebe fashion, he played his heart out at this tiny school in a tiny town, and he played hard. Invited to the NFL Scouting Combine, Beebe caught more than a few eyes by running a 4.25-second 40-yard dash in a torn sneaker, beating the fastest official 40-yard dash of 4.31 seconds. By the time his plane landed back in Chadron after the combine, the Bills and the Packers were knocking at his door. The Buffalo Bills drafted Beebe in 1989, and he would go on to play six Super Bowl games, four with the Buffalo Bills and two with the Green Bay Packers.

This was his third Super Bowl with the Buffalo Bills. It would also become a defining moment for both Beebe and Lett.

Dallas Cowboy Leon Lett has one hundred pounds and seven inches on Don Beebe. Lett **looks** like a football player. Beebe is 5'11" and weighs 185 pounds.

But Beebe is fast as hell. And when the fans start cheering, they are not cheering for Leon Lett. They are cheering for the scrawny guy in the Buffalo Bills uniform who came out of nowhere.

Four yards. Three yards.

Bystanders can tell you that the cheers are not solely from Buffalo Bills' fans. Team spirit goes out the window as Cowboys' fans watch proof of the human spirit and start celebrating, not because their team is about to win, but because they see a tiny little guy from the opposing team making the play of his life.

This is so much more than just a game. This will be recorded as among the greatest moments in Super Bowl history. Fifteen years later, Don Beebe will tell me that this moment defined him as a player, as a man, as a husband, as a businessperson, as a coach, and as a father.

"At least five times a week, someone tells me how much that moment meant. Just the other day, a sixteen-year-old told me that moment inspired him to be an athlete of character, to work hard, to stay in the game," said Beebe, who now owns House of Speed, a training facility that teaches athletes to build character through sports.

Two yards. One yard.

A split second later, and it would have been too late. But fast-as-hell Don Beebe knows that a split second is all it takes, and before Leon Lett can touch his foot to the endzone, scrawny Don Beebe smacks that ball to the ground.

Don Beebe has prevented a touchdown when the Bills had already lost, when no one would have blamed him for simply walking off the field, when it no longer mattered.

The crowd goes wild.

Though the scoreboard accurately reflects a 52-17 Bills' defeat, Buffalo Bill Don Beebe did not lose that day, and Dallas Cowboy Leon Lett did not win. And contrary to what the scorecard says, Beebe's play **did** matter. Anyone watching that game will tell you the same thing: Don Beebe was a hero that day. He reflected the kind of character we so desperately want to find. The kind of character an employer wants in his employees. The kind of character a woman wants in her husband. The kind of character a person wants in his friends. The kind of character a parent wants in a child.

Indeed, athletes **are** wanted.

BENEFITS OF ATHLETICS

SURELY, YOUNG FOOTBALL PLAYERS across the country watching Super Bowl XXVII remember Don Beebe and the play that stripped Leon Lett of the goal line on that fateful Sunday in 1993. They dreamt of the glory of professional status, heroic feats of accomplishment, and Super Bowl victories. And these children are not alone. Young athletes of all nations, whether they swim, run, golf, skate, or play baseball, soccer, lacrosse, football, or basketball, all dream of greatness. They dream of swimming in the Olympics, winning the Masters, hitting the game-winning homer in the World Series, or holding the Larry O'Brien NBA Championship Trophy.

Percent of high school athletes who will play at a professional level	
Football	0.09%
Men's basketball	0.03%
Women's basketball	0.02%
Ice hockey	0.4%
Baseball (minor and major leagues)	0.5%

But in all truth, the numbers are less than encouraging. Not everyone will be recruited to the NFL like Don Beebe, and those who do play professionally last no more than three seasons on average. Only 0.09 percent of high school football players go on to play for the NFL. A scant 0.03 percent of high school basketball players make NBA rosters. Fewer than 1 percent of high school athletes are fully funded at the Division I college level, and just 3.04 percent of high school athletes receive even partial funding for college sports at any level. Of the nation's 7.3 million high school athletes, fewer than 7 percent will play at a college level, and most of these opportunities will come from smaller, less-recognizable schools than they might have imagined.[1]

»« FAST FACT »«

NFLers Jerry Rice and the late Walter Payton failed to receive a single scholarship offer from Division IA college programs. Chicago Bull Scottie Pippen—who was named NBA All-Defensive Team eight times and All-NBA First Team three times—was forced to walk on at an NAIA school after failing to receive a single scholarship offer.

Student-athletes are not alone in their visions of glory. Every parent believes that his child has all-star potential—the future Peyton Manning, Candace Parker, and Michael Phelps. Although blue-chip players are among us, once student-athletes leave the safe confines of high school, they must compete not only against the cream of the crop from the 7.3 million high school athletes spanning the country, but also against athletes from Asia, Africa, South America, Europe, and Australia.

---

1 Statistics from the National Collegiate Athletic Association, the National Collegiate Scouting Association, and the National Federation of High School Associations.

FOREIGN COMPETITORS

Because few countries abroad allow students to compete at an amateur level while pursuing an education, overseas students jump at the opportunity to travel to the United States to receive a college degree while playing a sport. These athletes are attracted to the high-level coaching, facilities, competition, culture, and education that are integrated on American campuses, and this makes them appealing candidates for some coaches, who consider overseas athletes more disciplined than their American counterparts.

According to *The Chronicle of Higher Education*, the proportion of foreign players has doubled in many Division I sports since the beginning of the decade. In the 2005-2006 school year, foreigners accounted for:

- **23 percent of male hockey players.**
- **14 percent of female golfers.**
- **13 percent of all skiers.**
- **10 percent of all male soccer players.**
- **30 percent of male tennis players.** Half of the top 125 singles players in Division I are foreign, a big jump from 1970, when only eight NCAA men's singles champions came from outside the country.

Despite increased competition, the good news is that opportunities are increasing as well. The NCAA reported that more than half of high school students now play a sport, and between the 1981-1982 school year and the 2005-2006 school year, team membership increased by 51 percent. The number of female teams increased by 4,462, and the number of male teams increased by 1,416. During the same time frame, the number of athletes playing on NCAA teams increased by 65 percent. The number of female athletes increased by 98,230, and the number of male athletes increased by 61,421.

NCAA Athletic Team Opportunities: 1981-82 school year to 2005-06 school year

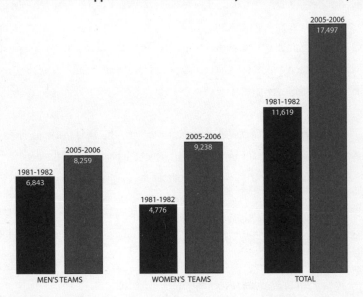

SOURCE: *NCAA Executive Summary: 1981-82—2005-06 NCAA Sports Sponsorship and Participation Rates Report*

Though most of the opportunities are at Division II, III, NAIA, and junior college levels, the true benefits of sports remain the same regardless of whether the athlete is playing at a Division I or Division III level. Participating in sports **can** help an athlete build critical lifelong skills, skills that build character, and skills that allow the student to win a quality education, job opportunities, and networks that stay with him a lifetime, regardless of whether he plays second-string on a junior college team or is the star of a Division I college team. In other words, every athlete can be just like Don Beebe in the ways that matter—athletes of all levels can build integrity, character, and dedication through sports.

THE TICKET TO A BETTER EDUCATION

Ask Crystal Smith, a high school track and field athlete from Wisconsin, about the benefits of athletics, and she will tell you that college would have been unaffordable were it not for her ability to throw the discus.

"I could have never afforded the $40,000-a-year tuition to Wagner College," confirmed Smith's mother, Cindy. A single mother dedicated to her daughter's future, Cindy said that her daughter's ability to attend college was entirely a result of her participation in track and field.

«« FAST FACT ««

According to the Department of Education's National Center for Education Statistics, the average student loan debt among college seniors was a little over $19,000 in 2004. Today, 42 percent of college students graduate more than $25,000 in debt, according to the Center for American Progress, and graduate school students have nearly $46,000 in debt. Adding to the financial stress, one-third of graduates have more than $5,000 in credit card debt by the time they graduate.

Crystal admitted that she rarely thought of college while in high school.

"Little focus was put on college, so I never realized how important furthering my education could be," she said.

Because Crystal excelled in discus, she earned a full scholarship to Wagner College in Staten Island, New York. Smith is now a senior with hopes of graduating on the horizon. After earning her bachelor's degree in chemistry with a concentration in biochemistry and minors in math and biology, Crystal intends to earn a PhD in pharmacological sciences.

How many people in her hometown have a PhD in pharmacological studies? She will be the first.

While undoubtedly inspiring, Smith's story is certainly not unique. Athletes who compete in Division I revenue sports like men's basketball also have been unsure of their path to getting an education. Jay Straight grew up in the Robert Taylor Homes in the South Side of Chicago. During this time, almost 100 percent of the housing development's residents were unemployed, and 40 percent of households were occupied by single-mothers earning less than $5,000 each year. Originally intended for eleven thousand people, the homes' number of occupants had expanded to nearly three times that capacity. Gang violence and drug use were commonplace.

Fortunately, Straight was raised by his grandmother, who saw sports as a way out of the impoverished life. From the time Straight was a young child, his grandmother found opportunities for him to play, teaching him to ride the bus across town to attend different basketball practices and clubs on his own. By the time Straight graduated from high school, he was among the best scorers in the country. Recruited by Notre Dame, Marquette, Boston College, Iowa State, and St. Louis, Straight chose to attend the University of Wyoming, graduating from college in three and one-half years.

Today, Straight is a professional basketball player who had a seat in the EuroCup. He has played for teams in Israel, Croatia, Ukraine, France, and Poland.

"Not bad for a kid from the Robert Taylor Homes," said Straight.

For kids like Smith and Straight, attending college is becoming more and more of an obstacle, unless tuition costs are lessened by scholarships and aid. The College Board, a non-profit membership association composed of fifty-four hundred schools, colleges, universities, and educational organizations, reports that despite an increase in tuition prices, federal student aid is decreasing, making college seem out of reach for even children of middleclass families.

According to *U.S. News & World Report*, the average sticker price for a typical four-year university is about $16,400 a year—which includes room and board, tuition, books, and ancillaries. The year-to-year increase in college tuition and fees is outpacing the general inflation rate. Aggravating matters, the normal public university student now takes more than six years to graduate, which means the average public college degree is close to $100,000.

But when compared to the student-athlete average scholarship/grants-in-aid package of $12,850 per year for those who attend public schools and $21,266 for student-athletes attending private colleges and universities, these tuition prices become within reach.

AVERAGE COLLEGE TUITION AND FEES
(Including Room, Board, and Other Fees), 2007-2008 Academic Year*

TYPE	Average Tuition per Year	Other Charges per Year	Annual Total	Increase Over 2006-2007	Average Grants and Benefits per Year	Average Student-Athlete's Scholarship / Grants-in-Aid per Year**
In state, public, four-year	$6,185	$7,404	$13,589	5.9%	$3,600	$12,850
Out of state, public, four-year	$16,640	$7,404	$24,044	5.4%	$3,600	$12,850
Private, four-year	$23,712	$8,595	$32,307	5.9%	$9,300	$21,266

*SOURCE: *The College Board*
**SOURCE: *NCSA Survey of 6,000 Student-Athletes Reporting from 2006 and 2007 High School Graduating Classes*

> ### «« FAST FACT ««
> **Most parents and athletes do not know the techniques for appealing their financial aid package. A simple act can award a student with an extra $12,000 to $20,000 over a four-year college career.**

THE KEY TO INCREASING THE ODDS

Other students, of course, are positioned financially, but not academically. Even though I had a 3.8 grade-point average, my ACT score of 21 certainly would not have allowed me to enter Vanderbilt University were it not for my ability as a football player. Vanderbilt, known to produce more Nobel Prize winners than Heisman winners, competes in the toughest athletic conference in the nation and is the best academic institution in the Southeastern Conference. Ranked eleventh in the Division I NCSA Collegiate Power Rankings and first in the Southeastern Conference, Vanderbilt's academic reputation is top notch. Because it needed a linebacker with strong character and work ethic, it welcomed me, despite an ACT score that was at least eight points below the average score of Vanderbilt students, which ranges from 29 to 32.

Though I am a strong proponent of an attitude in which academics trump athletics, the truth of the matter is that some students, despite their best efforts, simply do not have the grades to enter a top-ranked college based on academics alone. However, universities will make exceptions for students they want on their campus. Student-athletes are wanted because they bring leadership, work ethic, character, and determination. And if a student-athlete helps a team win, brings positive public relations and name recognition, and sells tickets, he is wanted even more.

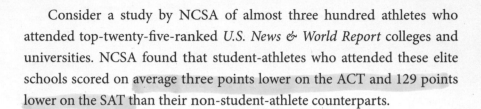

Consider a study by NCSA of almost three hundred athletes who attended top-twenty-five-ranked *U.S. News & World Report* colleges and universities. NCSA found that student-athletes who attended these elite schools scored on average three points lower on the ACT and 129 points lower on the SAT than their non-student-athlete counterparts.

«« FAST FACT ««

An NCSA survey found that some student-athletes were accepted to *U.S. News & World Report's* top twenty-five ranked universities and colleges with GPA's as low as 2.8, ACT scores as low as 21, and SAT scores as low as 920.

And statistics from College and Beyond confirm the NCSA findings, as reported in *The Game of Life: College Sports and Educational Values* (Princeton University Press, 2002). At Division I, Ivy League, and liberal arts colleges, intercollegiate athletes scored almost 120 points lower on the SAT than the student body at large. When considering single sports, the difference can be even more drastic. Basketball students scored about 307 points lower on their SAT scores than the student body at large. Football players scored 292 points less. In fact, fencing was the only sport in which student-athletes scored higher, and crew the only sport with no significant difference. For all other sports—cross-country, ice hockey, swimming, lacrosse, soccer, tennis, golf, volleyball, wrestling, baseball, football, and basketball—it pays to be an athlete. In 1999, an athlete had a 53 percent higher admissions advantage than a student with the same SAT score who was not an athlete, minority, or legacy. Minorities had only a 20 percent advantage, and legacies a 24 percent advantage.

This is not to say that student-athletes are less academically strong than their non-athletic counterparts. According to the NCAA Graduation-Rates Summary, student-athletes graduate at a rate 1 to 2 percent higher than the general student body. So while their admittance statistics are lower, student-athletes fare better in the end than the general student body.

THE CHARACTER-BUILDER

Perhaps more than anything, sports provide a framework for character development during early critical years when students are tempted by peer pressure and searching for their place in life.

LISA'S STORY

Had I not been a hockey player, I would have been lost during my high school years. As a teen, my identity revolved around the sport I loved. The first day of high school, most girls worried about their clothes and whether the "in" crowd would accept them, but I was busy preparing for hockey tryouts. As the only female hockey player, my identity was defined as "the girl who played hockey."

I had to be twice as good as the boys to prove I belonged. I carried a dedication to hard work with me in the classroom, where I pushed myself to be at the top of my class. Playing on two hockey teams—the varsity high school boys' team and a travel-club girls' team—was demanding, but I always completed my homework because otherwise I would face the consequences of a missed practice or, even worse, a missed game. I also knew that the better grades I achieved, the more opportunities I would have to play college hockey. Nothing was going to stand in the way of my dreams, so I practiced and studied relentlessly.

I also remained cautious in social situations because I did not want to compromise my ability to play in the next game. Time and time again, I made one good decision instead of one bad decision. I look back and know that these small decisions meant that I avoided some of the big setbacks many teenagers faced. Every move was guided by my love of hockey. I spent Friday nights resting so I was fresh for early morning skates. Summers were my time to attend camps and showcases. Rather than attend my own homecoming, I sat by the bonfire at Dartmouth College during its homecoming and my official visit.

I did not attend these events alone, nor would I have attended any of them were it not for two extremely supportive parents. My dad devoted all of his free time to chaperone me from rink to rink. Hockey enabled me to spend hours upon hours of quality time with my dad. Even if I never skated a day past high school, I would be grateful to my sport for the time I spent with my dad.

But it didn't end there. I was offered a scholarship to several schools, though I chose to attend Yale University, where I was eventually named captain of the hockey team. From the moment I walked onto Yale's campus, I had a built-in family of students who valued discipline and goal-setting. In fact, the summer before my freshman year, I received letters from many of my new teammates, so when I started, I already had a tight-knit family of athletes.

After college I was invited to play professional hockey in Switzerland. I was fortunate to participate in several developmental camps at the Olympic Training Center in Lake Placid, New York, and I currently coach girl's hockey in Chicago's North Shore community.

—Lisa Strasman, NCSA Director of Recruiting Coaches

Across the board, including coaches, players, teachers, parents, executives, employers, and students, people of all walks of life say that student-athletes have a unique experience to develop character skills they might not otherwise develop, especially when their athletic experience is coupled with strong parenting.

"I try not to laugh when someone asks a student-athlete about discipline, commitment, and leadership," said Kevin Carroll, author of *Rules of the Red Rubber Ball*.

NCSA Recruiting Coach Joyce Wellhoefer agreed, noting that students who play sports are required to learn how to manage their time appropriately, keeping a careful balance that allows time for both practice and their academic obligations. Owning up to responsibility is a big benefit of athletics, said Wellhoefer, who has coached basketball and softball at NAIA, NCAA Division I, and Division II levels.

"A student-athlete learns that there are consequences to the choices she makes," said Wellhoefer. "If she fails to study for class, she will earn poor grades, and she will not be allowed to play. Likewise, if she does not execute or play well, the results are not going to be positive. But if she studies and plays hard, she earns favorable outcomes. One way or another, the consequences are up to the student-athlete."

"If you play a position like fullback in soccer, no one other than you is going to prevent the other guy from making a goal," agreed Andy Petranek, owner of Petranek Fitness, a CrossFit-affiliated gym that trains elite athletes in Southern California. "The entire team is relying on you to do your job."

By every measure, high school student-athletes perform better than the general population, and this is particularly true in inner-city schools, said Arne Duncan, former CEO of Chicago Public Schools, who added that student-athletes have higher grade-point averages than their non-athlete counterparts.

«« FAST FACT ««

NFL players with college degrees have NFL careers that last 33 percent longer than those who do not earn college degrees.

Because of sports, Kevin Carroll earned a scholarship, authored several books, became a community leader, and addressed the United Nations. Sports afforded Carroll an opportunity to move away from the restraints of his neighborhood, which offered little in terms of education and opportunity.

"In my neighborhood, if you did not believe that you had a gift or a talent, you were done. The gang members and drug dealers put their nasty hooks in you and pulled you into their abyss," he said.

For Carroll, discipline is among the biggest benefits of athleticism, but it certainly does not stop there.

"Athletes have to possess a certain level of competitiveness or they would not advance to a collegiate level," said Howie Jacobson who, along with his partner Ross Lerner, founded Athletes to Business, an organization that connects student-athletes with employers in the business sector. "Employers want competitiveness. They also want organizational skills, and athletes would not get through college if they could not manage classes, games, homework, and practice schedules."

Jacobson said that his corporate clients are attracted to the idea of hiring student-athletes because they are results-oriented.

"Athletes always walk onto the field with a result in mind, whether it be winning the game, season, conference, or championship," agreed Lerner. "And almost all athletes have bounced back from some sort of adversity or defeat, so they are considered a resilient bunch, and employers like that."

ATHLETES WANTED IN BUSINESS

The National Collegiate Scouting Association conducted a survey of more than one hundred CEOs from the Entrepreneurs' Organization* to learn about their attitudes toward student-athletes:

- Of those CEOs randomly surveyed, 94 percent played in either high school or college sports.

- A full 100 percent said they would be more likely to hire a student-athlete than a non-student-athlete.

- More than 60 percent said they would hire a student-athlete with a B or C average before a non-student-athlete with an A average.

- In order of most named, CEOs listed the following as characteristics of the college student-athlete, and one-third said they consider all of these traits to be associated with the collegiate athlete:

1. Competitive
2. Hard worker
3. Coachable
4-7. Tie among the following:
   - Leader
   - Dedicated
   - Team player
   - Works well under pressure
8. Goal-setter
9. Assertive
10. Reliable
11. Communicator
12. Clutch performer

*Membership in the Entrepreneurs' Organization is limited to founders, co-founders, owners, and controlling shareholders with businesses with a minimum of $1 million in annual gross sales and who join before their fiftieth birthday.

"I learned a lot more on basketball courts than in classrooms," said Duncan, a Harvard graduate who was co-captain of his basketball team. "I learned so many life lessons and values that transferred later in life: hard work, loyalty, teamwork, and all of those things that have been instrumental in my work outside the athletic field."

The networks Duncan has built have stayed with him, and Strasman, Wellhoefer, Carroll, Petranek, and everyone else interviewed, echoed this sentiment. Michel Balasis, the head of visual communications at Loyola University and a former kicker from Michigan State University, said the notoriety of being an athlete, and the subsequent client base he was able to secure, allowed him to start a business as a graphic designer before he even graduated. Bridget Venturi-Veenema, the 1990 American Gladiator champion, traveled to Holland, Belgium, France, Japan, Canada, and Taiwan, building a network of amazing people along the way. Strasman was recently a bridesmaid for a woman she first met through sports when she was twelve years old.

"My network of friends includes a lot of former collegiate athletes," confirmed Duncan. "We have a bond and a camaraderie that would be hard to form in a chemistry lab or math class."

"You can take all the English classes in the world, and you are never going to learn the social skills or build the networks that an athlete builds," agreed Bob Chmiel, former football coach at Notre Dame, Michigan, and Northwestern, who added that athletes fly together, eat together, practice together, and socialize together.

The Department of Defense conducted a study in the 1980s on how to bridge different cultures and age groups for better social interchange. In the final analysis, the best and most common denominator for mixing cultures was an involvement in sports. Bypassing night clubs, restaurants, social events, and entertainment, sports broke through differences in age, race, religion, and gender.

"From an employer's perspective, the ability to get along with just about anyone is a very attractive trait," Chmiel said.

Duncan agreed, saying that a candidate's athletic experience is "absolutely a factor" when it comes to hiring.

"I know that former student-athletes often have leadership skills that others do not have. They have the ability to get along with folks who are different from them, and they have a work ethic that is pretty remarkable," said Duncan.

A fifty-hour work-week is a piece of cake for a student-athlete accustomed to spending seventy hours a week training, attending classes, studying, and competing in games.

Larry Wert, president of NBC Local Media, Central and Western Regions, echoed this sentiment. A high school and collegiate swimmer and diver, Wert said that goal-setting and discipline are themes that have spilled into his personal and professional life. All the training and competitions contributed to his identity and self-confidence, giving him a healthy paradigm to live inside during his formative years. And before Wert's résumé expanded to include titles such as sales manager, general manager, senior vice president, and president, his background gave potential employers two bits of information they could assume from his involvement in sports: He was competitive, and he was disciplined. These job skills landed him a job

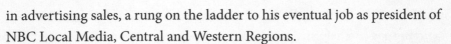

in advertising sales, a rung on the ladder to his eventual job as president of NBC Local Media, Central and Western Regions.

"If you want to be successful in sports, you have to be committed. You have to be committed to nutrition, to educational studies, and to everything else that goes into the sport. You have to be committed to having successful life habits," said Augie Maurelli, the director of strength and conditioning at Georgetown University.

THE BENEFITS OF STARTING EARLY

The earlier a child is introduced to sports, the better. When I was in fourth grade, my next-door neighbor was a basketball player. He unwittingly became my mentor. He tolerated my endless questions, played ball with me in the backyard, and counseled me about grades, friendship, and sports. He worked out every day and ate his Brussels sprouts. He became an All-State basketball player, then earned a full scholarship to the University of Illinois, and is now a college coach. I wanted to be just like him.

I wanted to be an athlete.

At the time, being an athlete primarily consisted of playing in the back yard with my friends. It was also a reward for positive behavior.

"Do your homework, or you cannot play ball," my parents would say.

"Keep your grades up, or you cannot play ball," they would say.

Athletes come in all ages—some are born into an athletic family, others do not discover sports until they reach fifty. Some mature early and are passed by later in life, while some late bloomers do not mature physically until college. Some elite athletes are naturally gifted; others make up for talent by pouring their heart into the game. One thing is certain: Athletes who start early are at an advantage. They learn how to set goals, manage their time, and practice every day. They benefit from positive mentors and role models.

New skills are more easily formed during the younger years. Like learning a language, early development of athletic habits and abilities embeds these skills into a person's DNA. Whether learning to swing a bat, work hard, deal with a loss, or be gracious after a win, engaging in sports at a young age can help shape children in a positive way and determine their later success, not only in athletics, but also in life.

Athletes Wanted is designed as a resource to assist in maximizing a child's athletic scholarship and life potential. Because recruiting is a process, not a one-time event, it can start before a student-athlete enters high school, and it often lasts three or four years. As such, refer back to this book regularly for a refresher.

With the cost of college education increasing faster than the cost of living, the competition for scholarships is at an all-time high. The goal of this book is to give student-athletes an advantage. Combined with the *Athletes Wanted* website and interactive blogging community (www.athleteswanted.org), this book allows students to turn their dreams of playing collegiate sports into reality.

Synthesizing the best practices from more than ten thousand student-athletes who have gone on to play collegiately, this book serves as a complete resource full of Coach's Tips, Fast Facts, timelines, graphs, worksheets, and key point summaries at the end of each chapter. Remember to also check the *Athletes Wanted* website, which has downloadable forms, tutorials, and access to the latest rules, techniques, and success stories.

The pre-high school years mark the best time to begin preparing for college recruitment and guiding a child's abilities so that a student-athlete presents an attractive package to recruiters. If athletes do not start preparing until high school, they might not be too late, but they will definitely be forced to play another game: a game of catch up.

An early involvement in sports will help build the foundation for later success in all areas of life. Remember: The goal is not to be successful at athletics—the goal is to use athletics to be more successful.

Let's not forget, however, the physical benefits of sports. In a nation that is plagued by childhood obesity, early involvement in sports conditions a child for a continued dedication to physical fitness. For this reason alone, any parent interested in her child's longevity and health should incorporate some sort of athleticism into a child's life.

Yet, sports provide a way to condition more than the physical embodiment of a child. By participating in sports, a child will begin to draw larger lessons about life that speak to his mental, emotional, and intellectual character. By learning these kinds of lessons from athletics, a student-athlete will build the kind of character that will bring him success on and off the field. Indeed, as Coach Bob Chmiel is fond of pointing out, character is the top quality coaches look for in a recruit.

The following are nine ways athletics can build a young child's character:

1. Athletics help a child learn to deal with authority.

Imagine that a young college graduate enters the workforce. Because academia was always his focus, this is his first experience as a subordinate. Though he is well schooled and competent, he has questions about how to best fulfill the responsibilities associated with the job. Fresh on the job, he is not comfortable approaching his boss and admitting his uncertainties. He has a brilliant idea about running the office more efficiently, but he is worried about stepping on toes. Should he approach his boss, or just toe the line?

Now imagine that "the dragon lady" hires the young man. She runs a tight ship, demands much, and pays little. She is quick to snap and unwilling to forgive. By the end of his first week, the young graduate feels a tight knot in his stomach each time he steps foot into the door. He wonders whether he should confront his boss or toe the line.

Regardless of a student's career choices, one thing is for certain: At some point or another, an athlete will need to contend with an authority figure without the safety net of Mom and Dad. Joining sports presents an opportunity for students to begin learning to take direction and to communicate with all different types of authority figures. Similar to bosses, coaches come in every size and shape. Some are intense and direct; others believe in positive reinforcement. Some are fair and righteous; others make mistakes often.

"Participating in sports allows a child an opportunity to approach an adult and express himself," said Venturi-Veenema, the athletic director of Regina Dominican High School in Wilmette, Illinois. "It's hard for a child to approach an adult and say, 'I have a problem,' but sooner or later, every child is going to have a problem that needs to be addressed. Why not allow him to do this in the safest environment? Let him stumble in the double safety net of parents and a school system so that later, when Mom and Dad are not there, he has experience with authorities."

2. Young athletes learn how to lose gracefully and win graciously.

When I was in the seventh grade, I played on a basketball team that was undefeated. We were on top of the world, a world we thought was owned by our seventh-grade basketball team. No one could beat us. I vividly remember my parents telling me that they wished we would lose a game. At the time, I did not understand.

Now I do. Eventually, we lost a game, ending the season with a 39-1 record. Over the course of my life as an athlete, I would go on to lose many, many more games. I learned that a team can work and work and work and still lose in the end. I learned that a seventh-grade basketball team doesn't own the world. I learned to take it one game at a time—that just as easily, a winning team can become a losing team. I also learned to respect my competitors, recognizing that regardless of a team's record, every competitor has his strengths and weaknesses.

No purer analogy for life's victories and spills exists than this.

3. Young athletes learn to be team players and manage conflict.

I would be lying if I said sports are not accompanied by conflict. Young athletes get hurt, they fight with their teammates, and they feel overlooked by their coaches. But with proper parenting, these athletes work through adolescence and become mature adults, confident to handle and manage conflict, which they accept as a part of life. Because they had parents, a team, and a coach supporting them, they aren't paralyzed when conflict rears its head. After all, they have likely dealt with something very similar in the past.

A child who has experienced teamwork enters adulthood much more equipped, said Coach Chmiel.

"So many things a person experiences while a member of a team are seamless to the workplace: the ability to get along with others, the ability to move forward in a group setting, hard work, and dedication. And let us not forgot one of the greatest byproducts: You cannot compete in athletics in this day and age if you are not color blind," he said.

Coach Chmiel uses the football huddle as an analogy for business.

"In a huddle, orders given are unequivocally followed, and if one person does not carry out his assignment, there is immediate failure," Coach Chmiel said. "An athlete cannot look to the left and challenge someone because of her socioeconomic status. An athlete cannot look to the right and challenge some-one because of his race. An athlete cannot go to committee with the play, and there is no room for discussion. An athlete has thirty-five seconds to listen to the instructions, and then he must take them and carry them out."

Does this teach a kid to be a team player? Absolutely, and this is a big triumph down the line when it comes time to apply for a job. In fact, almost all of the skills a student-athlete learns—time management, leadership, team work, commitment, goal-setting, competitiveness—are traits employers look for.

4. Along with teamwork, athletes learn personal responsibility.

Because each member is a vital part of a team's success, young athletes learn that other people are relying on them. When a young athlete drops the ball, he learns to accept responsibility and vows to make a stronger effort. In the end, athletes learn to never pass the buck when they drop the ball.

Andy Petranek—who participated in four cycles of the Eco Challenge, a round-the-clock, three hundred-mile expedition adventure race regarded by athletes as among the greatest challenges ever—said he knows two things immediately about people who push themselves athletically: They are reliable, and they are responsible.

"They have to be," he said. "If an athlete is competing at a higher level, he has to be 100 percent committed and 100 percent accountable, so when I am hiring for a position, the athlete will always have a leg up. The athlete knows what it takes to be a champion. He knows how hard it is to be the best, and I want that person on my team."

Add to that enthusiasm, teamwork, and leadership skills, said Petranek, and an employer considers the student-athlete an all-around attractive package. Student-athletes are rewarded favorably: A study by College and Beyond reported that former athletes who entered the workforce earned about 15.4 percent more than their non-athlete counterparts.

While this personal responsibility is critical, athletes also learn not to dwell on mistakes. Imagine what would have happened to the Green Bay Packers had its running back, Ryan Grant, focused on his two early fumbles in the 2008 divisional playoffs against the Seattle Seahawks. Going into the game, the Packers were the favored team, but within the first quarter, Grant's fumbles put the team in a two-touchdown hole. Instead of collapsing into the fetal position or allowing his spills to distract him, Grant ran for 201 yards and three touchdowns. As any Packers or Seahawks fan can tell you, the Packers went on to crush the Seahawks, 42-20.

To this end, when a student loses a game, parents and coaches must encourage the athlete to lose the game without passing the buck. If parents or coaches blame the loss on a coach or another teammate, the athlete will learn to shift responsibility, which might temporarily stroke his ego, but will not serve him later in life. Sports teach student-athletes to stop pointing their fingers at other people and start pointing their thumbs at themselves.

5. Athletes learn leadership skills.

Throughout the course of their athletic careers, most young athletes will play many different roles. At some point, whether an athlete is team captain of the soccer team or section leader of the cheer squad, the team will rely on the athlete to take a leadership position. Like learning to deal with authority, being a leader provides an athlete with an opportunity to interact with a broad spectrum of personality types. As well, it teaches the athlete to be fair, to listen, and to make judgment calls, all skills that are needed later in life.

Leadership means doing the right thing when no one is watching, even if it is not popular. I can remember when some of my teammates decided to cut corners while the coaches were not watching. As team captain, I decided we should all do extra pushups to make up for the lack of effort. The decision was unpopular with many of my teammates, but the team became much more respected (and respectful) that day. Colleges and employees know that athletes who are leaders on the court will be leaders in life.

»« FAST FACT »«

According to a study by the University of Virginia, 80 percent of female Fortune 500 top executives describe themselves as former athletes.

---

6. Young athletes learn the value of hard work.

As a child, Larry Wert wanted to be an Olympic diver. He set goals and worked hard. In the end, Wert fell short of his goal, but along the way, he won state and national competitions, became team captain of his high school and college diving teams, and was sent to college on a full athletic scholarship. Later, he was afforded jobs at least in part because of the assumptions employers made based on Wert's experience as an athlete. Wert and the employers both knew the same thing:

Hard work does not guarantee success, but success guarantees hard work.

The discipline it takes to master a trade is not something commonly found in a child, and a person takes notice of a student able to embrace this kind of regimented commitment. When a student is able to embrace this kind of discipline, he will be noticed.

Basketball taught Kevin Carroll traits that he carries with him through life. When a student rises at 5:30 every morning for a 6:00 a.m. practice, he starts learning the discipline necessary to master a skill. He carries that discipline with him, and thirty-five years later, when he starts a new job, or picks up a hobby that begins to frustrate him (Carroll is reacquainting himself with the cello, an ambitious instrument for an adult learner), he reflects back and draws from his skills. He remembers how many times he shot the basketball and ran drills before it became second-nature. He remembers that nothing ever comes without practice.

7. Athletes learn to set goals.

To succeed at anything, from business, to health, to life as a whole, athletes learn that they must have goals clearly defined. During junior high, I began looking to high school. What would I need to do to play high school football? What about college? What sort of physical condition would be required of me? What sort of grades did I need?

Goals motivate. They enable us to set priorities, to set a long-range course, to deal with setbacks, and to measure our achievement. When a student reaches middle school and starts making independent and important choices about what he wants out of life, he can begin cementing a life-long commitment to goal-setting by constructing major athletic and academic goals, as well as the action steps needed to achieve them.

The key to goal-setting is to use the SMART formula—goals should be **S**pecific, **M**easurable, **A**ttainable, and **R**ecorded over **T**ime.

SMART GOALS

A detailed description = **SPECIFIC**

A number or other objective standard can be tied to the goal = **MEASURABLE**

Realistic = **ATTAINABLE**

Written down = **RECORDED**

A specific date or timeframe (years, months, hours, minutes, or seconds) is set as a deadline for achieving the goal. = **TIME-BOUNDED**

If an athlete's goal is to simply improve speed or GPA, how will he measure this goal? When does he want to improve his endurance? This year? This month? This decade? Without concrete, actionable goals, students will not make a connection between the activities in which they participate and the achievement of the goal. (For more about goal-setting, download our SMART goals article, available online at www.athleteswanted.org.)

For example, quarterly goals might look something like this:

Goal 1: *Maintain at least a 3.0 GPA for the upcoming quarter.*

Actions:

- *Complete homework the evening it is assigned by 9:00 p.m. and go over with Mom.*

- *Read at least one chapter over the weekend.*

- *Review class notes the following day during study hall.*

Goal 2: *Run 55-minute 10K.*

Actions:

- *Run ten 100-yard hill sprints under twenty seconds each three times each week.*

- *Run three miles once a week in less than twenty-five minutes; two miles once a week in less than fifteen minutes; and four miles once a week in less than thirty-two minutes between now and the next cross country meet.*

- *Lift weights, three sets of eight, ten, twelve, each body part, three times a week.*

One athlete might be hard-pressed to do his homework, much less run one mile, while another athlete might an over-achiever. Regardless of the starting point, goals simply move a person forward. By setting athletic goals, students begin to see that success is not a mysterious, luck-driven concept. Rather, they see that moving forward in life only requires small, actionable, measurable, specific steps that they can track over time, a valuable concept that, when applied, can help them throughout life.

GOAL-SETTING

A student-athlete should create a written schedule each week based on his goals. Here are the basic steps:

STEP 1: Identify all mandatory items, such as school hours, scheduled practices and games, dentist appointments, and the like.

STEP 2: Student-athletes should set aside sufficient time for activities such as their homework load, upcoming projects, and papers. These activities should be as specific as possible.

STEP 3: With the remaining time, a student-athlete should fill in optional activities, such as additional practices, recreation, and time with friends, referring back to his SMART goals to make sure that he includes activities that propel these goals forward. Eventually, a child should also include time for researching colleges and attending sports camps. Be sure to include blocks of free time. A schedule should be an aid, not a burden.

By preparing a schedule this way, an athlete recognizes that increased demands from his sport must be shifted from optional activities, not from schoolwork.

With the schedule in hand, parents and coaches can monitor athletes, not only to make sure they are sticking to the schedule, but also to make sure the schedule is accurate and realistic. For instance, if a student-athlete regularly crams on Sunday nights to complete his assignments, he has not blocked enough time for schoolwork during the week.

8.   Athletes learn to manage their time effectively.

Middle school is the first time a student-athlete has to deal with the challenge of balancing the demands of schoolwork and the demands of athletics. As he becomes more serious about sports, his top priority must be on receiving a good education. Parents and coaches can use the child's participation in sports as incentive. By setting firm rules for participating in athletics, parents and coaches can require the child to make his best efforts in the classroom before he is granted the opportunity to walk onto the field.

Though most schools mandate a required grade-point average for participating in sports, my parents reinforced this system by setting requirements higher than the school's established standards. Each parent requires a different level of academic achievement. For some parents, a 3.8 grade-point average might be the cutoff for participating in sports. For others, a 2.5 grade-point average is sufficient. My job is not to counsel parents, coaches, and athletes on the importance of academia, but simply to show them that athletics can be used to strengthen time management and academic goals, whatever they might be. My parents used this incentive to great success. I was not a "natural" student, and my interests were not in academia. But were it not for sports, my grades would have suffered. The threat of having sports taken away from me was too much, and I kept my grades high because my parents made it a condition of walking onto the field.

Recognizing that education is a priority is not enough. Even a child who genuinely desires to succeed in school and in sports will face difficulties because knowing how to balance competing demands on one's time is an acquired skill.

9. **Athletes naturally pick other athletes as role models and mentors.**

Children of all ages need healthy role models to flourish, and athletes naturally look to other athletes as role models and mentors. Remember that throughout a student's school years, she will be subjected to peer pressure. The need to be accepted is profound during these years, so children exposed to athletes who are self-confident, assured, well-mannered, and disciplined can combat the negative influences that might creep into life.

KEY POINTS

_1._ More than 7.3 million student-athletes are walking the halls of the nation's high schools, and millions of foreign athletes want to compete for coveted spots on American college teams. Fewer than 7 percent of the nation's athletes will play at a college level, and just 3.04 percent will receive any athletic scholarship funding. That said, opportunities have increased in the past two decades. NCAA's membership has grown by 2,574 collegiate men's teams and 3,845 collegiate women's teams.

_2._ More than 80 percent of athletic opportunities are at the NCAA Division II, III, NAIA, or junior college levels, with these schools often providing more playing time, a strong academic department, and a better fit for the student-athlete.

_3._ The average sticker price for a typical four-year college is $16,400 a year, and the average college student graduates more than $25,000 in debt. A student-athlete can offset this cost by aggressively positioning himself for scholarships.

_4._ High school student-athletes who compete in college win on average more than $12,850 per year (for in-state, public school students) to $21,266 per year (for private school students) in scholarships, grants, and financial aid to play sports at a collegiate level for four or five years.

_5._ Admissions standards are often lowered for athletes. In a study of three hundred athletes who attended some of the nation's top universities, the National Collegiate Scouting Association found that student-athletes scored on average three points lower on their ACT and 129 points lower on their SAT than their non-student-athlete counterparts.

_6._ College athletes graduate at a rate 1 to 2 percent higher than the general student body.

7. Student-athletes develop critical skills, such as:

- Character development
- Goal-setting
- Responsibility
- Time management
- Camaraderie
- Teamwork
- Leadership
- Discipline
- Commitment
- Self-reliance
- Cultural awareness
- Competitiveness
- Reliability
- Enthusiasm
- Hard work
- Ability to work under pressure
- Confidence
- Communication
- Loyalty

8. A survey of CEOs found that 100 percent of employers would be more likely to hire a student-athlete than a non-student-athlete. And 60 percent would hire a student-athlete with a lower grade-point average than a non-student-athlete with an A-average.

9. The student-athlete carries with her a network of friends and a commonality that can be leveraged for career and life opportunities.

10. Student-athletes build successful life habits such as proper nutrition and exercise!

11. It's never too early for children to start playing sports. Regardless of how old or young an athlete is, athletics can help a student learn to:

- Deal with authority
- Lose gracefully and win graciously
- Manage conflict and become a team player
- Have personal responsibility
- Develop leadership skills
- Value hard work
- Set goals
- Manage time effectively
- Benefit from the wisdom of mentors and role models

HISTORY OF
COLLEGE RECRUITING

IN 1852, HARVARD UNIVERSITY received a challenge from Yale University's boat club to "test the superiority of the oarsmen of the two colleges." This event marked the beginning of intercollegiate athletic competition in the United States, and on August 3, 1852, collegiate sports were borne when Harvard's *Oneida* crew beat Yale's *Shawmut* by two boat lengths.

This event marked a cultural change in academia: Sports emerged as a signature of a college's reputation and a source of its pride. In 1859, Amherst College beat Williams College by a landslide thirty-four points in the first intercollegiate baseball game. The first soccer match was a decade later, and in 1874, Harvard beat McGill University in the first game of football.

By the 1930s, the trend was rampant. Recognizing the importance of sports, college athletic programs were recruiting with gung-ho enthusiasm. Coaches recruited athletes with the sole intention of restricting their competitors' access to talented athletes, and it was not uncommon for a college team to have one hundred new freshmen as athletes. This Wild West attitude created a clear separation of the *haves* from the *have nots* whereby a small number of college teams housed all the athletes. The bigger the school's budget, the more athletes it could confiscate.

With such large numbers of athletes sitting on the bench, only a select few of these athletes were awarded opportunities to play, and few women and minorities were recruited, if any at all.

Clearly, the rules had to change. The playing field was not level.

By the 1950s, the National Collegiate Athletic Association (NCAA), the National Association of Intercollegiate Athletics (NAIA), and the National Junior College Athletic Association (NJCAA) emerged as leaders in the field of collegiate sports' regulation. These organizations began dictating the rules for fair competition in recruiting, limiting the number of new recruits a school could have, as well as the methods a coach could use to recruit new student-athletes.

In 1972, Title IX of the Educational Amendments was enacted, mandating the following:

"No person in the United States shall, on the basis of sex, be excluded from participation in, be denied the benefits of, or be subjected to discrimination under any education program or activity receiving Federal financial assistance."

President Carter in 1976 would interpret Title IX to mean, among other things, that athletic opportunities must be substantially proportionate to the student enrollment. If 40 percent of the student body was female, 40 percent of athletic opportunities must be for women.

These regulatory bodies—the NCAA, NJCAA, NAIA, and Title IX—changed the face of sports, creating greater opportunities for a more diverse student body. From 1981 until 2006, the number of student-athletes under the purview of the NCAA increased by 65 percent, and the number of teams by 51 percent. The number of female athletes more than doubled: 74,239 women played NCAA sports in the 1981-1982 school year; by the 2005-2006 school year, this figure increased to 172,469.

NCAA ATHLETIC OPPORTUNITIES:
1981-82 SCHOOL YEAR COMPARED TO 2005-06 SCHOOL YEAR

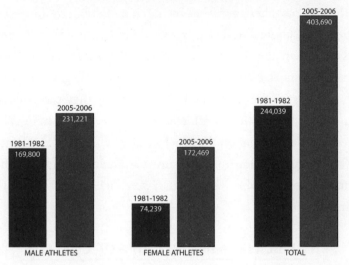

Source: *NCAA Executive Summary: 1981-82—2005-06 NCAA Sports Sponsorship and Participation Rates Report*

While the opportunities for student-athletes have increased, one thing has never changed: College coaches are hungry to identify and secure the best student-athletes before competition sweeps in. With restrictions on the number of spots per team and facing greater competition, every college coach has a different angle for quickly identifying, evaluating, and securing student-athletes. Though this new environment might indicate that recruiting is becoming easier for the student-athlete, the reverse is true. Coaches play a confusing game. They cast the net wide, showing interest in as many athletes as possible in hopes of whittling the candidates down to the best of the best. They attract attention from as many student-athletes as possible, only to leave the bulk of these athletes in the cold come Signing Day.

Unfortunately, this hungry and hurried attempt to secure athletes is not patient, organized, or consistent. Coupled with a large number of athletes to sort through, coaches are rushed by the tremendous amount of competition from rival schools. Add to this a turnover of more than 30 percent of coaches each year, and the process is riddled with giant cracks. With variables based on sport, coach, division, and school, colleges and universities find talent as fast as they can and in whatever way they can. To make sure a coach notices them, student-athletes must also cast the net wide and do whatever they can to land on the coach's radar, wherever it is pointed.

Before discussing *how* to make sure a student-athlete is on the radar, let us take a look at the *who, what, where, when,* and *why* of college recruiting.

WHO ARE THE PLAYERS IN THE GAME OF COLLEGE ATHLETIC RECRUITING?

The athletes competing in the game of recruiting include students not only from cities across the nation, but also from countries across the world. The competition for spots on college teams has never been stronger. Over 7.3 million high school children are involved in sports in the U.S. alone, with millions more playing in other countries. Just look at the Final Four of the 2008 NCAA Men's Basketball Tournament for a sample of the foreign student-athletes competing at the highest level of collegiate athletics. Among the countries represented in the Final Four were Russia (Kansas University's Sasha Kaun), Africa (UCLA's Alfred Aboya and Luc Richard Mbah a Moute), and Serbia (UCLA's Nikola Dragovic). Southern Methodist University's twenty-member swim team roster included nine students from abroad in the 2007-2008 school year, and DePaul University's tennis team had only two American players. At Arizona State University, four of the five starters on the women's golf team were foreign.

Clearly, in this competitive environment, it takes more than athletic ability and luck to land a coveted spot on a college team. To win the game of recruiting, athletes must understand the rules and know how to play so they can bypass the competition. *Athletes Wanted* will help you understand who governs the world of college recruiting, providing an intimate look at the rules and regulations specified by the respective governing body.

Depending on the college, three associations preside over the rules of college recruiting:

- **The National Collegiate Athletic Association (NCAA) is** the world's largest collegiate athletic association, governing the athletic programs of more than one thousand colleges and universities and more than 400,000 student-athletes. The NCAA provides different recruiting, scholarship, and academic standards for each of the three NCAA-designated categories: Division I, Division II, and Division III schools.

- **The National Association of Intercollegiate Athletics (NAIA)** comprises about 280 colleges and universities overseeing about forty-five thousand student-athletes. NAIA schools are separated into Division I and Division II. Generally, NAIA schools are smaller with lower budgets than their NCAA counterparts.

- **The National Junior College Athletic Association (NJCAA)** provides the rules and regulations for approximately five hundred junior colleges and fifty thousand student-athletes.

As well, thirty-five thousand college coaches are involved in the recruiting process, not to mention the guidance counselors, high school coaches, academic tutors, and parents who play critical roles in the recruiting process by acting as a student-athlete's support staff.

WHAT IS COLLEGE RECRUITING?

The answer to this question depends on the person you ask. Every coach, every school, every sport, and every division is different. For some, college recruiting is the process of sending a questionnaire to hundreds or thousands of athletes, and then sorting through the responses. For schools with big budgets, college recruiting means purchasing lists of the top-ranked high school and middle school athletes. Some coaches attend club tournaments, others send letters to high school coaches looking for recommendations, and still others subscribe to recruiting services and scouting services. Some make a ton of phone calls, and others make home visits. Though some sort through hours and hours of tapes and DVDs, many savvy and progressive coaches rely on enhanced streaming videos that spot-shadow the athlete and sequence best plays in high-definition quality. Some use a combination of techniques, including emails, social networking websites, and new technology offered through the National Collegiate Scouting Association.

The biggest complication of the college recruiting system is that no standard system exists. No one can define exactly what recruiting looks like. Because budgets, coaches, and programs are varied, the recruiting process is haphazard: College recruiting is twenty different things. Just when a coach's recruiting system becomes identifiable, the coach, like more than 30 percent of the nation's coaches each year, transfers schools, changes positions, or retires, creating a hole a new coach will fill, revamping the school's entire recruiting system!

«« FAST FACT ««

A program's recruiting process is most often a direct reflection of the coaching staff's history. The relationships they built in the past help them identify potential future prospects. For example, University of Illinois's head football coach, Ron Zook, formerly coached at the University of Florida; his former offensive coordinator, Mike Locksley, is from Washington D.C. Under their direction, the team at the University of Illinois had twenty-one players from D.C. and Florida.

Complicating matters is a huge discrepancy in recruiting budgets. Only fourteen Division I colleges have more than $1 million to divide among all their programs to locate talented student-athletes. If a superstar athlete from North Dakota wants to play for Florida A&M University, the recruiting pipelines might be clogged by A&M's less-than-desirable $50,000 recruiting budget, which it divides among all men's and women's athletic teams.

Consider the statistics:

- About fifty of the nation's Division I colleges and universities have recruiting budgets of less than $100,000. Only twenty-two Division II and III schools have more than $100,000 earmarked for recruiting. These budgets are then split among all the school's athletic programs, which might include men's and women's tennis teams, swim teams, golf programs, football, basketball, lacrosse, baseball, and the like.

- Though Title IX effectively increased opportunities for women, women's teams most often receive a disproportionate percentage of a college or university's recruiting budget, with only about 7 percent of Division I schools offering at least half of the recruiting budget to women's teams.

- The average college coach has less than $500 to recruit athletes.

Two things are certain about college recruiting. First, the process changes from school-to-school, coach-to-coach, and sport-to-sport. Second, all recruiting systems rely on personal interaction with the student-athlete. Since colleges have limited budgets and limited personal relationships with high school coaches, student-athletes must take the initiative, casting a wide enough net to be noticed, no matter what a coach's specific recruiting system looks like.

WHERE DO COLLEGES FIND TALENT?

The recruiting process varies by sport, institution, program, and coach. As such, college coaches find talent through a variety of sources, including:

- **Purchased lists from reliable sources, including student-athlete scouting services**—In football, Tom Lemming's *Prep Football Report* is considered one of the top sources of high school talent. Lemming travels thousands of miles each year to identify the best high school ball players, and some football coaches recruit exclusively from this list. Rich Kern does the same for volleyball. And the Collegiate Sports Data is a comprehensive list of the nation's top athletes.

    Depending on the sport and level, coaches use a variety of national, local, and even international lists, such as Rob Meurs's international scouting report, which includes the statistics of top players in Europe, Africa, and Asia. Scouting services such as the National Collegiate Scouting Association, Randy Taylor Recruiting, and Bob Gibbons All Star Report (basketball), find the nation's talent, rating prospects on ability and potential. Colleges subscribe to these services to save time and identify talented athletes early. College programs with large recruiting budgets often subscribe to dozens of local, national, and international lists and information services.

Most student-athletes identified by these lists are tracked and begin receiving recruiting letters as freshmen. The athletes who do not appear on the relevant lists must do more work on their own.

- **Recruiting services**—With limited time and budgets, especially in a tight economy, college coaches are becoming increasingly dependent on assistance from recruiting services with verified scouting reports. Recruiting services are similar to scouting services with one major distinction: Student-athletes hire recruiting services such as the NCSA, College Prospects of America, College Sports of America, and the National Scouting Report to promote the athletes to coaches.

»« FAST FACT «»

Scouting services and recruiting services both provide college coaches with lists of student-athletes, but they do have one major difference. Scouting services are hired by college coaches to find talent while recruiting services are hired by student-athletes to promote the student.

- **Recruiting websites**—Internet-based sites and databases are now available to college coaches and are growing in popularity. These, coupled with video services, create video libraries to which colleges can subscribe to view high school athletes' highlight or skills videos. Other databases and video services include the NCSA Recruit Match and Be Recruited. Some coaches turn to popular social networking sites like Facebook.com or TAKKLE.com to attract student-athletes to a program, as well as media sites like Rivals.com and Scout.com, which are used primarily to track recruitment and rank of the nation's most highly recruited athletes. These sites are visited primarily by college sports' fanatics to see how their favorite teams are doing in the recruiting wars.

»« FAST FACT »«

College coaches find value in websites that verify data. The rule of thumb is this: If any athlete can join a website, a college coach will be less likely to use the website. The more verification requirements necessary, the more likely the college coach will use the website.

- **Athlete-initiated communication**—Direct contact via phone or in-person visit is the best way for students to develop personal relationships with coaches. Students—not parents—who initiate relationships with coaches or submit questionnaires on a college program's web page increase the chances of getting on that coach's radar.

- **Incoming "mom and pop" mail packages**—Coupled with athlete-initiated communication, a targeted mail campaign can be effective, especially when the coach requests the athlete's résumé and highlight or skills video.

Smaller programs sometimes rely on this source of information, but the bigger the program is, the less likely it is to rely on unsolicited packages. Randy Taylor, former recruiting coordinator for UCLA, said that some coaches will ask their graduate assistants to sort through packages to identify "walk-on" prospects or to be sure a prospect does not slip through the cracks.

- **Mailers**—Some coaches send thousands of questionnaires to candidates, assuming that those who do not respond are not interested. (Coaches can send these at any time in the recruiting process.) Questionnaires narrow the pool into a more manageable size. If a student-athlete does not receive a letter from a college coach accompanied by an athlete questionnaire, the athlete is most likely not on that school's initial recruiting list.

- **Tournaments, clubs, camps, and combines**—Some college coaches will attend or host tournaments and camps in hopes of evaluating student-athletes. Most often, coaches do not discover talent at these tournaments; instead, they are given an opportunity to evaluate students already on their radar. That said, coaches who attend these camps, tournaments, club events, and combines might purchase lists of attendees to add to their mailing list. Coaches often place the names of underclassmen attending tournaments, clubs, camps, and combines on a list of student-athletes to watch.

- **Recruiting education programs**—Offered by clubs, high school programs, camps, and top combines, recruiting education programs provide student-athletes, high school coaches, and parents with information about the collegiate recruiting programs. Often, coaches add the names of attendants to their initial mailing lists or cross-reference with their active recruiting list.

Recruiting education programs are a new trend that emerged due to the constant changes in the recruiting process and the NCAA rules. To keep students, parents, and high school and club coaches abreast of changes and developments, more and more high schools hire educational consultants to provide workshops. The Nike and U.S. Army All-American combines, which feature five hundred of the country's best football players, have both implemented recruiting education into their curriculum, hiring former college coaches and experts to teach families, students, and high school and club coaches about the rules of the recruiting game. These programs also provide an opportunity for college coaches to collect information for initial scouting evaluations.

- **Other trusted sources**—College coaches may turn to trusted referral sources, such as alumni, club coaches, or high school coaches with a long history of recruiting involvement and success, to identify students for their mailing lists.

  Because the rules and methods of recruiting swing so wide, the key to a student-athlete's success is to become known by as many sources as possible. The plain fact is this: Recruiting changes so rapidly, with competition popping up from every corner, that a family's awareness and involvement in the process is critical to a student-athlete's future.

> **«« FAST FACT ««**
> While a recruiting coordinator at Notre Dame, Bob Chmiel only recruited student-athletes who appeared in at least four of the national publications to which he subscribed.

WHEN SHOULD A STUDENT-ATHLETE GET STARTED?

Student-athletes should start early if they want to be considered in the running. Hundreds of students have been offered scholarships as early as the seventh or eighth grade, like Michael Avery, a 6'4" guard from Ascension Middle School in Thousand Oaks, CA, who received a verbal scholarship offer from Billy Gillespie, head basketball coach at the University of Kentucky, before he even walked through the doors of a high school.

Due to more aggressive recruiting strategies, most major college programs have been forced to start the recruiting process one or two years earlier than in years past. If student-athletes are not starting the game early enough, they can trust their competitors are!

«« FAST FACT ««

A survey by the National Collegiate Scouting Association (NCSA) of more than one thousand college coaches found that 84 percent of all coaches identify prospects during or before the end of the athlete's sophomore year.

WHY DO COLLEGES RECRUIT?

Athletics have always been used to boost awareness of colleges and universities, and when Title IX was adopted in 1972, women's sports strengthened this vehicle of creating publicity. Homecoming games, fundraising boosters, front-page headlines, and ESPN highlights have become great branding opportunities for colleges and universities. Even Division III games are staples of ESPN and local affiliates.

Today's college athlete and athletic programs have been overhauled so that the student-athlete is now noticed by coaches, professors, and employers as a hard working, motivated, and success-oriented individual. The NCAA, the organization charged with the oversight of the majority of college athletic programs, has set rigorous standards to assure student-athletes do not fall prey to college programs that focus only on athletics. The NCAA has adopted an academic progress rate (APR) that tracks the success of a team by the number of student-athletes it graduates. If a team's APR does not meet NCAA standards, the school's ability to award athletic scholarships is restricted. As such, not only does the student-athlete contribute to the student body's coffers, exposure, and public relations, but he also develops character that makes him wanted by academia and employers.

Successful student-athletes act as human billboards for those colleges and universities that trained them. Former athletes who become business-people, doctors, lawyers, teachers, and even professional athletes give years of positive public relations and brand affiliation to their alumni, donating to the schools' fundraising ability. The NCAA has even adopted a public service announcement noting that "almost all student-athletes are going pro in something other than sports."

KEY POINTS

1. With restrictions from the NCAA, NJCAA, and NAIA on the number of students and when they can be recruited, college coaches frantically search for athletes during small windows of opportunity. This, coupled with the lack of consistency in recruiting methods, has created giant cracks in the system through which many otherwise-qualified athletes fall.

2. The average college coach has a recruiting budget of less than $500.

3. No standard recruiting system exists. Coaches find student-athletes through a variety of sources.

4. The responsibility falls primarily on student-athletes and their parents. Because the rules and methods of recruiting swing so wide, the key to success is the student-athletes' ability to become known by as many sources as possible.

5. The earlier student-athletes begin promoting themselves, the better. In fact, some student-athletes receive verbal scholarship offers as early as their seventh-grade years.

»« FAST FACT »«
Eighty-four percent of verbal scholarship offers are extended before the end of an athlete's sophomore year.

THE *HOW TO* GUIDE DURING HIGH SCHOOL

BY NOW, YOU KNOW *why* a student should be an athlete—sports will open the doors to opportunities, help make college affordable, create critical skills, build character, and strengthen networks. Next comes the question of *how* to leverage athletics.

During high school, students will begin maneuvering through the world of collegiate recruiting, dedicating hundreds of hours to promoting their athletic abilities. They will buy uniforms, pay for camps and clubs, and spend hard-earned money traveling to and from out-of-town games.

At times, this might seem like a huge expenditure, but the return on investment in an athlete's future is even bigger. The National Collegiate Scouting Association reports that high school student-athletes who compete in college win on average more than $15,500 a year in scholarships, grants, and financial aid to play sports at a collegiate level for four or five years at public or private schools. At the upper end of the scale, athletes receive $200,000 in scholarships and grants-in-aid—not bad considering the average college student graduates with more than $25,000 in debt.

A student and parent's investment in athletics continues to pay later in life, as well. As reported by *The Game of Life: College Sports and Educational Values* (Princeton University Press, 2002), athletes earned 15 percent more than their non-athlete counterparts upon graduating.

«« FAST FACT ««

Among the most overlooked opportunities are those at Division III programs. Student-athletes and their parents miss out because they fall prey to the technicality that Division III programs do not offer athletic scholarships. While this is true, it is also a technicality. Division III schools offer grants-in-aid and non-athletic scholarships that often make the cost of attending less than that at their Division I and II counterparts. Of all the divisions, Division III has the largest number of athletic programs and the highest concentration of top-ranked academic programs.

Some parents think that opportunities are reserved for only elite athletes, and indeed, some opportunities are. More than seven million high school athletes of both genders are vying for only about $1.4 billion awarded in athletic scholarships. If this pot were awarded proportionately, each of the nation's athletes would receive less than $200 to help pay for tuition. Only about 6.76 percent of high school athletes will play at a college level, and only 1.68 percent will receive a full or partial athletic scholarship to an NCAA-affiliated school. Only 0.98 percent will make the cut to play on a Division I college team.

But guess what isn't a Division I school? Williams College. Neither is Amherst, or countless other colleges that offer world-class education. Only about 15 percent of collegiate athletic opportunities are at the Division I level. More opportunities are available through Division II and III schools, NAIA programs, and junior colleges.

And while athletes might have their eyes turned toward big-name programs, they might find that the smaller programs offer bigger opportunities and more prestige. The smaller programs are often a much better fit, both academically and athletically. Consider, for instance, the University of

Chicago and Chicago State University. One is a Division I school, one is a Division III school. One is consistently ranked among the top fifty universities in the country by *U.S. News & World Report*. The other is not.

Guess which is which?

You might be surprised. The University of Chicago, a Division III school, shows up ninth on *U.S. News & World Report*'s 2008 list of the best colleges. Chicago State University, a Division I school, does not make *U.S. News & World Report*'s top 50 percent of colleges.

Earlier, you learned about average athletes who attended world-class universities, elite athletes who turned down Division I offers to attend smaller, more intimate schools, and great athletes who flew under the radar and were passed over simply because they did not know how to play the collegiate recruiting game.

Opportunities are available, regardless of an athlete's level, but the opportunities might pass by if students and their parents do not learn how to play the recruitment game. If parents and their athletes learn how to play the game, they can position a student-athlete for success, not only in athletics, but also in academics, relationships, career, and life.

Before we begin discussing the *how to's*, consider two things:

1. The rules change depending on whether a student-athlete is in high demand. Contrary to popular belief, most high school athletes do not choose the school they attend. The schools choose them. Because only a select few of heavily recruited athletes have multiple schools fighting for them, most students are given an opportunity to play at only a handful of schools from which they must find the best fit. Throughout, we will discuss how students who are heavily recruited, lightly recruited, or not-at-all recruited can leverage their talent for eventual success. Specifically, see Chapter 1 and Chapter 2. As well, to determine a student-athlete's level of recruitment, visit www.athleteswanted.org and complete the

Recruiting Action Plan questionnaire (RAP). Based on a athlete's level of recruitment, this questionnaire also provides action steps that can help build the necessary relationships with college coaches to earn scholarship dollars.

2.   The rules change depending on how early or late in the process an athlete starts. Because most parents, athletes, and high school and club coaches do not start the process until an athlete is in high school, the rest of this book assumes that the athlete is in the ninth, tenth, eleventh, or twelfth grade, unless otherwise noted. However, college recruiting can start while a student is in junior high school, and the NCAA course requirements start the moment a child begins taking classes his freshman year. As we discussed earlier, a student-athlete's involvement in sports and dedication to goal-setting can start when that child is in elementary school.

COACH'S TIP

Complete the Recruiting Action Plan questionnaire (RAP) at www.athleteswanted.org for specific steps a student can take to increase his level of recruitment based on his sport and grade level.

With this in mind, parents and coaches of young athletes can help by preparing children for future collegiate athletic careers in elementary or junior high school, whenever possible. Even something as simple as picking out the correct core classes before high school can make the difference between winning and losing the game of recruiting.

If a student-athlete is in elementary or junior high, preparing for her college career when she cannot even drive a car might seem strange. But remember that top student-athletes are given verbal scholarships as early as their seventh-grade years in junior high school. College coaches, who know their jobs and salaries are tied to a team's ability to win, are hungry to secure talented athletes, so they start looking early, hoping they can snatch the best athletes before a competing school sneaks in and scoops talent away. Though it is not impossible for student-athletes to start during their senior year, most recruiters start looking at students the minute they begin as freshmen. Five of the top seven basketball players graduating in 2010 gave verbal commitments in the spring of their sophomore year.

As well, most athletes can confirm that they started dreaming of college careers early. I knew in the fourth grade, so setting goals was appropriate when I was nine.

In short, it is never too early to get a child started on the path, and the earlier the better, especially since only limited students are offered scholarships. The more student-athletes practice their skills, and the more experience they have for exposure, the better chance they will have of being recruited by the college of their choice.

COACH'S TIP

Parents and athletes should start learning the game of recruiting as early as possible, said Chris Ducar, the women's soccer coach for the top-ranked University of North Carolina. Ducar starts the recruiting process with this year's pool of the top seventh and eighth graders.

Leveraging statistics from thousands of student-athletes who have made the leap from high school to college in twenty-five different sports, the following chapters provide realistic advice on:

- Evaluating an athlete's potential to play in college;

- Positioning a student to build relationships with coaches;

- Becoming educated on opportunities; and

- Ultimately finding a college that not only allows a student to play sports, but also earns a child a top quality education that opens doors after college.

Remember that student-athletes cannot redo the recruiting process. They cannot take a mulligan. The recruiting process is a once-in-lifetime experience that requires both the parents and the students to jump in full-steam ahead.

High school consists of only about 720 days. How will the student-athlete make the most of this small window of opportunity?

KEY POINTS

__1.__   Almost 85 percent of collegiate athletic opportunities are available through Division II and III schools, NAIA programs, and junior colleges.

__2.__   The rules of the game change depending on whether an athlete is highly recruited, moderately recruited, lightly recruited, or not-at-all recruited. To determine a student-athlete's level of recruitment, complete the Recruiting Action Plan questionnaire (RAP) at www.athleteswanted.org.

__3.__   The rules of the game change depending on how early or late in the process the athlete starts, as well as the sport the student-athlete plays. For sport- and time-specific information, complete the RAP questionnaire at www.athleteswanted.org.

__4.__   It is never too early to start packaging a student for recruitment. Some coaches start recruiting students as young as the seventh or eighth grade.

RECRUITING TIMELINE

THROUGHOUT THIS BOOK, you will learn that a student's ability to be recruited will be based on:

- Character.

- Athletic ability, athletic profile (size, strength, speed, skill), and "projectability" (the athlete's expected future potential).

- Academics, which include coursework, GPA, ACT/SAT, and class ranking.

- Work ethic (which applies to academics and athletics).

- Desire to compete.

- Willingness to travel wide and far to play at a college level.

- Willingness to consider playing for any level college (Division I, II, III, NAIA, or junior college).

The stronger student-athletes are in each of these seven areas, the more likely they will be recruited, and the more leverage they will have for negotiating for a bigger scholarship package to the school of their choice, as discussed in Chapter 9. Though all seven of these are critical, they are far less important than the eighth criterion:

- **The student-athlete's ability to play the game of college recruiting.**

Remember: The best offers do not necessarily go to the best all-around candidates. Sometimes, the best offers go to the student who knows how to best play the game of recruiting. Just being a good student-athlete does not mean that a student will receive a scholarship offer.

The key to a successful recruiting process is knowing what to do and when and how to do it. Too many parents and students get lost in the shuffle. They had no recruiting plan, failed to complete the homework, and did not play the game of recruiting. Signing Day comes and goes, and they are left scratching their heads.

«« FAST FACT ««

Also known as National Letter of Intent (NLI) Day, "Signing Day" is a specific date set by the Collegiate Commissions Association in which a student-athlete, an athlete's parent, and an athletic director sign an "Inter-Conference Letter of Intent" binding a student-athlete to a specific university or college. Generally, the athletic director will also indicate the type and amount of financial aid being extended to the student. Once a student-athlete has signed an NLI, other universities and colleges must stop recruiting the student. Different sports have different signing days, and some sports have early signing dates and final signing dates.

This section will serve as a basic timeline of activities in four categories—academics, recruiting, competition, and summer activities. Keep in mind that recruiting starts the minute a student enters high school as a freshman, and preparation can start even earlier.

PRE-HIGH SCHOOL

The pre-high school years are preparatory years student-athletes can use to develop habits and character traits that will help them earn a spot on a college team. Goal-setting, dedication, and time management are all learned skills a young athlete can use to move forward.

During eighth grade or earlier, a student should check out the core course requirements and create a list that ensures these general courses will be fulfilled during high school years. More information on selecting core courses, as well as the NCAA's List of Approved Core Courses (also known as Form 48H), can be found at www.athleteswanted.org.

Be sure, too, that a student-athlete's sport is offered at the local high school. If a student-athlete plays football or basketball, the high school likely offers this sport, but what about lacrosse or swimming? Some smaller schools may not have these programs, which means the student should consider attending a different school, or search aggressively for club opportunities.

But most importantly, this can be the beginning of a student-athlete's relationship with the high school coach. Prior to high school, the student-athlete should visit the high school coach and ask about the coach's philosophy and expectations. Student-athletes might ask questions like:

- *What is the school's history of producing athletes who go on to college and play on an athletic scholarship?*

- *What do I need to do to earn play-time or to start?*

- *How quickly do your athletes generally move up to varsity?*

- *What is your style of play?*

- *What are your views on being a multiple sport athlete?*

- *What club opportunities are available?*

- *What is the policy on getting game videos?*

- *What is the program's recruiting philosophy?*

- *Who is responsible for recruiting?*

- *What specifically do the coach and athletic program do to promote the student-athletes to college programs?*

- *Does the athletic department provide recruiting education?*

When asking these questions, the student-athlete should have two objectives in mind. First, by uncovering information early in the process, the student-athlete will develop a plan for future success and avoid hurdles down the road. By setting clear expectations early, the student-athlete will not be disappointed later. Second, an athlete's high school coaching staff can make or break the student when a college coach calls for a recommendation prior to extending an offer. By expressing an interest in a successful high school athletics career, a young student-athlete can begin the critical processes of goal-setting and of establishing deep and memorable relationships with high school coaches.

ADVICE FOR PARENTS
OF YOUNG CHILDREN
SERIOUS ABOUT ATHLETICS

Augie Maurelli, Georgetown University's director of strength and conditioning, said a parent should look to make his child stronger and faster. But when is it "too early" to start lifting weights? And outside of natural talent, what can be done?

Maurelli suggests starting strength training in the fourth grade, but he cautions parents to make sure it is supervised.

"First, parents need to realize that biological age and physical age do not always coincide," said Maurelli.

If a parent wants to see whether a child can begin strength training, the child should have a complete evaluation by a certified strength specialist who can tell a parent where the child is developmentally.

"Generally speaking, in the fourth grade, a child can always improve speed mechanics, improve flexibility, and build coordination. Take care of motor coordination and motor patterns first, then functional strength, then maximal strength, in that order. By doing that, a child will build good habits progressively through his pre-collegiate career."

Consider also taking young children to high school games so they can begin to see what they need to do to compete at a higher level.

FRESHMAN YEAR

Academics

Student-athletes should make sure they are taking the right classes by reviewing lists of approved core courses. Athletes should check with the guidance office and research the NCAA and NAIA guidelines. Visit www. athleteswanted.org for the NCAA's List of Approved Core Courses (also known as Form 48H).

Enough emphasis cannot be placed on the importance of good grades for student-athletes. Though collegiate athletes have a reputation for being less than stellar students, this reputation is undeserved in today's environment. Today's college athletic programs have been overhauled to require athletes to achieve rigorous academic standards. The NCAA has even adopted an academic progress rate (APR) that tracks the success of a team by the number of student-athletes it graduates. If a team's APR does not meet the NCAA's standards, the school's ability to award athletic scholarships is restricted. Coaches, fearful of having crucial scholarship monies taken away, are not interested in recruiting students who cannot maintain the minimum required grade-point average.

Students should set SMART academic goals before the first day of high school to maintain at least the minimum grade-point average. In truth, students should try to exceed this minimum by as much as possible. Every tenth of a point will make a difference when negotiating for a scholarship. The higher a student-athlete's GPA, the larger the base of universities willing to recruit him, and the more he will stand out from the crowd.

Student-athletes should know:

- The minimum grade-point average requirements for their favorite colleges.

- The core course requirements (totaling sixteen credits) they must complete while in high school to satisfy the NCAA requirements for playing collegiate level sports in Division I and II, though Division III and NAIA might have different requirements. They should know this before walking through the doors as freshmen. Having this knowledge upfront will position student-athletes for more immediate fulfillment of these requirements. See www.athleteswanted.org for more information about core course requirements.

An athlete's freshman year sets the stage for the remainder of high school. By getting good grades now, a student will not be forced to play catch up as a sophomore, junior, or senior.

High School and Additional Athletic Competition

In addition to setting academic goals, student-athletes should start setting goals that specify what they would like to accomplish to become better athletes. Now is the time for student-athletes to develop a strong work ethic and commitment to their sport, even if they are not varsity athletes as freshmen.

Students should talk to their coaches to identify areas where improvement is needed. They might want to consider finding weight training, speed, and/or conditioning programs to steadily improve their athleticism. Do not forget about the opportunities to play outside of the high school programs in clubs or camps.

Athletes should follow the blueprints of those they want to emulate. Different programs have different guidelines, so athletes should understand the benchmarks associated with each program. When I was a child, I reviewed the recruiting section of the paper every year and learned how big, strong, and fast the Division I-recruited linebackers were. I memorized the statistics: 6'2", 220 pounds, and a 4.7-second 40-yard dash. I knew that this—the DNA of the Division I linebacker—was where I needed to be to have a shot at recruitment. A Division II linebacker had less stringent guidelines: 6'0", 210 pounds, and a 4.8-second 40-yard dash.

Every sport has objective numbers than can be used to determine how an athlete compares to the rest of the world—invaluable information for setting realistic goals. See www.athleteswanted.org for sport-specific benchmarks that will help gauge a student-athlete's ability and goals.

COACH'S TIP

Student-athletes should shake hands with the opposing coach after every game, regardless of whether they win or lose. Coaches from rival schools usually have a hand in naming the all-conference, all-area, and all-state teams, so a student-athlete should be respectful of rival coaches and conduct himself with class. As well, a college coach might have a relationship with a high school coach from a rival school. If an athlete makes a positive impression on every high school coach, the athlete's chances of being recruited increase.

Recruiting

An athlete can never begin the recruiting process too early or receive too much assistance. A child becomes a prospective college athlete upon entering high school and might begin receiving some correspondence from colleges and universities.

Though Division I and II college coaches cannot call underclassmen, they can send questionnaires, camp brochures, and general admissions material. A student's commitment to reply to all correspondences is extremely important as it allows the student-athlete to get or stay on the college coaches' radars.

An athlete who does not receive mailings during her freshman year should not worry. While this **does** mean that the student-athlete is not included in the small cadre of athletes recruited at the elite level (fewer than 1 percent), the process is still early. Student-athletes should take the

Initial Target List

College Name					
Location					
Distance From Home					
Nearest Major City/Airport					
Tuition					
Setting (Urban vs. Rural)					
Size					
Major Offered					
Fraternities/Sororities					
Division					
Conference					
Notes On Coach					
Perceived Playing Time					
Notes On Team					
General Notes					

initiative by contacting coaches and asking for admissions material and questionnaires, which can be found on most college websites. In doing so, the athlete's name will likely be added to that coach's recruitment list as long as the athlete submits questionnaires from programs that are realistic both athletically and academically.

In particular, an athlete might want to concentrate on those schools that are on student-athlete's Initial Target List, a register of schools that have made their way onto the athlete's radar early in the process. This list, which can be downloaded from www.athleteswanted.org, represents a starting point for an athlete's recruiting efforts.

Student-athletes should start building relationships with Division III and NAIA coaches, who are not restricted from initiating phone calls to or returning phone calls from freshmen. (Most are too busy recruiting juniors and seniors to initiate calls, but they will enthusiastically return or accept incoming calls from interested freshmen.) Even if student-athletes have their eyes set on a Division I or II school, communicating with coaches from Division III, NAIA, and junior colleges early in the process allows them to develop and practice their communication skills. As well, because these coaches are not restricted from communicating with underclassmen, student-athletes will have a much easier time getting in touch with coaches from Division III, NAIA, and junior colleges.

> ## «« FAST FACT ««
>
> Though Division I and II coaches cannot call freshmen, Division III, NAIA, and junior college coaches can. Student-athletes should connect with these coaches as freshmen. Even if student-athletes have their eyes set on a Division I or II school, communicating with coaches from Division III, NAIA, and junior colleges early in the process allows them to develop and practice their communication and relationship-building skills.

Do not assume that the rule prohibiting Division I and II coaches from calling a student-athlete is reciprocal. A huge loophole in the rules allows a ton of recruiting to take place during the freshman and sophomore year so long as the student-athlete initiates the communication. This is the loophole that allows elite-level recruits to receive offers during their freshman or sophomore year. Regardless of level, a student-athlete can use this loophole to develop relationships early in the game.

If a student calls a Division I or II coach, the coach can accept the phone call at any time! Though a Division I or II coach cannot return a phone call from a freshman or sophomore athlete, the coach might answer the phone, giving the student-athlete an invaluable opportunity to get an early foot in the door. Taking advantage of this loophole gives athletes the competitive edge.

Regardless of whether they are in contact with Division I, II, III, NAIA, or junior college coaches, student-athletes should work to foster these relationships by keeping the coaches updated through emails, letters, or phone calls.

Ideally, a student-athlete will develop relationships with many different coaches as a freshman. The details of each conversation and correspondence might be hard to remember, so a student-athlete should keep a Correspondence Log (download a template at www.athleteswanted.org) to track interactions with coaches.

«« FAST FACT ««

The NCAA annually updates its regulations on when and how coaches can contact student-athletes, so review the *NCAA Guide for the College-Bound Student-Athlete* and refer to Chapter 5.

Summer Activities

Student-athletes should plan at least one unofficial visit to meet a coach at a local college campus. If that athlete is targeting Division I or II colleges and universities, he should set up at least two unofficial visits during the summer following freshman year. Keep in mind that unless he is playing varsity sports, Division I and II coaches will likely not be interested in meeting with the student-athlete. Instead, the athlete should focus on Division III and NAIA coaches. (See Chapter 6.)

An athlete should call at least six college coaches: two should be from Division III and NAIA "backup" schools, two from schools likely to recruit the athlete, and two from top picks. (See Chapter 5.) Depending on whether the athlete is a varsity player, he might consider asking the following questions during unofficial visits or telephone calls with coaches:

- *What would I need to do to earn an opportunity to compete for your program?*

- *Am I on your recruiting list, and if not, how do I make your recruiting list?*

- *What GPA do I need to attend your program? What about my ACT/SAT score?*

- *Have you had a chance to see me play? If not, would you like to see my highlight or skills DVD?* (This question is most suited if the student-athlete plays varsity.)

- *What would I need to do to be offered an official visit to your school?* (Again, this question is appropriate only if the athlete plays varsity.)

Student-athletes should be prepared to answer questions the coach might ask as well. Be aware that college coaches might make verbal scholarship offers to top student-athletes who are freshmen or sophomores. If these students fail to initiate calls, however, the coach will have no way of communicating with them, and opportunities will pass by.

Following is the freshman student-athlete's recruiting checklist. This checklist can be downloaded from www.athleteswanted.org.

KEY CODE
Red: Mission critical!   **Grey:** Proactive communication with college coach needed.

The Freshman Student-Athlete's Recruiting Checklist		
COMPLETED?	**WHEN?**	**ACADEMICS**
	Fall	Order or download and print a copy of the *NCAA Guide for the College-Bound Student-Athlete* and read thoroughly.
	Fall	Use Division I core course worksheet inside *NCAA Guide* to set specific academic goals and plan the core course schedule. (www.athleteswanted.org). Use the Division I worksheet, even if you do not expect to play Division I athletics. After all, things might change!
	Fall	Meet with high school guidance counselor to inform him/her of your goal to play college athletics and to review your core course curriculum to make sure it matches with the NCAA approved core courses.
	Fall	Fill out Initial Target List with twenty-five colleges you want to pursue (five Division I, five Division II, five Division III, five NAIA, and five junior colleges, if applicable).
	All	Maintain a minimum of a 3.0 grade-point average. Take honors classes only if an A or B average is possible.
	All	Seek help from your teacher or a tutor if you are struggling in any subject area.
COMPLETED?	**WHEN?**	**ATHLETIC COMPETITION**
	Fall	Research athletic benchmarks to set specific athletic goals (www.athleteswanted.org).
	In Season	Ask an objective qualified third-party (such as a high school or club coach) for honest feedback about your strengths and weaknesses.
	In Season	Join a club or team outside of the high school that will provide more competition and better coaching (if applicable for your sport).
	In Season	Alert high school and/or club coach(es) of goal to play in college.
COMPLETED?	**WHEN?**	**RECRUITING**
	Fall	Begin building student-athlete résumé or scouting report to present to college coaches.
	Fall	Introduce yourself to three to five college coaches at levels you realistically qualify for based on recruiting benchmarks (www.athleteswanted.org). Start at junior college, NAIA, or Division III as you can always move up to other divisions.
	Fall	Do a spot check of personal outgoing voicemail messages and any social networking sites to which you subscribe (e.g., MySpace, Facebook, TAKKLE). Make sure you always appear mature and that no inappropriate information is on public display.

COMPLETED?	WHEN?	RECRUITING (CONT.)
	Fall	Add folders in inbox to organize emails from college coaches. Organize folders by division, recruiting category, and college.
	Spring	Call two college coaches from your Initial Target List. Once you are comfortable on the phone, call at least two coaches from top-choice programs where you qualify academically and athletically.
	Summer	Prepare for phone conversations by role-playing with your parents or a recruiting consultant. Review the questions the coach is likely to ask.
	In Season	Get recruiting assessment from a reputable scouting service.
	In Season	Start to accumulate game or skills footage according to sport-specific video guidelines (www.athleteswanted.org).
	In Season	Demonstrate good sportsmanship after every contest/game/match. Win or lose, shake hands with all opposing coaches and officials. Look them in the eye and say "nice game."
	All	Create and update a log of correspondence with college coaches (www.athleteswanted.org).
	All	Respond to all communication from college coaches at all levels. Add all contacts to your Correspondence Log (www.athleteswanted.org).
	All	If interested in a specific college that did not send recruitment information, contact the coach, introduce yourself, and fill out a questionnaire if you meet the minimum academic and athletic qualifications. Remember that academic requirements might be different because you are an athlete.
	All	Email at least ten college coaches from your Initial Target List. Start with two coaches from local colleges, followed by four coaches from Division III, NAIA or junior colleges. Always have your emails proofread.

COMPLETED?	WHEN?	SUMMER ACTIVITIES
	Summer	Plan at least one unofficial visit to a local college campus. Contact coaches in advance to schedule a meeting.
	Summer	Plan at least two unofficial visits to a Division I or II campus, if interested in attending a Division I or II program, and visit at least two Division III, NAIA or junior college campuses. Regardless of division, always contact coaches in advance to schedule a meeting.
	Summer	Attend local camps/combines to see how you compare with other high school athletes.
	All	Steer clear of situations that could jeopardize your goals. Always make responsible choices.

SOPHOMORE YEAR

Academics

By now, student-athletes should have a good idea of what track they are on academically. They should be making sure that they are on pace to achieve academic goals, and to set new ones. Grades are the first priority, and a student-athlete who is struggling with a specific class or subject should seek help from a teacher or a tutor. A student-athlete who can handle the extra workload might also ask for extra credit.

Now is a good time for an athlete to take the PLAN (Pre-ACT) and/or the PSAT (Pre-SAT), tests to prepare for the ACT and/or SAT. In fact, a student can even take the ACT or SAT as a sophomore to prepare for taking the test as a junior.

> **«« FAST FACT ««**
> A child can take the ACT and SAT as many times as necessary, reporting only the best score.

Student-athletes need to behave appropriately at all times and in all forums. They should be particularly aware of social networking sites, such as MySpace, Facebook, TAKKLE, or other emerging technologies. In fact, enough cannot be said about the importance of being aware of these emerging technologies. Anyone can post a picture of another student, and an athlete whose exploits are publicized on Facebook might lose a scholarship offer.

Billy Porter, a former tennis coach at the University of Dubuque, said that he has stopped recruiting prospective student-athletes due to inappropriate content posted by their peers on Facebook. And in 2008, a backup lineman was kicked off his college football team for posting an offensive message on Facebook. Remember that most cell phones have cameras, and friends can easily upload information about a student-athlete's behavior to a social networking site that the whole world can view. One mistake, such as being caught on camera holding a can of beer at a party, can cost a student-athlete an athletic scholarship. In the same spirit, an athlete's outgoing voice mail should be appropriate.

High School and Additional Athletic Competition

Student-athletes should keep working hard and staying focused, setting new goals each time previous goals are met. Athletes need to ask for feedback from a high school or club coach. Student-athletes should be getting stronger, faster, and more powerful, and high school and club coaches can offer specific guidance to help them develop athletic abilities.

College coaches will look for students who love to compete, so student-athletes need to pursue organized competition outside of high school, looking for a club that will provide the best opportunity to play against strong competitors, improve skill level, and receive coaching.

Athletes should be developing positive relationships with high school and club coaches, who will be asked to serve as references to college coaches.

Recruiting

As a sophomore, an athlete is still allowed only to receive general correspondence from NCAA Division I and II schools, though Division III, NAIA, and junior college coaches can call the athlete at any time. If a student has returned questionnaires from athletic departments, the athlete's name might be on athletic departments' mailing lists. Do not be fooled into thinking that tons of general mail will translate into recruitment. Coaches send thousands of mailers in the initial student-athlete initiation process.

Student-athletes should continue building and maintaining relationships with college coaches, being sure to respond to all questionnaires, brochures, and admissions materials by calling or sending personal letters to coaches. Though Division I and II coaches are not permitted to call or send personal emails at this point, an athlete can call and email coaches from all divisions and levels with updates about pertinent information. In fact, a student-athlete should take advantage of a questionnaire or general letter that invites a phone call with verbiage such as: *If you have any questions, feel free to call me on my home or cell phone.* This creates a perfect opportunity for a student-athlete to stand out from other athletes who are not confident enough to initiate calls.

An athlete should maintain the Correspondence Log to keep track of the details of each conversation or correspondence with a coach.

Student-athletes need to avoid the "Name Game"—that is, they should not judge universities based solely on name recognition. Over eighteen hundred colleges are in Division I, Division II, Division III, NAIA, and junior college levels. At this point, students do not know enough about these colleges to start ignoring schools based only on their name or the size of their program.

COACH'S TIP

If an athlete fails to respond to a coach, the coach might think that athlete is not interested in the program. To stay on the coach's recruiting list, student-athletes need to be prompt, thorough, and personal when responding to correspondences.

Now is the time for a student-athlete to:

- Start researching institutions to get a feel for the different types of campuses. A student-athlete should be directed to evaluate a wide range of schools, understanding that bigger is not always better, and Division I schools do not always offer better playing time, opportunities, or education than Division III or NAIA schools.

- Contact coaches to set up at least two unofficial visits, which include meeting with the coach on campus. Start with Division III, NAIA, and junior colleges to develop sea legs before working up to Division I and II schools.

- During these visits, athletes should be prepared to meet with the coach. Prior to the visit, the student-athlete should create a written list of questions to ask the coach about the college and the team. Top recruits might receive verbal offers during these meetings as early as their freshman or sophomore year!

- Visit local colleges, even if they do not offer the athlete's sport. The more campuses a student becomes acquainted with, the more aware of likes and dislikes the athlete will become.

- Schedule a meeting with a high school guidance counselor. The counselor can help direct the student-athlete toward activities and goals that will help the athlete be a more attractive prospect. Most guidance counselors have an average of 250 students to help and do not have much experience in navigating through the athletic recruitment process. They might not understand all of the NCAA rules. This responsibility falls on the student and the student's parents, not the high school guidance counselor.

Summer Activities

No matter what level of institution an athlete is targeting, the goal should be four unofficial visits for the summer with local colleges and universities. Getting comfortable visiting college coaches will pay big dividends later in the process, as well as allow a student-athlete to build relationships, learn interpersonal skills, and build confidence.

If scheduling permits, an athlete might want to round out a résumé and demonstrate character by volunteering in the community.

Following is the sophomore student-athlete's recruiting checklist. This checklist can be downloaded from www.athleteswanted.org, where dates can be assigned to each of the activities.

KEY CODE
Red: Mission critical!   **Grey:** Proactive communication with college coach needed.

The Sophomore Student-Athlete's Recruiting Checklist		
COMPLETED?	**WHEN?**	**ACADEMICS**
	Fall	Order or download and print a new copy of the *NCAA Guide for the College-Bound Student-Athlete* and read it thoroughly. Look for any new rule changes.
	Fall	Use Division I core course worksheet to review and update specific academic goals and track core course progress (www.athleteswanted.org). Be sure core course requirements are being fulfilled.
	Fall	Meet with high school guidance counselor to review your academic progress, core course requirements, and get national ACT and SAT testing dates.
	Fall	Review and update Initial Target List and continue to research colleges to get a feel of different types of institutions. The Initial Target List should include at least forty schools across all divisions you are qualified for (Division I, II, III, NAIA, and junior college, if applicable).
	Winter	Schedule and take the Pre-ACT (PLAN) and/or Pre-SAT (PSAT).
	All	Consider taking SAT II test if you complete an AP class and feel strong with the subject matter.
	All	Maintain a minimum of a 3.0 grade-point average.
	All	Take honors and AP classes only if an A or B average is possible.
	All	Seek help from your teacher or a tutor if you are struggling in any subject area.
COMPLETED?	**WHEN?**	**ATHLETIC COMPETITION**
	Fall	Review athletic benchmarks and use recruiting benchmarks to re-evaluate specific athletic goals (www.athleteswanted.org). If you have achieved some of your goals, set new ones.
	In Season	Ask an objective qualified third-party (such as a high school or club coach) for honest feedback about your strengths and weaknesses. Ask if you have progressed since freshman year.
	In Season	Join a club or team outside of the high school that will provide more competition and better coaching (if applicable for your sport).
	In Season	Remind high school and/or club coach(es) of goal to play in college and be sure to inform any new coaches. Maintain positive relationships with all coaches.
	Fall	Begin to create priority list and rank your Initial Target List.

COMPLETED?	WHEN?	RECRUITING
	Fall	Review NCSA Power Rankings (www.athleteswanted.org) and cross-reference against Initial Target List.
	Fall	Get recruiting assessment from reputable scouting service.
	Fall	Update student-athlete résumé or scouting report.
	Fall	Introduce yourself to five to ten new college coaches at levels you realistically qualify for based on recruiting benchmarks (www.athleteswanted.org). Be sure to add these contacts to your Correspondence Log.
	Fall	Screen outgoing voicemail messages and any social networking sites (e.g., MySpace, Facebook, TAKKLE). Make sure you always appear mature and no inappropriate information is on public display.
	Fall	Manage folders in inbox to organize emails from college coaches. Organize folders by division, recruiting category, and college.
	Spring	Call five to ten new college coaches from your Initial Target List. If coaches send letters or emails inviting you to call their cell phones, do it!
	Summer	Continue to prepare for phone conversations by role-playing with your parents or a recruiting consultant. Review the questions the coach is likely to ask.
	In Season	Schedule a follow-up meeting with your coaches and athletic director to discuss your recruiting progress and ask if there is anything specific they think you should be doing to improve your chances of playing at the next level. Remember, it is important to keep these key people involved in your recruiting process, but they may not have all the answers.
	In Season	Start to create a highlight or skills video using sport-specific video guidelines, and continue to collect footage (www.athleteswanted.org).
	In Season	Demonstrate good sportsmanship after every contest/game/match. Win or lose, shake hands with all opposing coaches and officials. Look them in the eye and say "nice game."
	All	Maintain your Correspondence Log (www.athleteswanted.org).
	All	Respond to all communication from college coaches at all levels. Add all contacts to your Correspondence Log (www.athleteswanted.org).
	All	If interested in a specific college that did not send recruitment information, contact the coach, introduce yourself, and fill out a questionnaire if you meet the minimum academic and athletic qualifications.

COMPLETED?	WHEN?	RECRUITING (CONT.)
	All	Email all coaches from your Initial Target List. At this point, you should introduce yourself or update the coaches on your progress. Remember to establish relationships. Always have your emails proofread.
	All	Keep coaches up to date on your progress through email.
COMPLETED?	WHEN?	SUMMER ACTIVITIES
	Summer	Determine your Estimated Family Contribution (EFC) to familiarize yourself with the collegiate financial aid process (www.athleteswanted.org).
	Summer	Volunteer over the summer break, if possible.
	Summer	Visit at least four college campuses at levels you realistically qualify for. Always contact coaches in advance to schedule a meeting.
	Summer	Consider attending camps and combines to build skills, speed, or strength, and see how you compare with other high school athletes.
	All	Steer clear of situations that could jeopardize your goals. Always make responsible choices.

JUNIOR YEAR

Academics

Grades should still be a student-athlete's top priority. If student-athletes are not achieving the grades needed for admittance, they should seek additional academic assistance from teachers or a tutor.

COACH'S TIP

It is never too late to be a good student, said Coach Chmiel. An upswing in a student's grade-point average in later semesters can give a coach the ammunition to make a case for an otherwise-unqualified student-athlete to gain admissions to a college. For this reason, a student's GPA in later semesters is more important than the GPA in early semesters.

The fall semester brings with it the standardized tests: SAT and ACT. The SAT and ACT allow students graduating in 2010 or later to test several times and submit just their highest scores to colleges. All other scores will not be reported, unless the student chooses otherwise. To take advantage of this strategic advantage, student-athletes should try to take at least one of these tests twice during their junior year. If students plan to apply to highly selective institutions, they should check with the college coach to determine whether to register for the SAT Subjects Tests (SAT II), one-hour tests in academic subjects required by a few elite schools.

By now, student-athletes should be well aware of the grades and scores needed for admittance into all top-choice colleges. Understand that the required GPA and test scores for student-athletes might differ from those required by the rest of the student body, so a student-athlete should ask a coach for input into the academic requirements for athletes. Remember that recruited athletes often receive preferential treatment in admissions. This does not mean that an athlete should slack. Student-athletes want as much leverage as possible, and the higher their grades, the harder a university will fight for them, and the bigger financial aid package they will receive.

Once a student has completed six semesters (or the quarter/trimester equivalent), the athlete should register with the NCAA Eligibility Center. Unless registered with the NCAA Eligibility Center, athletes will not be able to take official visits during their senior year, nor will they qualify for athletic scholarships. The Eligibility Center will require that a student-athlete prove he is not a professional athlete by completing an "amateurism certification process," which can be done early in the junior year (if not sooner).

> «« **FAST FACT** ««
>
> Student-athletes must take the ACT and/or SAT on a national testing date for their scores to qualify for the NCAA Eligibility Center, which allows them to qualify for athletic scholarships and take official visits. You can find ACT/SAT national testing dates at www.athleteswanted.org. Athletes can register with the NCAA Eligibility Center at https://web1.ncaa.org/eligibilitycenter/common/.

High School and Additional Athletic Competition

Junior year is the most important in the recruiting process, particularly if an athlete is a Division I or II prospect. During the junior season, interested college coaches will seriously evaluate a child's development, performance, achievements, strength, and speed. If an athlete has caught a coach's eye, the coach might come to see the student-athlete compete in person, though most coaches will be restricted from off-campus visits due to NCAA rules. Others will request a transcript or résumé and a highlight, skills, or game video.

Recruiting

The recruiting process generally becomes more intense after September 1 of the junior year, especially if an athlete is a Division I or Division II prospect. (Division III, NAIA, and junior college recruiting generally occurs later.) Top recruits will usually receive scholarship offers in writing during their junior year.

Division I coaches can start to contact a student via personalized written correspondence, and they can call once a week beginning junior year. Dates depend on the sport and can change annually. For sport-specific dates, see *NCAA Guide for the College-Bound Student-Athlete.*

Student-athletes should continue to send periodic email updates to the coaches in their Correspondence Log and record all interactions with these coaches, being sure to respond to every coach that initiates contact, whether it be through an email, phone call, or questionnaire.

By now, student-athletes should be focusing only on those colleges that have expressed interest in recruiting them. They should try to visit as many of these colleges as possible during the summer, holidays, and spring break. No limits are set on the number of unofficial visits a student can take. Athletes should target colleges that they are interested in and that have expressed an interest in them. Coaches are typically more than happy to meet with a student-athlete, especially if they are interested in the athlete, but be sure to contact the coach prior to the visit.

COACH'S TIP

A good indicator of a coach's interest is whether the coach and staff actively accommodate an athlete during an unofficial visit. Colleges and universities often leverage the school's athletic program to drive a student's interest in the school. If the coach does not spend time with a student-athlete, safely assume that the coach is not interested in recruiting that athlete. (But keep reading. The student-athlete might be able to pique the coach's interest with a few tactical moves!)

A good indication that a coach is interested in recruiting a student-athlete is if the coach extends an invitation for a game-day visit. According to NCAA guidelines, a college coach can offer three complimentary tickets to student-athletes invited for a game day visit, which is considered an unofficial visit.

Remember that anytime student-athletes contact a coach, they gain an advantage over competition. Coaches appreciate student-athletes who are proactive and mature.

Some questions an athlete might ask when meeting with the coach include:

- *Have you had a chance to see me play? If not, would you like to see my highlight, skills, or game video?*

- *What would I need to do to earn an opportunity to compete for your program?*

- *Am I on your recruiting list, and if so, where do I stand on the list?*

- *Will you be inviting me for a game day or official visit?*

College coaches are not technically allowed to visit a student-athlete in person off-campus until June 15 following the junior year. Instead, most coaches will want to evaluate a student-athlete by watching a skills or highlight video, then seeing the student-athlete in person, if possible. A student's junior year marks the perfect time to put this DVD or enhanced streaming video together.

Video evaluations will be the foundation of a student-athlete's recruiting campaign, so an athlete should keep playing hard at every opportunity to build a highlight video. Athletes whose sports rely more heavily on skills video than highlight videos should make arrangements to record footage in a controlled environment where quality, close-up footage can be obtained from proper angles so that a coach can get a true feel for the recruit's skill level and potential. Parents and athletes should remember that coaches will critique videos much differently. An objective third-party service can make sure that the video has been sequenced and enhanced so that the video footage captures an athlete's strongest abilities in the proper format. Nothing can hurt an athlete's chances more than a substandard highlight or skills video that does not allow the coach to easily identify or evaluate the athlete. Enhanced streaming video with high definition, spot-shadowing, and proper performance-sequencing can give a prospect a tremendous advantage in the recruiting process. See Chapter 8 for more information about videos and www.athleteswanted.org for sport-specific guidelines.

COACH'S TIP

If an athlete is not being recruited by his or her junior year, one of two things is happening: 1) the student is not a good enough athlete/student; or 2) the colleges do not know about the athlete. If an athlete has initiated contact with coaches and followed all the rules of the game but is still not being recruited, the athlete should expand the search to include less competitive programs at Division II, III, NAIA, or junior colleges. As well, a student-athlete might want to seek help from a reputable professional recruiting service.

Summer Activities

The summer before a child's senior year is critical in the recruiting process. Remember that Division IA college programs will make the majority of their offers to the top sophomore and junior prospects before January of the prospect's junior year. If a student-athlete does not have an offer by the summer following the junior year, the athlete should shift focus to more realistic programs. Consider Division II, Division IAA, Division III, or NAIA schools, as well as junior colleges.

Student-athletes should use the summer to take more unofficial visits and to narrow down the list of colleges they are considering. Coaches are allowed to call athletes during this summer (generally once a week starting June 15, but the rules change depending on the sport and most recent NCAA guidelines), and student-athletes should make coach communications a priority.

Athletes should:

- Have a list of the colleges they communicate with the most.

- Reference the NCSA Collegiate Power Rankings (www. althleteswanted.org) to determine which colleges rank best in academic, athletic, and graduation rates.

- Cross-reference these lists with the colleges that are most likely to accept them and show high interest, invite them for an official visit, and offer a scholarship. Critical to this is an athlete's ability to gauge where he stands at his colleges of choice. Student-athletes should not be afraid to simply ask: "Where do I stand on your list of recruits?"

If invited by a college coach, especially a coach they are trying to impress, student-athletes might consider going to camps to improve or demonstrate their skills. Camps are a good opportunity for student-athletes to experience campus life, evaluate a college, or continue developing a relationship with coaches who are already recruiting them; however, student-athletes are rarely discovered at camps. See Chapter 12 for more information about the role of camps in a student's recruiting potential.

An athlete invited to a prospect camp or a one-day visit camp has a strong indication that the student-athlete is being recruited and evaluated by the camp's coaching staff. On the other hand, if an athlete is not invited to such camps by the end of the junior year, a student should shift expectations and expand the search to programs that are more realistically compatible with the athlete's competition level.

> ## «« FAST FACT ««
>
> While attending a camp to evaluate a student-athlete, coaches often verify a prospect's recruiting information—height, weight, strength, or speed. A coach can analyze a student-athlete's skills and make a determination on where the prospect stands, generally assigning one of three categories to a student-athlete: 1) make a scholarship offer; 2) invite as a walk-on; or 3) wait to see the athlete's senior year performance before making a final determination.

Following is the junior student-athlete's recruiting checklist. This checklist can be downloaded from www.athleteswanted.org, where dates can be assigned to each of the activities.

KEY CODE

Red: Mission critical! **Grey:** Proactive communication with college coach needed.

The Junior Student-Athlete's Recruiting Checklist		
COMPLETED?	WHEN?	ACADEMICS
	Fall	Begin ACT/SAT preparation.
	Fall	Order or download and print a new copy of the *NCAA Guide for the College-Bound Student-Athlete* and read it thoroughly. Look for any new rule changes.
	Fall	Use Division I core course worksheet to review and update specific academic goals and track core course progress (www.athleteswanted.org). Be sure core course requirements are being fulfilled.
	Fall	Meet with high school guidance counselor to review your academic progress and core course requirements.

COMPLETED?	WHEN?	ACADEMICS (CONT.)
	Fall	Review and update Initial Target List and continue to research colleges to get a feel of different types of institutions. Target List should include at least forty schools across all divisions you are qualified for (Division I, Division II, Division III, NAIA, and junior college, if applicable). Maintain relationships with coaches at each school. If school is not on your Correspondence Log, re-evaluate if it should remain on your Target List.
	Winter	Take the ACT and/or SAT. Request the test scores be sent to the NCAA Eligibility Center by marking "9999" in the code box where indicated. Take the SAT II test if considering highly selective schools.
	Spring	Register with the NCAA Eligibility Center and make sure your high school counselor sends your transcripts at the end of junior year.
	Spring	Begin the "amateurism certification process" questionnaire on the NCAA Eligibility Center's website.
	All	Maintain a minimum of a 3.0 grade point average. Take honors or AP classes only if an A or B average is possible.
	All	Seek help from your teacher or a tutor if you are struggling in any subject area.
COMPLETED?	WHEN?	ATHLETIC COMPETITION
	Fall	Get phone numbers and email addresses of all coaches and ask them to be references.
	Fall	Review athletic benchmarks and use recruiting benchmarks to re-evaluate specific athletic goals (www.athleteswanted.org). If you have achieved some of your goals, set new ones.
	In Season	Ask an objective qualified third-party (such as a high school or club coach) for honest feedback about your strengths and weaknesses, and what they feel you should focus on in order to achieve your goals.
	In Season	Join a club or team outside of the high school that will provide more competition and better coaching (if applicable for your sport). Play at the highest level possible and look for a team that competes at major tournaments and showcases (if applicable for your sport).
	In Season	Remind high school and/or club coach(es) of goal to play in college and be sure to inform any new coaches. Maintain positive relationships with all coaches.
COMPLETED?	WHEN?	RECRUITING
	Fall	Review the recruiting timeline for each division in your sport (www.athleteswanted.org) and make sure your recruiting process matches the levels you are targeting.
	Fall	Schedule game day visits (if applicable for your sport).

COMPLETED?	WHEN?	RECRUITING (CONT.)
	Fall	Update priority list and re-rank Initial Target List. Consider how interested the coaches seem in you.
	Fall	Review College Power Rankings (www.athleteswanted.org) and cross reference against Initial Target List.
	Fall	Get recruiting assessment from reputable scouting service.
	Fall	Update student-athlete résumé or scouting report.
	Fall	Screen outgoing voicemail messages and any social networking sites (e.g., MySpace, Facebook, TAKKLE). Make sure you always appear mature and no inappropriate information is on public display.
	Fall	Manage folders in inbox to organize emails from college coaches. Organize folders by division, recruiting category, and college.
	Spring	Start to plan travel for unofficial visits during spring break and summer.
	Spring	Take at least two unofficial visits. Target schools where the coaches are recruiting you.
	Spring	Look for invitations from coaches to call in their letters and emails. If a coach gives you a home or cell phone number, use it!
	Summer	Continue to prepare for phone conversations by role-playing with your parents or a recruiting consultant. Review the questions the coach is likely to ask.
	In Season	Finish highlight or skills video and spot shadow, if possible. Send video to college coaches. Always notify coaches prior to sending video and follow up to see if they have watched it. Once you know they have viewed your video, ask what they thought.
	In Season	Meet with coaches and athletic directors to assess progress toward goals. Implement their suggestions. Remember, it is important to keep these key people involved in your recruiting process, but they may not have all the answers.
	In Season	Continue to capture footage using sport-specific video guidelines (www.athleteswanted.org).
	In Season	Demonstrate good sportsmanship after every contest/game/match. Win or lose, shake hands with all opposing coaches and officials. Look them in the eye and say "nice game."
	All	Be aware of all important recruiting dates (including call dates) for your sport.
	All	Ask coaches where you stand and always be prepared with a list of questions (www.athleteswanted.org).

COMPLETED?	WHEN?	RECRUITING (CONT.)
	All	Maintain your Correspondence Log and call every coach in the log to continue to maintain relationships. Your Correspondence Log should include every school from your Initial Target List at this point. You may keep up to five schools on the Initial Target List who you have not communicated with. Consider these your "reach" schools academically and/or athletically. Maintain consistent email contact with every coach, notifying them of updates, tournament play, etc.
	All	Respond to all communication from college coaches at all levels. Add all contacts to your Correspondence Log (www.athleteswanted.org).
	All	If interested in a specific college that did not send recruitment information, contact the coach, introduce yourself, and fill out a questionnaire if you meet the minimum academic and athletic qualifications.
	All	Keep all coaches up to date on your progress through email.
COMPLETED?	WHEN?	SUMMER ACTIVITIES
	Summer	If you have not connected with any college coaches, contact a reputable recruiting service immediately!
	Summer	Create a log to track application deadlines of your top ten to thirty schools.
	Summer	Ask coaches which camps or combines they recommend and why.
	Summer	Consider attending top showcases if applicable for your sport.
	Summer	Attend camps and combines if invited by a coach who is heavily recruiting you or who invites you for a one-day pro-rated recruiting camp as a prospect.
	Summer	Take at least five unofficial visits to meet coaches at schools you are seriously considering.
	Summer	Continue ACT/SAT prep and register to re-take test(s) if needed.
	Summer	Consider whether or not you want to accept any verbal offers you may receive.
	Summer	Call any coaches you have not communicated with. Ask all coaches where you stand on their recruiting list and what their recruiting timeline is.
	Summer	Get a head start on applications and write first draft of all application essays (if necessary).
	Summer	Meet with family accountant/specialist to make adjustments and maximize EFC (www.athleteswanted.org).
	Summer	Volunteer over the summer break, if possible.
	All	Steer clear of situations that could jeopardize your goals. Always make responsible choices.

SENIOR YEAR

Academics

Again, grades should be a student's first priority. Student-athletes have worked hard for three years. They should not give up now! By now, a student-athlete should be able to target colleges that are an academic fit based on grades and test scores. If an athlete needs to retake the ACT or SAT, he or she should do so early in the school year. And if students are looking into highly selective colleges, they should ask the college coach if it is necessary to take the SAT II or advanced placement achievement tests.

Student-athletes should update the NCAA Eligibility Center with their test scores if they improve. Mark "9999" on the code box to have the results sent to the NCAA Eligibility Center (formerly the NCAA Clearinghouse).

High School and Additional Athletic Competition

Student-athletes should continue to play and build skills during their senior year. College coaches are impressed with students who show leadership skills, so a student-athlete should aim to be named team captain.

Athletes should continue to get strong grade-point averages, stay out of trouble, and finish with high class rankings. Student-athletes should avoid contracting "senioritis." A lapse in judgment during the senior year could cost an athlete a scholarship. Too many kids lose scholarships because they are in the wrong place at the wrong time with the wrong people. It is not enough that student-athletes make good decisions—athletes must also be aware that the actions of those people with whom they associate might make or break their college careers. A student-athlete has come too far to lose an opportunity due to a lapse in judgment.

"TELL ME WHAT COMPANY YOU KEEP, AND I'LL TELL YOU WHAT YOU ARE."

Jon was a 6'3", 190-pound wide receiver who ran a consistent 4.5-second 40-yard dash. Not only did he earn a 3.8 grade-point average and an ACT score of 34, he was also involved in community service. In other words, he was the total package.

At the time, I was a football coach for a Division IA school, and I invited Jon, a junior in high school, for an unofficial visit on game day. Jon's demeanor impressed each and every coach, including the head coach, and all knew he could contribute plenty to the program. He was a natural fit.

Later in the season, Jon returned for another game day visit. After the game, we met with Jon and told him he would be offered a full-ride athletic scholarship to play for our program.

"From here on out, your job is simple," we told Jon. "Return to your high school and keep exhibiting the great character you have already displayed. Excel in the classroom and in the community, and play hard."

In other words, Jon was told to keep doing what he was doing.

We told Jon that after the second game of his senior year, we would offer him an official visit, during which time we would present him with a written scholarship offer. Later in the season, we met with Jon's high school coach, who confirmed what we already knew: Jon was a coach's dream athlete. We would be lucky to have him.

It was a done-deal, or so we all thought. Jon was sitting on the cusp of a full-ride athletic scholarship to play football at a Division IA school that would set the stage for the next forty years of his life.

That's right: forty years. A child's four-year collegiate experience will set the stage for the next forty years. And based on his past performance, Jon's future was bright. He had the opportunity of a lifetime.

The season passed, and we continued to keep in touch with Jon within the rules dictated by NCAA. All was in place to confirm his spot on the roster.

During the early weeks of Jon's senior year, I called Jon's high school coach to request a transcript of his classes. The request was met with dead silence.

"Coach, please tell me everything is okay," I begged, holding my breath. Something was not right.

"I can send you a copy of Jon's transcript," said his high school coach, "But I am afraid he doesn't have a game tape. He no longer plays football for us."

I was in shock. Was he hurt? Did he quit the team? Transfer to another school?

Jon's high school coach went on to explain. Two days before his senior year, Jon and nine other football players were arrested at 2:00 a.m. while attending a beach party with alcohol and marijuana.

"We had to start the year by throwing ten seniors off the team," reported his coach, sadly.

I was shocked. I had been a coach for twenty years, and I had met my fair-share of student-athletes. The partiers were easy to spot. Jon simply was not the type to drink or take drugs. Jon's high school coach felt the same way.

"Jon was the designated driver," said the coach. "But he was arrested for being in possession of alcohol and drugs. We have a no-tolerance policy at our school, and any student caught knowingly in the presence of alcohol or drugs is immediately suspended from athletics and extracurricular activities."

His high school coach and I knew something that Jon did not yet know. The company Jon chose to keep cost him a college scholarship. If unable to play during his senior year, he would be ineligible for our program. And it was too late in the process for Jon to find a spot on another comparable Division IA team.

One night changed the course of Jon's life. His future, his education, and experiences most people can only dream of were in the palm of his hand, but he was in the wrong place at the wrong time with the wrong people. He cried when we told him the scholarship offer would not be extended.

"What can I do?" he said. We shook our heads. Overnight, he went from a highly recruited athlete to someone Division IA coaches wouldn't touch with a ten-foot pole.

One bad decision can forever change the course of an athlete's future. A student-athlete should make sure that the rewards of his investment are not squandered by one bad decision, or by the company he keeps.

— Bob Chmiel, former football coach Notre Dame, Michigan, and Northwestern

Recruiting

This is the home stretch. Coaches can call once a week except during dead periods, quiet periods, and evaluation periods. (See the *NCAA Guide for the College-Bound Student-Athlete.*

A student-athlete's goal this year is to have fifteen schools in the queue, five of which are a stretch, five of which are solid possibilities, and five of which are backups. During the course of the year, a student-athlete will ideally have five top choices who waive the application fee, offer official visits, and ultimately extend offers, which the student-athlete can leverage to increase the scholarship package offered by the athlete's top choice.

This is when the relationships an athlete has forged with the coaching staff will pay off. A student-athlete should keep in contact with coaches on the Correspondence Log and update them through emails and phone calls. Remember that recruiting is a process, not a one-time event.

In Division I, II, and III recruitment, student-athletes are allowed five official visits their senior year, so they should use them wisely, visiting those schools that they want to attend. More information about official visits is included in Chapter 6, but be aware that official visits cannot exceed forty-eight hours. Unlike unofficial visits, the college program pays for official visits. This includes the cost of transportation, lodging, and food expenses.

«« FAST FACT ««

An invitation for an official visit is a strong precursor to a scholarship offer. One rule of thumb in recruiting is that if an athlete is not offered an official visit, that athlete likely will not be offered a scholarship.

Most scholarship offers are finalized (athletic, academic, grant, financial aid, etcetera) during the senior year, and each sport has a National Letter of Intent Signing Day, which is listed at www.athleteswanted.org.

Student-athletes need to make sure to work with the college coach during the admissions process, submit college applications early, and pay attention to deadlines. They should ask the coach for an athletic application and fee waiver of the $50 to $250 non-refundable application fee. Many top academic colleges have deadlines between November and January. Others have a rolling deadline where applications are accepted until the enrollment class is full. From time to time, coaches can extend deadlines for student-athletes who are highly recruited. Some offers are made as late as August.

Some coaches might pressure an athlete to apply early, a process called "Early Decision Enrollment." Student-athletes should avoid Early Decision to a college unless they are 100 percent sure they want to attend the college. Athletes accepted as Early Decision students sign binding contracts that close doors for other opportunities. At a minimum, students who accept an Early Decision lower their negotiating potential.

Summer Activities

Most likely, a student-athlete has committed to a college by this point. The athlete should ask the new college coach for the summer workout plan and follow the program closely.

Following is the senior student-athlete's recruiting checklist. This checklist can be downloaded from www.athleteswanted.org, where dates can be assigned to each of the activities.

KEY CODE

Red: Mission critical!   **Grey:** Proactive communication with college coach needed.

The Senior Student-Athlete's Recruiting Checklist		
COMPLETED?	**WHEN?**	**ACADEMICS**
	Fall	Ask coaches when and how you should apply. Decide if you will submit any early applications. Obtain application waivers from coaches.
	Fall	Complete FAFSA form.
	Fall	Re-take the ACT and/or SAT. Request the test scores be sent to the NCAA Eligibility Center by marking "9999" in the code box where indicated. Take the SAT II test if considering highly selective schools. Update improved test scores and grades with the NCAA Eligibility Center.
	Fall	Order or download and print a new copy of the *NCAA Guide for the College-Bound Student-Athlete* and read it thoroughly. Look for rule changes.
	Fall	Use Division I core course worksheet to review and update specific academic goals and track core course progress (www.athleteswanted.org). Be sure core course requirements will be fulfilled by the end of the school year.
	Fall	Meet with high school guidance counselor to review your academic progress and core course requirements.
	Fall	Review and update Initial Target List. Narrow down Target List to ten to twenty schools you are seriously considering. Do not include more than five schools where the coach is not heavily recruiting you. Target List should include at least five schools where you know you will be accepted and the coach has offered you a scholarship and/or spot on the team (depending on division and personal situation).

COMPLETED?	WHEN?	ACADEMICS (CONT.)
	Winter	Finalize and submit all applications.
	Winter	Discuss financial aid with college coaches and fill out aid applications with direction from coaches.
	Winter	Submit FAFSA form on January 1.
	Spring	Review Student Aid Reports (SAR) to determine best package. Consider appealing through financial aid office.
	Spring	At the end of the school year, ask the high school guidance counselor to send a copy of your final transcript and proof of graduation to the NCAA Eligibility Center.
	All	Apply for outside scholarships.
	All	Maintain a minimum of a 3.0 grade point average. First semester of senior year grades are critical. Take honors or AP classes only if an A or B average is possible. Finish off your high school career on a high note!
	All	Seek help from your teacher or a tutor if you are struggling in any subject area.

COMPLETED?	WHEN?	ATHLETIC COMPETITION
	Fall	Update references if necessary.
	Fall	Review athletic benchmarks and use recruiting benchmarks to re-evaluate specific athletic goals (www.athleteswanted.org). If you have achieved some of your goals, set new ones.
	In Season	Ask an objective qualified third-party (such as a high school or club coach) for honest feedback about your strengths and weaknesses. Remind them that they are on your list of references for college coaches.
	In Season	If you have fewer than ten legitimate coach relationships, ask college coaches where you can compete to showcase yourself. Seek out any opportunity to play at the highest level possible and look for a team that competes at major tournaments and showcases (if applicable for your sport).
	In Season	Remind high school and/or club coach(es) of goal to play in college and be sure to inform any new coaches. Maintain positive relationships with all coaches.

COMPLETED?	WHEN?	RECRUITING
	Fall	Schedule official visits (five Division I and II and unlimited Division III, NAIA, and junior colleges), unofficial visits, and game day visits. If a coach at the top of your Target List and Correspondence Log has not offered an official visit, call coaches and ask if official visit will be extended.

COMPLETED?	WHEN?	RECRUITING (CONT.)
	Fall	Consider what you will say if offer is extended during official visit.
	Fall	Prior to Signing Day, ask top coaches where you stand on their recruiting list. Revise search to include more realistic schools if necessary.
	Fall	Begin scholarship negotiation early in senior year.
	Fall	If you are not comfortable with your options, or if your Correspondence Log includes fewer than fifteen schools, call at least ten new coaches at levels where you are receiving attention. Introduce yourself and ask if they are still recruiting.
	Fall	Review the recruiting timeline for each division in your sport (www.athleteswanted.org) and see where you stand.
	Fall	Update priority list and re-rank Initial Target List. Consider how interested the coaches seem in you.
	Fall	Review College Power Rankings (www.athleteswanted.org) and cross-reference against Initial Target List.
	Fall	Get recruiting assessment from reputable scouting service.
	Fall	Update student-athlete résumé or scouting report.
	Fall	Screen outgoing voicemail messages and any social networking sites (e.g., MySpace, Facebook, TAKKLE). Make sure you always appear mature and that no inappropriate information is on public display.
	Fall	Manage folders in inbox to organize emails from college coaches. Organize folders by division, recruiting category, and college.
	Spring	Look for invitations from coaches to call in their letters and emails. If they give you their cell phone number, use it!
	Summer	Continue to prepare for phone conversations by role-playing with your parents or a recruiting consultant. Review the questions the coach is likely to ask.
	In Season	Continue to capture footage using sport-specific video guidelines (www.athleteswanted.org).
	In Season	Ask coaches if they'd like you to create a new highlight or skills video or if they want you to send game footage. Always notify coaches prior to sending video and follow up to see if they have watched it. Once you know they have viewed your video, ask what they thought.
	In Season	Meet with coaches and athletic directors to assess progress toward goals. Remember, it is important to keep these key people involved in your recruiting process, but they may not have all the answers.
	In Season	Demonstrate good sportsmanship after every contest/game/match. Win or lose, shake hands with all opposing coaches and officials. Look them in the eye and say "nice game."

COMPLETED?	WHEN?	RECRUITING (CONT.)
	All	Be aware of all important recruiting dates (including call dates) for your sport.
	All	Ask coaches where you stand and always be prepared with a list of questions (www.athleteswanted.org).
	All	Maintain your Correspondence Log and call every coach in the log to continue to maintain relationships. Your Correspondence Log should include every school from your Initial Target List at this point. You may keep up to five schools on the Initial Target List who you have not communicated with. Consider these your "reach" schools academically and/or athletically. Maintain consistent email contact with every coach, notifying them of updates, tournament play, etc. If your Correspondence Log includes more than fifty schools at this point, you may start to trim down by not initiating contact with schools you are not interested in or graciously declining offers from coaches at schools you are 100 percent positive you will not consider.
	All	Respond to all communication from college coaches at all levels. Add all contacts to your Correspondence Log (www.athleteswanted.org). Even if you are not interested in a school, never ignore any correspondence.
	All	If interested in a specific college who did not send recruitment information, contact the coach, introduce yourself, and fill out a questionnaire if you meet the minimum academic and athletic qualifications. Ask if they are still looking for prospects at this stage.
	All	Keep all coaches up to date on your progress through email.
COMPLETED?	WHEN?	SUMMER ACTIVITIES
	Summer	Congratulations! You are now ready to prepare for your collegiate athletic career! Follow your summer workout schedule closely and meet with a trainer if you need help.
	Summer	If you do not have contact with any college coaches, contact a reputable recruiting service immediately!
	Summer	Ask coach for playbook and film if possible.
	Summer	Contact your new teammates if you have any questions.
	Summer	Set collegiate academic and athletic goals for college.
	Summer	Schedule orientation and meet new guidance counselor and prepare schedule if possible.
	Summer	Contact roommate and coordinate dorm room necessities.
	Summer	Set up bank account.
	Summer	Get campus map and study key points.

COMPLETED?	WHEN?	SUMMER ACTIVITIES (CONT.)
	Summer	Save athletic résumé or scouting report and continue to add to it throughout collegiate career. This will become your professional résumé, and as a collegiate athlete, you already are ahead of your peers.
	Summer	Volunteer over the summer break, if possible.
	All	Remember where you came from and those who helped you achieve your goals. Be sure to thank your coaches and guidance counselor and keep them informed of your progress throughout your college career.
	All	Stay involved in your community, give back, and encourage younger student-athletes to reach their goals. Tell your story to inspire others!
	All	Steer clear of situations that could jeopardize your goals. Always make responsible choices.

GAUGING A STUDENT-ATHLETE'S LEVEL OF RECRUITMENT

IN HIGH SCHOOL, Izell Reese was a negligible five pounds shy of the average Division I linebacker. His other stats were spot on. He was 6'2" with a 3.2 grade-point average and a 4.4-second 40-yard dash. On top of that, he was one hell of a great ball player, making the varsity team his freshman year.

College coaches took notice of Reese. During practice his junior year, Reese's high school coach handed him piles of recruitment letters from college coaches; each letter assured him that he would not only have a spot on a Division I football team, but also win a full athletic scholarship.

Reese was certain he had a place on a college team. And in retrospect, he should have been a sure thing. After all, he would go on to play for the Dallas Cowboys, Denver Broncos, and Buffalo Bills for seven years. But Signing Day came and went, and Reese, who was later an NFL draft pick, was not offered a spot.

Compare Reese with Heather Geck. Her junior year in high school, Geck's eighteen-hole golf average was 106.4, way too many strokes for even the Division III average golfer. Her grade-point average was 2.2. But Geck received nearly a full scholarship to a private university, a dream come true for her parents.

Why the vast difference? Why was Geck, an average athlete with average grades, given nearly a full ride while top football prospects with good grades are overlooked? You might guess that football is more competitive than golf. True, but when Izell Reese walked on as a freshman at University of Alabama at Birmingham, he noticed that teammates with less ability and lower grades had been given full athletic scholarships while he, clearly a superior student and athlete, was paying out of pocket.

And Reese's story is not rare. Hall of Famer Jerry Rice, a first-round draft pick, was not recruited by any Division IA programs, even though he grew up only seventy miles from the University of Alabama and, as a college athlete, would go on to set records that stood for more than twenty years. As a high school player, Walter Payton was one of the state's top running back prospects, but he too would not receive a single Division IA scholarship offer, though he also would go on to become a first-round draft pick for the Chicago Bears. Tony Eason, a first-round pick in the famous 1983 NFL Draft, was not recruited out of high school; after junior college, he was offered only one scholarship.

Far too many athletes miss out on collegiate opportunities or, like Reese, Payton, and Rice, pay out of their own pockets simply because they do not know how to play the recruiting game. In every high school community in every town across the country sits an aging athlete reliving his glory days as the high school quarterback. This scenario has become a token joke in movies, but in truth, the situation is heartbreaking. Those athletes **should** have been awarded scholarships, but they did not know the rules. These athletes, their parents, and high school coaches operated under myths, unaware of the five things they needed to know to open the doors to college opportunities, namely:

1. When does the recruiting process begin?

2. Where do college coaches find talent?

3. How do college coaches evaluate talent?

4. Where should student-athletes find colleges?

5. Who is responsible for what?

THE FIVE THINGS YOU NEED TO KNOW

#1: When does the recruiting process begin?

The myth is this: *The recruiting process begins when a student-athlete is contacted by a college coach during the athlete's junior or senior year of high school.*

The reality is this: *Due to the rise in athletic scholarship need and the increase of available information for college coaches, the recruiting process is now started earlier than ever. According to the NCAA, college coaches are starting to identify seventh and eight graders as recruits and are even starting to offer scholarships to prospects before their freshman year.*

The recruiting process starts during a student's freshman year at the latest. The NCAA requires a specific number of core courses be completed for a student to compete at NCAA colleges and universities. These core classes begin the athlete's freshman year. Failure to meet these requirements can eliminate a student-athlete's scholarship hopes, regardless of how talented the child might be. Every freshman student-athlete with serious hopes of playing collegiate athletics should visit www.ncaa.org and read the *NCAA Guide for the College-Bound Student-Athlete*.

College coaches begin identifying prospects as early as seventh grade in some sports, including men's basketball. For Division I programs in every sport, college coaches begin compiling their lists of potential recruits when student-athletes are freshmen. College coaches are able to offer scholarships to student-athletes at any point, as evidenced by the recent trend in sports such as men's basketball, where many student-athletes commit to a college prior to their first day of high school.

Randy Taylor, former recruiting coordinator for UCLA, tells the story of J.D., an eighth-grader from Louisiana. Taylor attended a practice in Shreveport to evaluate a senior recruiting defensive end when he noticed J.D. standing on the sidelines playing catch.

The year was 1999. "At that moment," said Taylor, "we had our first offer for the class of 2004, and to the best of my knowledge, that was J.D.'s first offer while in the eighth grade."

In most cases, college coaches will begin the recruiting process by sending letters and questionnaires to the student-athletes on their lists during freshman year. Relationships are developed by student-athletes who take advantage of their ability to call, write, and take unofficial visits to these college coaches at any time.

Waiting to connect with a coach might be the biggest mistake a young student-athlete can make! Coaches from Division III and NAIA schools can call a student-athlete at any time, though some opt to follow the Division I and II rules. Division I and II coaches are prohibited from calling under-classmen, but student-athletes who are smart enough to initiate contact with the coach can start the recruitment process well before their junior year. If a student-athlete calls any coach, regardless of the coach's division, the coach can accept the call and talk to the prospect at any time.

As well, college coaches can send the student-athlete a letter and questionnaire any time, even in grade school, in some cases. Those letters might ask the athlete to call the coach if the student has any questions regarding the university. This is the green light for the student-athlete to initiate a phone call!

These letters, however, do not necessarily indicate real interest. An athlete, as well as thousands of other high school athletes in the United States, Japan, Canada, Spain, Kenya, China, Australia, and Germany, could be receiving recruitment letters from the very same college coaches. If student-athletes receive letters—even hundreds of letters—from college coaches, they are not necessarily being heavily recruited. Chances are good that they simply made their way onto a prospect list and were identified as student-athletes. Coaches from schools with big athletic programs will send ten to fifteen thousand letters to start the recruiting process, but they will only offer about twenty to twenty-five scholarships.

THE RECRUITING FUNNEL

A college football staff might send 10,000 to 15,000 letters

And watch 1,000 to 2,000 videos

Before making 500 phone calls to potential recruits

Verbally offering between 65 and 200 scholarships

Extending up to 85 offers for official visits

Before signing a maximum of 25 players per year

For many high school athletes, receiving that first letter of inquiry from a college is the most exciting, but do not mistake an initial letter from a college as an indicator of high interest. My first five letters came from Michigan, Tennessee, Notre Dame, Arizona, and Brigham Young University, none of which made offers. Coaches and athletic directors purchase lists of high school athletes, so an athlete's name is likely just one on a list. A letter means a school knows who the athlete is, and in many cases, all it means is that the school has seen the student's name in some sort of database. Remember: Mail is just the initial stage; recruitment occurs when a student and coach talk, build a relationship, meet personally, and schedule an evaluation. Do not confuse the two.

The top indicators of a coach's level of interest, in declining order, are:

1. Full scholarship offer in writing.

2. Full scholarship offer made verbally.

3. Partial scholarship offer in writing.

4. Partial scholarship offer made verbally.

5. Offer of an official visit.

6. Phone calls from the head coach on the first day of the contact period, which varies by sport.

7. Hand-written weekly letter from head coach or assistant coach (the former indicates higher interest).

8. Athletic application with fee waiver.

9. Letter from head coach or assistant coach with an invitation to call or email (the former indicates higher interest).

10. Offer of an unofficial visit or game day visit.

11. Request for game, highlight, or skills video.

12. Invitation for pro-rated one-day summer camp visit.

13. Questionnaire and letter inviting the student-athlete to correspond or call.

This list merely denotes interest. Without exception, official commitments are signed into action only on Signing Day. Unless an athlete has signed on the dotted line, no guarantees exist, no matter how many phone calls, letters, FedEx packages, or written offers the student-athlete receives. Also remember that the scholarship offer is for one year only; student-athletes will need to renew their scholarships for their sophomore, junior, senior, and sometimes fifth year of college, so the recruiting process continues even after they have signed on the dotted line.

«« FAST FACT ««

The following are not signs of recruitment:

1. Invitation to attend a camp.

2. A generic admissions letter.

3. A scout attending a game (unless the scout came to evaluate the student-athlete).

#2: Where do college coaches find talent?

The myth is this: *College coaches discover talent their junior or senior year by attending camps, combines, showcases, tournaments, and high school games.*

The reality is this: *College coaches depend on verified information from reliable sources, and they purchase lists of prospects as young as seventh grade. Most coaches attend tournaments, games, and camps with lists of student-athletes they intend to evaluate, not with hopes of discovering random prospects.*

Far too many student-athletes are lost because they think they are going to be discovered. But remember that college programs have a pool of talent that includes over 7.3 million high school athletes in more than twenty-five sports, and each coach has less than about $500 on average to sort through all these athletes. Just take a look at Williams College's recruiting budget. Williams College ranks first in *U.S. News & World Report's* list of best liberal arts colleges. It has the top-rated Division III program according to the Director's Cup, and for three years straight, Williams College has topped the NCSA's Collegiate Power Rankings. Williams was also ranked fourth in financial resources by *U.S. News & World Report,* yet the school has $12,400 earmarked to recruit for its women's teams, which include basketball, crew, cross country, field hockey, golf, ice hockey, lacrosse, skiing, soccer, soft-ball, squash, swimming, diving, tennis, track and field, and volleyball.

If Williams College has a restricted budget, imagine the problems faced by programs that are not as highly rated!

WILLIAMS COLLEGE RECRUITING BUDGET

SPORT	RECRUITING BUDGET DOLLARS	PERCENT OF BUDGET
Football	$16,700.00	43%
Men's Basketball	$5,800.00	15%
All Other Men's Sports	$4,000.00	10%
Combined Men's Sports	$26,500.00	68%
Combined Women's Sports	$12,400.00	32%
Total Recruiting Budget	$38,900.00	100%

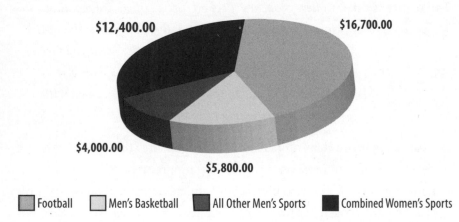

$12,400.00 $16,700.00

$4,000.00

$5,800.00

■ Football   ☐ Men's Basketball   ■ All Other Men's Sports   ■ Combined Women's Sports

Add to this all the rules and regulations of recruiting, and it is easy to see why otherwise-qualified students are simply passed by. And parents often add to the problem. If a parent believes his child is the next LeBron James or Mia Hamm, he likely thinks colleges would be crazy to overlook his son or daughter, so he stands on the sidelines waiting for the school to take notice. And then Signing Day comes and goes. Where are all the college coaches beating down the athlete's door to help ol' State U. win champion-ships? Where is the pot of gold at the end of the athletic rainbow—the free tuition, books, room, and board?

Perhaps the athlete **is** a superstar, but if the student-athlete does not initiate communication with coaches and convey an interest in competing in a program, the student will have a hard time finding a home at a college. The student-athlete must be prepared to call coaches, ask the right ques-tions, and take the initiative.

As well, remember that college coaches purchase verified recruiting lists and rely on credible third parties to begin their process of finding talent. These trusted sources save the college coach an enormous amount of time, effort, and money by providing the college coach only with poten-tial student-athletes they might be interested in.

College coaches rarely discover talent at events such as camps, combines, and showcases. (In fact, NCAA rules prohibit college coaches from attending combines.) Coaches attend most events with a list of student-athletes who they are already recruiting. If a student-athlete is not on the list, chances are that the athlete will not be on the list after attending a camp, combine, or showcase. The average college coach recruits from multiple lists. Student-athletes should take advantage of all credible oppor-tunities to get their name on as many of these lists as possible.

#3: How do college coaches evaluate talent?

The myth is this: *College coaches initially evaluate talent by attending high school games and watching unsolicited videos sent from students and families.*

The reality is this: *College coaches do a majority of their initial evalua-tions by looking at videos requested or received from reliable sources and delivered online or digitally. After watching a video, a coach may decide to make an in-person evaluation.*

Once the college coach has compiled his list of potential recruits, he will want to evaluate the athletes' ability.

College coaches begin their evaluation process as early as an athlete's freshman year. Coaches will send questionnaires requesting basic information, which helps the coaches narrow down their initial, broader recruiting list. If a student-athlete neglects to fill out questionnaires, the athlete will be removed from coaches' databases. The student-athletes who return questionnaires and fit certain criteria remain on the coaches' recruiting lists.

Once they have a list of potential recruits, coaches will request film. The film serves as a far more efficient method of evaluation than traveling to watch the athlete play in person. Most college coaches will review film only if they have requested it or it has been sent from a credible third party. A few coaches at schools with small recruiting budgets will review unsolicited film.

If the college coach evaluates the film and believes that student-athlete possesses the required level of skill, he will make a personal evaluation. Once the list of potential recruits has been narrowed, the college coach might attend a game or tournament to make a final decision.

#4: Where should student-athletes find colleges?

The myth is this: *NCAA Division I is the only option for collegiate athletic scholarships.*

The reality is this: *Over eighteen hundred colleges and universities sponsor collegiate athletes and are able to offer financial packages. Most opportunities fall outside of Division I programs.*

What student-athlete has not imagined being featured on ESPN? And what parent has not imagined Junior earning a full scholarship to the best school in the country? After all, parents have likely been preparing for recruitment since the day their daughter laced up her first soccer cleat. All those long, tedious parent meetings. All those practices that lasted well into the darkness. All those weekends on the road and dinners at the drive-thru window. All those lost holidays and summer vacations spent at sporting events. Don't forget all those checks written to support their mighty endeavors.

«« FAST FACT ««

According to Jack Renkens, former college athletic director at Division II school Assumption College, former college coach, and parent of a recruited student-athlete, parents can expect to spend on average $15,200 on their child's athletic career after paying for shoes, uniforms, equipment, camps, clubs, traveling, and medical expenses.

All those sacrifices were made with one goal in mind: a college athletic scholarship to the best school out there. But remember that fewer than 1 percent of student-athletes receive fully funded Division I scholarships. About 80 percent of opportunities are at Division II and III colleges, who provide need- and non-need-based scholarships, grant monies, and outstanding educations. For every Michigan, UCLA, and Duke, there are Williams, Amhersts, and Wellesleys not as well known for their athletic aptitude, but academically world class.

According to *U.S. News & World Report*, more than 50 percent of the top-rated colleges and universities do not have Division IA non-Bowl subdivision football programs. Only two of the top ten- and six of the top twenty-rated colleges have Division I football programs. Of the top liberal arts colleges, only about 8 percent have Division I football programs. And guess how many of the top fifteen have Division IA football programs?

Not a single one.

Refusing to play the "Name Game" will dramatically help a student's chances to parlay athletics into an outstanding education by taking advantage of athletic opportunities at schools that will prepare an athlete for a meaningful career. Remember that this process is about leveraging athletics to win academic scholarships, grants-in-aid, and eventually career opportunities. For most college athletes, sports are a means to an end.

With this in mind, we recommend that all student-athletes start by looking at Division III programs. Consider the facts:

- Division III is the largest division, with over 450 colleges and universities.

- Overall, Division III schools also have the highest level of academic programs.

- The biggest grants-in-aid packages are available at the Division III level.

- The Division III level of play is more realistic for most student-athletes.

In other words, a student-athlete will likely be awarded more money to receive a better academic education while seeing more playing time at a Division III school.

«« FAST FACT ««

The top of the top athletes can receive fifty offers by January 1 of their junior year. Most major Division I prospects will receive offers by the end of their junior year.

Sometimes the trickiest place for a student-athlete to be is that gray middle ground with enough talent to earn some cursory interest from schools but not enough to be pursued heavily. Most of these athletes lose out on potential scholarship money because they are unrealistic about their lot in the athletic world, and they believe they are being more heavily recruited than they really are. They sit by the phone or mailbox waiting to hear from coaches that are not going to call.

Often, these athletes will ignore overtures from Division II, III, and NAIA programs because they are certain they should be playing Division I athletics. Never mind that the education they would receive could be just as good, if not superior, at a smaller school, and that they could receive more playing time, making for a rewarding experience. Trouble is, by the time many of these athletes realize that the Division I scholarship is not coming, they are too late for a Division II or III school.

Take football, for example. Though the annual Signing Day is in early February, many commitments are made before the beginning of the athlete's senior year. Any player who has not received a verbal offer by Christmas likely is not getting one. Once those Division I verbal commitments are made, the cards begin to fall, as athletes who have not been offered Division I scholarships are scooped up immediately by Division II and III programs.

Student-athletes should not blow it by sitting around waiting for coaches to plead for them to come. Athletes should do their homework early and often, and not let ego get in the way of a fulfilling college experience.

#5: Who is responsible for what?

The myth is this: *A student-athlete's high school or club coach is responsible for getting the athlete a scholarship.*

The reality is this: *The average high school coach has contact with fewer than five college coaches, most of whom are local. Student-athletes and families are ultimately responsible for connecting with college coaches.*

The harsh reality is this: High school and club coaches most often cannot secure scholarships for student-athletes. The average high school coach knows no more than five college coaches. Fewer still have a personal relationship with college coaches, most of whom are local, though more than 99 percent of the opportunities for athletes will be from outside their geographic location.

Even if a student's coach is highly connected, the coach will likely have other student-athletes to help. High school coaches usually have neither the time nor the resources to commit enough energy necessary for an athlete to be recruited. Most high school coaches are not required to facilitate the recruiting process, and their budgets do not cover the expenses related to recruiting. The responsibility rests squarely on the shoulders of the student-athlete and parents.

If a student-athlete's high school coach tells an athlete otherwise, the athlete should express gratitude and accept any offers for help, but the athlete should **not** rely solely on the coach when it comes to a scholarship future. An athlete should provide her coach with all the information necessary to help her earn a spot on a college team and continue her own aggressive search. Even Frank Lenti, named Illinois Coach of the Century and the 1998 Nike USA High School Coach of the Year, agreed that a high school coach most often cannot negotiate a scholarship for a student-athlete. The student and the student's family must work proactively, consulting the high school coach about the realistic level of recruitment, but taking the reins themselves.

Incidentally, Frank Lenti, averaging seventeen players a year who go on to play football in college, is legendary. In the twenty-four years he has been head coach of Chicago's Mount Caramel High School football team, the team has been to the state championships thirteen times and won nine state crowns.

Consider also that high school coaches are most often physical education teachers. If student-athletes have aspirations that fall outside the purview of physical education, they should get help from educators in more related professions to find the correct fit for college.

COACH'S TIP

"Families needs to take responsibility for their own youngsters," said Coach Lenti.

A family's first job in the recruiting process should be to set these myths aside and accurately gauge two things:

1. An athlete's ability to play at a Division I, Division II, Division III, NAIA, or junior college level; and

2. Whether the student's current level of recruitment falls into the category of elite recruitment, serious recruitment, moderate recruitment, light recruitment, or no recruitment at all.

GAUGING THE ATHLETE'S ABILITY

Chris Ducar, the women's soccer coach for the University of North Carolina, once said that he has never met parents who thought their children were unqualified to play for Ducar's team. And Frank Lenti, legendary football coach from Mount Caramel High School, said parents almost always think their athletes can play at least one level above their actual ability.

Survey one hundred college coaches, and they will all tell you the same thing: Most students who come knocking are simply unqualified to play at that level. The same goes for parents. Part of a parent's job is to be a child's number one fan. Though this is the trademark of a good parent, it is not conducive to making an objective evaluation of a child's potential, especially when parents likely have little, if any, access to information about overseas and nationwide competitors.

Gauging an athlete's abilities **accurately** might be difficult for parents and athletes, but it is also critical. Students who believe they play at a Division I level might overlook opportunities from Division II or III schools that offer more realistic opportunities. Having an accurate gauge of an athlete's level of ability early in high school helps manage expectations and set goals. A freshman athlete playing at a Division III level in high school might very well set goals and become a Division I-level athlete by the senior year, but without a barometer advising what those goals should be, the athlete might fail to meet the recruitment requirements.

»« FAST FACT »«

Some recruiting and scouting services, like the NCSA, provide objective third-party evaluations that assess a high school student-athlete's ability to play at the collegiate level. For more information, visit www.athleteswanted.org.

Together, parents and their student-athlete should take a look at the recruitment requirements for the athlete's sport and position. When talking with a college coach, student-athletes should also ask what that particular program's recruitment requirements are, and ask their high school coach if they are likely to improve enough to meet those requirements. If an athlete runs a 16.5-second 100-meter hurdle, she should consider whether she can realistically shave a second or two off her time and be recruited to a particular school.

A SAMPLE OF THE RECRUITMENT REQUIREMENTS PER SPORT AND DIVISION			
SPORT	DIVISION I	DIVISION II	DIVISION III
Baseball, right-handed pitcher	80-90 miles per hour	85+ miles per hour	83+ miles per hour
Women's basketball, point guard	At least 5'8" tall	At least 5'7" tall	At least 5'5" tall
Men's basketball, shooting guard	At least 6'2" tall	At least 6'1" tall	At least 5'11" tall
Women's track, 100-meter hurdle	< 14.5 seconds	< 15.2 seconds	< 15.5 seconds
Men's track, 100-meter dash	< 10.5 seconds	< 10.9 seconds	< 11.0 seconds
Football, running back speed	< 4.5 second 40-yard dash	< 4.6 second 40-yard dash	< 4.7 second 40-yard dash
Women's golf, 18-hole average	< 78	< 85	< 95
Men's golf, handicap	< Scratch	< 2	< 3
Softball, pitcher's ERA	60+ miles per hour	58+ miles per hour	55+ miles per hour
Men's swimming, 50-meter freestyle	< 21.4 seconds	< 22 seconds	< 24 seconds
Women's swimming, 50-meter freestyle	< 24 seconds	< 25.5 seconds	< 28.0 seconds
Women's track, high jump	5'10" plus	5'4" plus	5'1" plus
Men's track, shot put	60'10"	50'	50'
Women's volleyball, average setter's block jump	9'10"	8'9"	8'7"
Height	5'10"	5'8"	5'7"
Men's volleyball, setter's average approach jump	10'8"	10"6'	10'6"
Height	6'3"	6'3"	6'1"
Wrestling	Four-time varsity letter-winner in high school	Three-time varsity letter-winner in high school	Two-time varsity letter-winner in high school

For a full listing by sport and position, see www.athleteswanted.org.

Parents and athletes should gauge the athlete's grades and other academic and extracurricular achievements as well. Though student-athletes often have little time to volunteer for the community or participate in extracurricular activities, students who promise to bring a bevy of talents to a school will be more easily recruited than adequate students with few highlights on their college application. The stronger the athlete is in athletics and academics, the less important other extracurricular activities will be.

GAUGING THE ATHLETE'S LEVEL OF RECRUITMENT

Keep this in mind: Having all the right stuff and doing the right stuff are not the same things. An athlete might meet or exceed all Division I criteria and still fall into the category of lightly or not-at-all recruited because the student did not play the game of recruitment properly.

A student-athlete's level of recruitment falls into one of five categories:

1. Elite recruitment

2. Serious recruitment

3. Moderate recruitment

4. Light recruitment

5. No recruitment

Elite Recruitment

If an athlete is a superstar athlete who knows how to play the game of recruitment, especially in the marquee sports of football and basketball, the athlete likely would already have offers. Coaches will start sending letters of inquiry as early as an athlete's seventh or eighth grade year, using every strategy within the rules—and some outside the rules—to sign an athlete on Signing Day. Even in the so-called Olympic, or non-revenue sports, such as lacrosse, soccer, swimming, and wrestling, the elite athletes will probably not go unnoticed.

Keep in mind that athletes recruited at the elite level comprise only about one hundred of the top kids in the world (note the word *world* and not *nation),* and only the top five in any position. Most athletes are unlikely to fall into this category. Athletes recruited at the elite level are those who start receiving FedEx packages their freshman year and have fifty to one hundred offers by the end of their junior year. These athletes will likely have their picks of the top schools providing they meet academic qualifications, progress athletically, and graduate on time.

Even if student-athletes fit into this category, parents and athletes will be far better off assuming they do not. If they are wrong, they will be pleasantly surprised with the results. But if athletes assume they are elite recruits and pass over great offers, they might miss out on outstanding opportunities. Our motto is this: Aim low and shoot high. Assume Division I is a reach. Athletes should apply for Division I schools (shoot high) but focus also on Division II, Division III, and NAIA programs that offer an abundance of realistic opportunities.

If an athlete has not received a scholarship offer by the beginning of the junior year, or even as early as the freshman year, that athlete does not fit into the category of elite recruits. These athletes should begin an aggressive and targeted marketing campaign so that the appropriate coaches will notice the athlete.

The Rest of the Recruitment Pool

Most likely, a student-athlete's recruitment level falls into one of four categories:

1. Seriously recruited

2. Moderately recruited

3. Lightly recruited

4. Not at all recruited

INDICATORS THAT AN ATHLETE IS AN ELITE RECRUIT

	FRESHMAN	SOPHOMORE	JUNIOR	SENIOR
Heavily Recruited	More than thirty letters/emails from different schools. Letters/emails include camp brochures, information about NCAA rules, and invite the student-athlete to call or email the coach.	Over sixty letters/emails from different schools. Letters/emails include camp brochures, questionnaires, information about NCAA rules, and invite the student-athlete to call or email the coach.	Over sixty emails immediately following September 1.	Student-athlete receives personal phone calls from college coaches immediately following July 1 (Division I) or June 15 (Division II). See NCAA recruiting guidelines for sport-specific call dates.
	At least one offer (depending on sport).	At least three offers (depending on sport).	Coaches say student-athlete is the top recruit.	
			Unofficial visit invites.	Three or more in home visits.
	College coaches call student-athlete's high school or club coach/director to inquire about the athlete.	College coaches call the student-athlete's high school or club coach/director to inquire about the athlete.	At least five offers on the table.	Ten or more offers on the table.
			Transcripts requested by college coach.	At least ten official visit invites.
	College coaches watch the athlete play at club tournaments and showcases (depending on sport).	College coaches watch the athlete play at club tournaments and showcases (depending on sport).	Depending on sport, head college coach begins to call after April 15.	Fifty plus phone calls from different schools.
		Video requests (depending on sport).		Weekly emails/phone calls.
		Head college coach begins to call June 15 (depending on sport).		

INDICATORS OF A CHILD'S LEVEL OF RECRUITMENT				
	FRESHMAN	SOPHOMORE	JUNIOR	SENIOR
Seriously Recruited	Over fifteen letters/emails from different schools. Letters/emails include camp brochures, questionnaires, information about NCAA rules, and invite the student-athlete to call or email the coach.	Over thirty letters/emails from different schools. Letters/emails include camp brochures, questionnaires, information about NCAA rules, and invite the student-athlete to call or email the coach.	Over forty-five emails immediately following September 1.	Student-athlete receives personal phone calls from college coaches immediately following July 1 (Division I) or June 15 (Division II). See NCAA recruiting guidelines for sport-specific call dates.
	College coaches call student-athlete's high school or club coach/director to inquire about the athlete.	At least one offer (depending on sport).	Coaches say the student-athlete is in the top five recruits.	At least one in-home visit.
	College coaches watch the athlete play at club tournaments and showcases (depending on sport).	College coaches call student-athlete's high school or club coach/director to inquire about the athlete.	Coaches invite student-athlete to games.	At least five offers on the table.
		College coaches watch the athlete play at club tournaments and showcases (depending on sport).	Coaches extend personal invitations for student-athlete to attend camps.	At least five official visit invites.
		Video requests (depending on sport).	Video requests.	At least thirty phone calls from different schools.
		Head college coach begins to call June 15 (depending on sport).	At least three offers are on the table.	Frequent emails/phone calls.
			Transcripts requested by college coach.	
			Depending on sport, head coach begins to call after April 15.	

	INDICATORS OF A CHILD'S LEVEL OF RECRUITMENT			
	FRESHMAN	**SOPHOMORE**	**JUNIOR**	**SENIOR**
Moderately Recruited	Fewer than fifteen letters/emails from different schools. Letters/emails include camp brochures, questionnaires, and information about NCAA rules. College coaches may watch the athlete play at club tournaments and showcases (depending on sport).	Fewer than thirty letters/emails from different schools. Letters/emails include camp brochures, questionnaires, and information about NCAA rules. College coaches may watch the athlete play at club tournaments and showcases (depending on sport). Assistant college coaches begin to call June 15 (depending on sport).	Emails from coaches in the fall. Might be personalized. Unofficial visit invites. Coaches invite student-athlete to games. Coaches evaluate student-athlete's team in person. Coaches call student-athlete's high school or club coach/director. Transcripts requested by college coach. Depending on sport, assistant college coaches begin to call after April 15.	Under five official visit invites. Ten or more college coaches call in July. Coaches tell the student-athlete to apply. Possibly one to three offers. Sporadic emails/phone calls.

INDICATORS OF A CHILD'S LEVEL OF RECRUITMENT			
	FRESHMAN	SOPHOMORE	JUNIOR	SENIOR
Lightly Recruited	Fewer than ten letters/emails from different schools. Letters/emails include camp brochures, questionnaires, and information about NCAA rules.	Fewer than fifteen letters/emails from different schools. Letters/emails include camp brochures, questionnaires, and information about NCAA rules. Assistant college coaches begin to call June 15 (depending on sport).	Form emails from coaches. Coaches invite student-athlete to games. Coaches evaluate student-athlete's team in person. Coaches may call student-athlete's high school or club coach/director. Depending on sport, assistant college coaches begin to call after April 15. Transcripts requested by college coach. School will send 1-800 number and the school's media guide.	No more than three official visit invites. No more than ten college coaches call beginning in July. Possibly one offer. Coaches invite student to walk on. Coaches act as if student is going to apply. Student receives a few emails/phone calls from coaches.

INDICATORS OF A CHILD'S LEVEL OF RECRUITMENT			
FRESHMAN	**SOPHOMORE**	**JUNIOR**	**SENIOR**
Athlete receives camp brochures and general admissions information only.	Athlete receives camp brochures and general admissions information only.	Athletes receive no more than ten form emails. Athletes continue to receive camp brochures. Athletes receive fewer than ten questionnaires.	Athletes receive no more than ten form emails. Athletes continue to receive camp brochures. Athletes receive fewer than ten questionnaires.

Not at all Recruited

Surprisingly, even those students who receive one hundred letters of interest do not fall into the category of elite recruitment. Unless a ton of offers are on the table, assume that an athlete needs to proactively market himself and search for a college. Even student-athletes in the "heavily recruited" category will not likely have their top choice of a college.

To some extent, whether a student is noticed can be a crapshoot. The size of the high school can make a difference. The location can make a difference. The high school's media exposure can make a difference. College coaching staffs do have limited budgets even at the highest levels, and programs are restricted by NCAA guidelines from engaging in certain recruitment activities.

But if student-athletes play the game right, even if they are average athletes or students, they can still leverage outstanding opportunities.

The athlete or her parents should also complete the Recruiting Action Plan questionnaire at www.athleteswanted.org, which will provide an evaluation of where the student-athlete stands, as well as a sport-specific action plan based on the athlete's grade level, ability, and level of recruitment.

KEY POINTS

1.   Far too many athletes miss out on college opportunities because they do not know how to play the recruiting game. In fact, the best athletes are often not offered scholarships, while far less superior athletes receive glamorous offers. Athletes, parents, and high school and club coaches should know five things to protect the athletes from falling through the cracks:

#1: When does the recruiting process begin?

The myth is this: *The recruiting process begins when a student-athlete is contacted by a college coach during the athlete's junior or senior year of high school.*

The reality is this: *Due to the rise in athletic scholarship need and the increase of available information for college coaches, the recruiting process is now started earlier than ever. According to the NCAA, college coaches are starting to identify seventh and eight graders as recruits and are even starting to offer scholarships to prospects before their freshman year.*

#2: Where do college coaches find talent?

The myth is this: *College coaches discover talent their junior or senior year by attending camps, combines, showcases, tournaments, and high school games.*

The reality is this: *College coaches depend on verified information from reliable sources, and they purchase lists of prospects as young as seventh grade. Most coaches attend tournaments, games, and camps with lists of student-athletes they intend to evaluate, not with hopes of discovering random prospects.*

#3: How do college coaches evaluate talent?

The myth is this: *College coaches initially evaluate talent by attending high school games and watching unsolicited videos sent from students and families.*

The reality is this: *College coaches do a majority of their initial evaluations by looking at videos requested or received from reliable sources and delivered online or digitally. After watching a video, a coach may decide to make an in-person evaluation.*

#4: Where should student-athletes find colleges?

The myth is this: *NCAA Division I is the only option for collegiate athletic scholarships.*

The reality is this: *Over eighteen hundred colleges and universities sponsor collegiate athletes and are able to offer financial packages. Most opportunities fall outside of Division I programs.*

#5: Who is responsible for what?

The myth is this: *A student-athlete's high school or club coach is responsible for getting the athlete a scholarship.*

The reality is this: *The average high school coach has contact with fewer than five college coaches, most of whom are local. Student-athletes and families are ultimately responsible for connecting with college coaches.*

 2. Having an accurate assessment of ability helps a student-athlete determine which schools might be a good fit. Athletes can start by learning the recruitment requirements for their specific sport (see www. athleteswanted.org). The student-athlete can ask college coaches for an evaluation of all potential opportunities and ask college coaches what their specific athletic requirements are. Athletes should consider their grades and set goals accordingly.

 3. In addition to ability, athletes should know their level of recruitment and take the Recruiting Action Plan questionnaire, available at www. athleteswanted.org, for a sport-specific action plan based on grade level, ability, and level of recruitment.

THE PARENT'S ROLE

FOR PARENTS, the recruiting process can be one of the greatest challenges—a test of patience, endurance, and discipline all wrapped into one exhilarating yet anxiety-plagued package. In some ways, parents have been preparing for this time since first enrolling their child in AYSO soccer, Little League baseball, or Pop Warner football. They have invested time, money, and sweat for a decade. It can feel as if Mom and Dad have almost as much at stake as the athlete does.

A parent's primary challenge is to walk the fine line between guiding the athlete through the process and becoming overbearing. Parents might be tempted to take full control, especially when they see how overwhelming the experience can be. A parent's goal is to find the middle ground between a "hands off" parent and one who micromanages every move the student makes. These parents offer a certain threat to their children. By taking complete control of the process, these parents jeopardize their children's ability to learn and grow from the experience. As well, they can annoy the living daylights out of college coaches. Bob Chmiel, NCSA Education Speaker and former football coach at Notre Dame, said he stayed a mile away from children of "we dads."

"You always know who the 'we dads' are because they start every sentence with the word *we*. '*We* are applying to Georgetown. *We* had a great season.'"

Chmiel goes on to explain that college coaches do not want to be distracted by overbearing, meddlesome parents, so a parent who seems too controlling might actually hurt an otherwise-qualified student's ability to be recruited.

Perhaps Chris Ducar, North Carolina's assistant women's soccer coach put it best. Ducar once told me that in his twelve years as a coach, he has never once recruited a mom or dad to play for him.

COACH'S TIP

"It isn't unusual to drop a prospect from the recruiting board because the parents are a problem," said Randy Taylor, former recruiting coordinator for UCLA.

Some parents, on the other hand, take a completely hands-off approach, even though the athlete is still a teenager and can lose focus. A gentle guiding hand is the perfect touch, though not always easy for a parent to produce.

THE PARENTS' GOLDEN RULES

RULE #1: Don't be a helicopter mom or we dad.

This rule applies regardless of how old a child is, and whether dealing with a child, athletic director, high school coach, college coach, or Pee Wee football coach. A *helicopter* parent hovers over the child, not allowing her to grow or act for herself. A *we* parent lives vicariously through the child's accomplishments.

Remember, in the parent/student-athlete relationship, the student-athlete must become the team captain!

The greater load the student-athlete takes and is able to handle, the better. This particularly applies to communicating with the coach. While a parent might be well spoken and articulate, a student-athlete might mutter, stumble over sentences, and shake at the thought of approaching a coach. The parent's first inclination might be to jump in and rescue a child from her fledgling attempts at communication. But consider the college coach's perspective. Who would the coach rather hear from: the parent, or the student-athlete who will play for the program for the next four or five years?

Coaches are impressed by students who initiate conversations. As difficult as it might be for students to muster the courage to call coaches, student-athletes' abilities to represent themselves is critical to the recruiting process.

And the earlier parents can loosen the reins, the better. By allowing children to communicate directly with elementary, junior high, and high school coaches, parents will allow their children to grow confident, which means the athletes will make great first impressions when they pick up the phone to call their first college coach.

"A parent actually detracts from a high school student's ability to learn a valuable skill set if she marches into the coach's office every time there is a conflict or every time she thinks her son is not getting enough playing time," said Joyce Wellhoefer, who has coached for high school and college basketball, softball, and volleyball programs.

A high school athlete will have only one chance to make a first impression on a college coach. Confidence will be critical to this interaction, so early opportunities to communicate with adults is critical to an athlete's success down the road.

From a recruitment perspective, Carmen Bucci, a former San Diego Padre, agreed. If a college coach receives phone call after phone call from a parent, the coach might start to think that the parent is a nuisance, which could cost the child his athletic scholarship.

Does this mean the best approach for parents is to send their child into an unfamiliar, sometimes-scary world completely alone? Of course not!

Don Beebe, a former member of six Super Bowl teams, now runs a program called House of Speed in which he teaches athletes to build character through sports. The most important role he sees for parents is to create an environment that fosters positive growth.

Beebe had the following advice for parents: "The biggest thing is to stop putting pressure on kids. If playing sports is her passion, back her and support her. If a child puts her heart and soul into a game and still loses, a parent should pat her on the back with as much enthusiasm as if she had beat a world record."

COACH'S TIP

The mark of a good parent is an athlete who succeeds even without parents looking over his shoulders, said Chmiel.

RULE #2: Teach humility.

On the flip side, young athletes—especially those who are talented—can receive too much support, develop attitude problems, and become less motivated in important activities outside of their sport.

Quality parenting can make the difference between a child who thinks he is king of the world and a humble, gracious child who works hard and excels as an athlete and a student, said Michel Balasis, the former kicker for Michigan State University and head of Loyola University's department of visual communications.

"Student-athletes are a mixed bag. Because they are great athletes, the pampered ones think they can skate by," said Balasis, noting they are easy to spot for their lack of work ethic.

But Balasis takes notice of the students whose parents expect more of them. These students are also easy to spot because of their rigorous work ethic and ability to go the extra mile.

Parents are primarily responsible for their children's attitude. Children who strut into class thinking they will sail by because they are student-athletes will learn a lesson later in life. Parents who teach their children early to work hard will save their children from years of suffering while in college and later during their careers.

"Teach your kids that they need to earn what they have," agreed Beebe, who knows a thing or two about hard work. "When they cross the line in sports or academia, step in and tell them they have to change."

To compete successfully in sports, a student must maintain an academic standard. Parents should insist on it now, and their child will be better prepared for the demands of college. If parents overlook it now, their student-athlete might not make it past freshman year in college. Like a good coach, a good parent will discipline their children who have stepped over the line.

What the student does off the field is just as important as what takes place on the field. As the recruiting process begins, maintaining good grades becomes more and more important. Performance in the classroom tells a coach plenty about an athlete's likelihood of reaching their potential on the playing field. Coaches know that good students tend to make the most of their abilities and stay out of trouble.

Michael Stonebreaker, two-time All American from Notre Dame, reports that his father made him go to summer school because he received a C on his report card. Stonebreaker was not happy with the requirement, but it was the only C he would ever receive. Later, his high GPA helped him earn a full scholarship to Notre Dame, so while he had to devote his summer to academics, he learned a valuable lesson.

We suggest the three-part **ACE** formula for teaching students to be accountable.

Academics: Remember that a college coach will not recruit a student-athlete who cannot compete in the classroom. Academic performance tells a coach a lot about a child's ability to manage time, set goals, and prioritize.

Character: Character is a big part of a sport. No coach wants to work with a sore loser or an ungracious winner. Remember that you can tell a lot about a child's character by the company he keeps. Parents need to make sure that their children know how to make good decisions and are accountable for the actions they take.

COACH'S TIP

College coaches want character, not characters, said Coach Chmiel.

Effort: Effort and work ethic are a big part of children's ability to be successful student-athletes. During summers and weekends, my parents had a rule: I either worked or I did housework. If I worked, I made money, so I chose the former. Having a paper route and working as a caddy at the local golf course taught me the value of hard work early, and when I left for college, I stood out from the crowd because I was accustomed to working hard to achieve my goals.

Win or lose, a coach wants to know that student-athletes did their best not only athletically, but also academically. So long as a student makes his best effort with every play and in every classroom on every homework assignment and in every practice, a coach will see that the athlete is a class act.

THE WELL-ROUNDED STUDENT-ATHLETE IS SUPERIOR AT ACADEMICS, ATHLETICS, AND INTANGIBLES

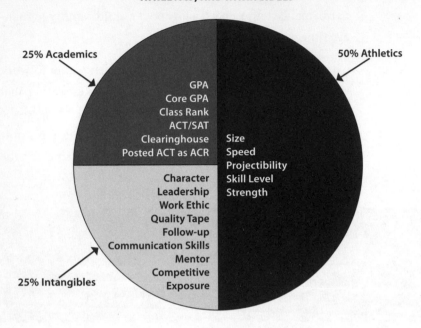

When considering whether to recruit a student-athlete, coaches weigh intangibles, as well as the student's athletic and academic ability.

RULE #3: Parents should be their child's assistant and mentor, not just the cheerleader.

A parent's primary role is to be the child's assistant and mentor. While a cheerleader simply offers encouragement and approval, the parent's job is to help the child.

I specifically remember asking my dad every week how I did in Pee Wee football. Finally, my dad turned to me and said, "Son, you will know you played well when you do not have to ask me how you did."

A parent's job is to teach children to stand on their own two feet. Eventually, the child should turn to parents for help, but not for approval. If parents act solely as their child's cheerleader, their child will constantly seek their approval, whereas if they support and help their child through the ups and downs, the child will learn to stand on his own two feet.

Parents should delineate their roles and give their athlete room to breathe and grow. While letting them make the decisions, Mom or Dad can do the most by serving as an assistant who keeps a level head, providing pragmatic help. As an assistant, a parent's role might include:

- Helping create the child's one-page athletic and academic résumé, as well as the highlight/skills video.

- Coordinating information about testing dates and time.

- Creating a filing system that includes each school of interest.

- Referencing this book and learning the rules of the college recruiting game.

- Helping children set academic and athletic goals, encouraging the child throughout the process.

- Maintaining the Recruiting Checklist, which can be downloaded from www.athleteswanted.org.

- Role-playing conversations with their child.

PREPARE THE STUDENT-ATHLETE BY ROLE-PLAYING

If a child is calling a coach, he will likely be nervous and stumble over his words. Parents can help by role-playing with their children, having them practice leaving voice mails and talking with coaches. For parents, who are confident and accustomed to making business transactions via phone, this might seem like a simple—or even silly—thing to do. Parents need to remember that most student-athletes have little experience initiating relationships with authority figures over the phone. Every impression counts, and parents want children to sound confident and capable.

Parents should start by having the child leave a practice voicemail, pretending as though the athlete is leaving a message for the coach. Parents should listen to the message with the athlete, and help the child eliminate "ums" from the message. As well, they should help their child sound enthusiastic. Often, a child who is timid leaving a message sounds bored, and a coach might misread this as lack of interest.

A parent can help a student prepare for calls with a coach by asking questions the coach might ask the student-athlete. Some sample questions include:

- *How was your season?*
- *What other colleges are you looking at?*
- *What do you consider to be your strengths and weaknesses?*
- *What other colleges have called you?*
- *What other colleges have made offers?*

Some coaches will ask questions specifically to get a handle on how highly recruited an athlete is. Parents need to prepare their child to be strategic by reading Chapter 5.

A student-athlete can start by practicing with schools he is less interested in so that he can learn from his mistakes. Far better for a child to fumble with a low-ranked school than his top choice, and this builds a student's confidence while teaching him how to communicate with coaches so that he is prepared when it really matters.

Remember: Coaches like student-athletes who take initiative and are proactive in the recruiting process. A student-athlete who takes charge off the field will do the same thing on the field!

Helping children with these rudimentary matters while letting them find their way will ensure that student-athletes will savor the process (and may even guarantee that Mom and Dad will get a call every Sunday once their children are out of the nest for the first time!).

The recruiting process can test a child's psyche. Rejection can deeply affect a teenager, and rejection will be part of this process. This is where parents can provide that loving, guiding hand. They should remind their children that they are immensely proud of their accomplishments and that the rejection does not diminish their efforts or alter their worth in any way.

Rejection is part of the educational experience, and it will happen again at some point. Parents should try sharing some of their experiences with rejection. Michael Jordan hit the nail on the head when he said, "I have missed more than nine thousand shots in my career. I have lost almost three hundred games. On twenty-six occasions I have been entrusted to take the game winning shot—and I missed. I have failed over and over and over again in my life. And that is precisely why I succeed."

(Incidentally, Jordan was cut from his high school basketball team.)

Everyone fails. It is not how many times athletes get knocked down, but how many times student-athletes get back up. A parent's role is to help a child deal with rejection and prepare the athlete for a future in the real world. Parents need to remind their child that the person who never quits can never be a loser.

COACH'S TIP

"There comes a point in time when a young person has to stand on her own two feet," said Chmiel. "She has to shake hands and socially interact and look people in the eye."

RULE #4: Parents need to create a specific plan and follow it.

This process can be daunting, but the early bird gets the worm. Those who act quickly and prudently have the most choices. Those who wait too long can miss opportunities. Parents should set an example for their child by emphasizing the importance of creating a plan to follow. Use the Recruiting Checklist and set SMART goals: Goals should be **S**pecific, **M**easurable, **A**ttainable, and **R**ecorded over **T**ime. This will be the roadmap and blueprint for success.

A parent's job is to help the child create and stick to a timeline. Parents should:

- Create a plan to incorporate each element from the Recruiting Checklist into a timeline. Complete the Recruiting Action Plan questionnaire at www.athleteswanted.org for sport-specific steps that will increase a child's likelihood of being recruited. Parents should remember that the overall plan consists of three components:

  1. The academic plan that tracks grade-point average, core courses, tests, and progress.

  2. The athletic plan for goal-setting (specific physical accomplishments to reach recruiting benchmarks) and tracking physical aspects of the child's progress as an athlete, such as height, weight, speed, and strength.

3. The recruiting plan to create the child's résumé, make a highlight or skills video, and build relationships with college coaches.

- Research websites and track progress using the Initial Target List and Correspondence Log, both of which can be downloaded at www.athleteswanted.org. Both parents and athlete should be familiar with the *NCAA Guide for the College-Bound Student-Athlete* and the admissions processes for the athlete's top schools. Again, a parent needs to empower the athlete to take control, make decisions, and initiate research, but as the more mature, experienced person, a parent should make sure the child is meeting deadlines and staying abreast of the recruiting process.

- Narrow the list of potential colleges, reminding the athlete that the first goal is to get an education.

- Make sure the athlete is communicating with coaches. Parents need to remember to use a Correspondence Log to track communication with college coaches.

- Carve time in the athlete's schedule to take unofficial and game day visits with local colleges and colleges of interest.

- Find an objective and credible third-party to provide an evaluation of the athlete's abilities.

- Map out the child's core courses and track GPA.

- Examine the *Media Guide of Potential College Programs* to realistically examine potential opportunities and set goals. The *Media Guide* usually appears on a school's athletic website and contains biographies of all the school's current players. The player's biographies reflect clues as to what accomplishments and statistics are necessary to be recruited by a particular program. Parents and athletes should pay attention to an athlete's size, strength, athletic, and academic honors.

- Help build a skills, game, or highlight video (see Chapter 8 and www.athleteswanted.org).

- Make sure that the athlete has a positive relationship with high school coaches. Though a high school coach cannot secure a scholarship for an athlete, a high school coach can make an offer disappear. Before making an offer, a college coach will always call the athlete's high school coach.

- When the time comes, make sure the child completes and submits college applications.

RULE #5: Parents should be realistic and get an honest evaluation of an athlete from a high school coach, club coach, or scouting organization.

Most student-athletes are dreamers. Though it is important to shoot high, it is equally important to have at least some grasp on reality. If an athlete is only five feet tall and plans to win a full-ride scholarship to play center guard for women's basketball, her parents might want to direct her toward some objective standards so she can set more realistic goals.

Likewise, parents should also be realistic about their child. Most parents are partial to their children and might not be the best judges of a student-athlete's ability. Parents should try to find objective statistics about their child. See www.athleteswanted.org for general statistics about student-athletes at Division I, II, and III levels for each sport so parents can see how their child stacks up.

The most successful student-athletes are the ones who aim low but shoot high. In other words, parents should not pressure their children to get into a Division I school, but allow and encourage them to apply to these schools, as long as they are also applying to schools where they realistically stand a chance of admittance. (Remember that the best schools do not always have great athletic teams, and that we recommend starting from the Division III level.) Parents should do their homework and have a good understanding of the NCSA Collegiate Power Rankings, available at www. athleteswanted.org, which compares academic records, athletic records, and graduation rates.

Parents need to be realistic about the financial side of their child's experience as well. Though many, many opportunities await, the majority of athletes will need to supplement their educational costs even if they receive athletic or need-based academic grants-in-aid. Parents should establish these parameters early and start doing research. Sometimes, the more expensive schools will offer the most in scholarship money, so a $40,000 school might cost only $10,000, while a $20,000 school might cost $15,000. Never evaluate a collegiate opportunity based only on a college sticker price.

RULE #6: Parents should know their Expected Family Contribution.

Critical to the financial side of a child's college opportunities is the Expected Family Contribution (EFC). The EFC determines how much the family can contribute, and understanding how this number is derived allows parents to make adjustments or allocate assets in such a way that best leverages their financial situation. Not knowing an EFC is like not knowing a credit score, or not knowing how much a person can afford for a down payment before buying a home. The EFC will allow a family to objectively compare collegiate opportunities. Remember that it can change year to year, and it is based on how many full-time dependents a family has in college. (See Chapter 9 for more information on the financial side of collegiate opportunities.)

Once parents have determined how much they can contribute, they should clearly communicate that the athlete must find a way to cover the gap through work-study programs, jobs, other grants, and student loans. Remember that being a college athlete is essentially a full-time job, and that maintaining another job, even if part-time, can be overly taxing and harm performance on the playing field and in the classroom.

RULE #7: The greater the distance, the greater the opportunities.

The process of discovering the right college for a child usually begins in earnest during his or her sophomore or junior year of high school. At this point, parents are basically staring at a blank slate, even if their child has picked out a so-called dream school of choice. Parents should avoid fixating on that one school.

"I have talked to a lot of parents who are blinded by ESPN and the Name Game," said Lisa Strasman. "They do not always take the time to investigate what different schools have to offer, and they end up finding out that the original image of a college was all wrong and not at all what they wanted."

Another big mistake, said Andrea Emmons, is to consider only colleges close to home. Wanting to keep children close to the nest is a natural instinct, but it eliminates many options. Children are better positioned for success if they can evaluate all options without restrictions on geography. This means that parents might not be able to see all of their child's games in person, a small sacrifice to pay for their child's long-term success.

The greater the distances the child will travel, the greater the opportunity for recruitment. A student with an average ability who is willing to travel will have more opportunities than the student-athlete who has very good athletic ability, but who wants to play close to home.

Parents and their children should go into this process with open minds, without any preconceived notions about a college or region of the country. The search should be from coast to coast, border to border, refusing to eliminate a part of the country based on a stereotype that might be an unfair broad brush. I once received a call from a coaching staff member from Coastal Carolina University, who reported that the women's tennis team had two full scholarship opportunities. The coach went on to explain that the team was housed in an ocean-front condominium. This sounds like a fantastic opportunity to me, but how many parents and student-athletes would overlook Coastal Carolina University simply because they had never heard of the school?

This can be an exciting yet unnerving time for many reasons. Ultimately, all of a parent's efforts in the process will end with the child elsewhere, in a new home, out of the nest for the first time. The athlete is about to become an adult, entering an unfamiliar world where Mom and Dad will not be an immediate safety net, even if the college of choice is close to home. Regardless of whether a child is a two-hour drive or a five-hour flight away, parents will worry. It will be an emotional time. They can count on it.

RULE #8: Parents should not risk their child's collegiate future by relying solely on the coach.

A parent's job is to assist the child in this process. The child's high school coach is not responsible for getting the athlete a scholarship, nor is the coach responsible for helping the student-athlete figure out how to pay for school.

"A child's high school coach will do everything he can to help a child become recruited, but it will not be enough," said Jack Renkens, the former coach of Massachusetts's Division II Assumption College. The entire senior class hopes to be recruited, as do juniors, sophomores, and freshmen getting an early start. The coach has a job, a family, and countless other obligations. And he will not get paid for helping a child win a scholarship or turn the head of a college coach.

« « FAST FACT « «

The average high school coach has personal contacts with an average of fewer than five college coaches, 90 percent of whom are local.

In addition, the typical high school coach has few strings to pull. Most college coaches do not know high school coaches, and vice versa. With almost two thousand colleges to consider, parents are unrealistic to think a student's high school coach has enough time to build relationships with college coaches. Likewise, how could a college coach possibly build relationships with the twenty-three thousand high schools in the nation?

If a family is lucky, the student-athlete's high school coach is a veteran with a handful of local contacts in the college sports world. But even in this ideal situation, the high school coach's help will not extend beyond a phone call or email.

KEY POINTS

1. When communicating with coaches, a parent should not be a "helicopter mom" or "we dad." Parents should loosen the reins and let the child take the lead. College coaches are not interested in dealing with their players' parents, so an overly involved parent might hurt a child's chance of being recruited.

2. The earlier the parent can loosen the reins, the better. By allowing a child to communicate directly with elementary, junior high, and high school coaches, parents will allow the child to grow confident in his communication skills, which means he will make a great first impression when he picks up the phone to call his first college coach.

3. Parents need to teach their children humility. To successfully compete in sports, a child must be willing to work harder than other students. If an athlete hopes to skate by on natural athletic ability alone, coaches will not be interested in recruiting him. In addition to athletic ability, a student-athlete will be judged on academia, character, and ethic.

4. Parents should be their child's assistant and mentor, not just a cheerleader. The parent's job is to prepare the child and assist with the recruitment process. The athlete should turn to the parent for help, but not for approval. Children who learn to stand on their own two feet will make better decisions and be more confident, capable people.

5. Parents can create SMART plans for athletic, academic, and recruiting goals. These plans should incorporate the Recruiting Checklist from pages 59 through 102. As well, parents should make plans to:

- Complete the Recruiting Action Plan questionnaire at www. athleteswanted.org.
- Research college websites, as well as the *NCAA Guide for the College-Bound Student-Athlete.*

- Help an athlete narrow the list of potential colleges.
- Make sure the child is communicating with coaches.
- Schedule time for official and unofficial visits.
- Stay on top of application deadlines.
- Find an objective third-party to evaluate the student-athlete.
- Map out the child's core courses and GPA.
- Examine the *Media Guide of Potential College Programs*.
- Help build a highlight or skills video.
- Encourage the child to build a strong relationship with the high school coach.

 6.   Parents should be realistic, and get an honest evaluation of the child from a high school coach, club coach, or scouting organization.

 7.   Remember that the greater the distance, the greater the opportunities. Parents should make sure the Name Game does not blind the child and encourage the athlete to search high and low, in every nook and cranny, for the right college fit.

 8.   Parents need to be aware that the high school coach is not responsible for getting the child a scholarship. Most high school coaches are also teachers who have families and other obligations. They have anywhere from fifteen to eighty other athletes for whom they are responsible. Their time is limited and precious.

ALIGNING A COLLEGE WITH A STUDENT-ATHLETE

WHEN MOST STUDENTS think of collegiate athletic scholarships, they imagine attending a Division I school with a world-class athletic department known throughout the country for its sports programs. For them, the definition of a "good school" rests on one criterion: the school's athletic reputation.

And for some students, this might be the right approach. But for other athletes, Big Ten schools are simply the wrong choice. This was the case with Jay Straight, the basketball player from the Robert Taylor Homes. Straight turned down other prominent offers from Division I schools to attend the University of Wyoming.

"I knew the University of Wyoming would allow me to walk away from all the distractions of the south side of Chicago," said Straight. "I went to a place where there was nothing to do but study and play basketball. I knew that I did not have to attend Duke or North Carolina to be a successful basketball player or a successful person. I was better off at Wyoming."

Straight would go on to be named *Parade Magazine's* Freshman All-America.

This chapter focuses on creating guidelines so that a student-athlete can find the right fit, leveraging his athletic ability to earn a great education. This might mean that an athlete turns down big name schools in favor of smaller schools that offer better scholarships or stronger career opportunities.

It all depends on the unique athlete's goals.

Ever heard of Ohio State? Most people know that the school's football team is consistently ranked among the best in the country. But have you ever heard of its English department? Is it any good? If a student wants to study creative writing, he should know the answer to this question.

And what about Mount Union College? Among the top private liberal arts programs, Mount Union also holds nine NCAA Division III football national championships.

Kenyon College has a 380-acre nature preserve on its campus. It also has a ten-to-one student-faculty ratio. Nearly one-third of the student body participates in Division III athletics, and 99 percent of its tenured teachers hold at least one PhD. Its swimming and diving teams have won twenty-nine consecutive men's national championships and twenty-two women's national titles.

Johns Hopkins produced eight Major League Lacrosse All-Star players for 2008. No other school produced more than three.

Mount Union, Kenyon College, and Johns Hopkins are all Division III schools. Do you know anything about their athletic programs?

Now consider the University of Oklahoma. If you have ever turned on the television during college football season, you know about the Oklahoma Sooners. The school has won seven NCAA football championships, and the team has the best winning percentage of any Division I team. It doesn't stop there: The school has won two national baseball championships, and the women's softball team won the national championship in 2000. Since 2002, the gymnastics team has won four national championships.

But what about its academic departments? You might know that in 2007, the school was named a "best value" college by *The Princeton Review*. It is ranked first in the number of National Merit Scholars per capita, and it is among the top five schools to graduate Rhodes Scholars.

But is it a research-intensive university? And how is campus life?

And do you know anything about Harvey Mudd? Athletes considering engineering careers should learn quickly about Harvey Mudd; it has one of the top engineering programs in the country.

NCSA COLLEGIATE POWER RANKINGS

The NCSA Collegiate Power Rankings are a yearly updated ranking of colleges and universities. The Power Rankings allow parents and student-athletes to evaluate the particular strengths of universities based on academic and athletic factors, as well as student-athlete graduation rates. Parents and athletes can use the NCSA Collegiate Power Rankings to investigate universities that send information to the athletes.

NCSA developed the Collegiate Power Rankings for each college at the NCAA Division I, II, and III levels by averaging the *U.S. News & World Report* ranking, the U.S. Sports Academy Directors' Cup ranking, and the NCAA student-athlete graduation rate of each university. For the latest NCSA Collegiate Power Rankings, see www. athleteswanted.org.

My point here is that depending on the student, more than just a few criteria must be considered when determining a school. I won a full-ride scholarship to play football at Vanderbilt University, the only private school in the Southeastern Conference, perennially the toughest conference in college football. I never played in a Bowl game, but I used my athletic skills to gain acceptance into an outstanding collegiate program that best fit my personal needs. *U.S. News & World Report* consistently ranks Vanderbilt in the top twenty-five schools, as does the NCSA in its Collegiate Power Rankings. Academic prestige was important to me. Today, no one asks me how many Bowl rings I have, or how many times I played on television, but people regularly comment on the great education I received.

This is probably the biggest decision a kid has to make, and it will not be a four- or five-year decision, but a decision that will have forty years of consequences. It should be made with the parents' support and guidance. Parents should ask many questions to help their children find a right fit, and they should consider several criteria.

SOLICITING AN OBJECTIVE OPINION

A student-athlete will have a tough time being objective about his own ability, and a parent might have even a tougher time. But given that only 0.09 percent of high school athletes go on to play professional football, and only 0.02 percent go on to play women's basketball, students and parents need to know how the athlete compares to other athletes. Without this knowledge, the student might be setting unrealistic and unattainable goals, considering colleges that are unlikely to accept him.

In Chapter 2, parents gauged their child's abilities and encouraged their child to solicit feedback, comparing this information to objective numbers that their child can use as comparisons to the rest of the world. Parents should also ask for feedback from objective third parties that might be more open with them than with their student-athlete.

Equally important to having measurable indicators is an athlete's ability to come to terms with reality and avoid being unnecessarily disappointed when the top-rated schools do not knock at the door. Student-athletes need to consider the answers to the following questions:

- *Have I received any recognition? All-League? All-County? All-State? Team starter? Varsity starter? Team MVP? Team captain? Did I lead the team in statistics and category?*

- *Have I performed at showcases, tournaments, or national camps? How did I stack up against the competition?*

- *Have I played on any summer, traveling, or club teams?*

- *What are this school's recruitment requirements, and do I meet them?*

- *Do I possess impressive physical attributes? If not now, will my gene pool work in my favor? Am I still growing? What is my shoe size? Am I a late bloomer?* (A student might be recruited if the coach thinks the athlete can develop into a great player over the next three or four years. College coaches will project where an athlete will be in two or three years, so a 5'7" center with a powerful three-point shot and outstanding ball skills might be recruited as a guard at the next level if both parents are over six feet tall.)

«« FAST FACT ««

Hall of Famer Scottie Pippin grew six inches as a walk-on basketball player for the University of Central Arkansas, an NAIA school.

"STUDENT, KNOW THYSELF!"

Athletes should answer some questions about personal interests, dreams, and goals. These questions should include:

- *What subjects do I enjoy the most?*

- *What subjects do I want to learn more about?*

- *What subjects have I excelled at to date?*

- *What career path do I want to take?*

  < *Am I interested in business, education, medicine, law, social work, sales, marketing, coaching, physical therapy?*

  < *Do I want to work inside or outside?*

  < *Do I want to work in an office or in the field?*

  < *Do I want to travel?*

- *What do I love?*

- *What do I loath?*

- *Which recreational activities or community services do I currently participate in and hope to continue in college?*

- *Am I shy or outgoing?*

- *Am I independent, or do I prefer a structured environment?*

- *Do I want to be far from home or within driving distance?*

- *Do I like the sorts of people I know from my high school, or am I hoping to meet new kinds of people?*

"What's the best college?" is a multiple-choice question with more than one right answer. Athletes should divide the enormous pie of American colleges into manageable slices, ranking them based on their values, scholarship packages, grants-in-aid packages, academic and career opportunities (internships, graduate school, job placement history, etc.), and playing opportunities. If the athlete can select slices that may be different flavors, but all flavors the student-athlete will enjoy, he will be on the way to making a good choice no matter which slice is ultimately selected.

Say that a student has decided on a medium-sized school, with a suburban campus, within driving distance from home, with a strong accounting program, and with a Division II softball team. Though hundreds of schools might be on the table at first, the athlete can narrow this down to only a dozen schools by finding the ones that fit all these criteria.

Student-athletes who know themselves will be able to eliminate schools so they can focus on those that look the most promising.

Remember that things can change quickly in a sport. The coach who recruited an athlete might leave. A student could sustain a career-ending injury. Another player could take over her position.

COACH'S TIP

Athletes are just one injury away from never playing again, so they should base their choice on academics, said Coach Lenti.

What if an athlete suddenly finds himself out of competitive athletics, at a college he selected only for its athletic program? He could look around and discover that he hates the place! Making matters worse, perhaps the college he wants to attend will not allow him to transfer because it is a competing school that restricts transfers? If a student chooses a school correctly the first time around, he will not need to transfer if something changes in his athletic opportunities.

Academics

Not many high school students are 100 percent sure what their major will be in college, but most at least have an idea what subjects interest them. If an athlete is a female lacrosse player, and she is interested in majoring in sports management, her options for a college that offers both that major and that sport could be narrow.

Does the school have a diversity of majors available? Remember that college is a time of exploration and discovery. Students should not limit themselves to majors and careers they have heard about in high school. They are sure to find out about majors and careers they never knew existed, and one of those may be the perfect fit!

Student-athletes should consider the following questions:

- *Does the school have a diversity of majors that interest me?*

- *Is the academic level at this college too demanding? Will I be in over my head, or will I be bored because it is not challenging enough?*

- *Are the admission requirements the same or more rigorous than the NCAA minimums for eligibility?*

- *Will I want or need tutoring, and if so, is there tutoring available for athletes?*

- *What is the school's graduation rate for scholarship athletes in my sport?*

- *Do former student-athletes have interesting careers and good jobs? Are they successful?*

- *Does the engineering department have ties with city and local engineering firms? Does the medical school have an affiliation with the hospital?*

- *Does the school have many internship opportunities?*

- *What percent of students go on to post-graduate opportunities?* (Remember, depending on a student's major, the student-athlete might want to consider looking forward to graduate opportunities.)

Jim Goranson is a successfully recruited student-athlete who found out the hard way about the pitfalls of choosing the wrong college. Jim started out with a full football scholarship to a Big Ten university. He graduated high school with a 23 ACT and a 3.2 GPA.

Even though Goranson played on a team that went to a Sugar Bowl, he was quickly disillusioned with the "business side" of being on such a high-profile team.

"My school wanted me to focus on football," said Goranson. "No matter what the sugarcoating was, I was playing at a high level, and my football team was a business with a bunch of money involved. The coaches were paid to have results on the football field, so they discouraged anything that might compromise this. I wanted to take a psychology class, but counselors told me not to because it would hurt my GPA, which might make me ineligible for the team."

If athletes want to succeed at a high level, they have to be okay dealing with the business side of the sport. Some players are, especially those who want professional careers, but Goranson was not one of those athletes. Goranson wanted an academic education, and when a coach told him that he should put more effort into football and less into classroom activities, he knew it was time to change. He sought help from a recruiting service and transferred to a college that placed a higher emphasis on academics.

Jim went on to graduate in 2005 with a degree in English, a concentration in journalism, and a minor in history. And he stresses, "I was able to write a book of poetry. I acted in plays. I had my own television show while I was there. I know I would have never been able to do that at my former college."

«« FAST FACT ««

The average student changes majors four times and will change jobs twenty-five times throughout life, which is why a good education support staff at a student's college or university can make such a huge difference.

Rural/Urban

If a student is from a rural town in the Midwest and decides to attend a school like the University of Southern California in Los Angeles or New York University in Manhattan, she might experience culture shock. Depending on the child, she might be extremely energized by stepping into a big city.

On the other hand, if a student-athlete is raised in New York City, imagine what she would think when stepping onto the Judson College campus in the small town of Elgin, Illinois.

A student-athlete might or might not relish the excitement of going to school in an environment completely different than the one she is used to. Students should consider these questions:

- *What sorts of new activities do I want to experience?*

- *What are the demographics of the student body? What is the male-to-female ratio? Am I considering any cultural organizations that the school offers?*

- *Is it a commuter campus, or is there campus housing?*

- *Is there a big Greek system?*

- *How involved is the university or college in the community?*

- *Does the school allow freshmen to have cars on campus?* (A lot of schools don't!)

Location

Location is a hugely important consideration when trying to whittle down a short list of colleges, but remember that a four-hour drive is not much easier than a two-hour flight, and that an athlete will have more opportunities by extending the college search beyond the confines of local universities.

That said, cost might be a factor. Out-of-state tuition might be too burdensome without a healthy scholarship or financial aid package, but more often than not, out-of-state tuition or private school opportunities for the recruited student-athletes become much better academic, financial, and athletic opportunities than those offered at local state schools. Most student-athletes find that it is far better to attend schools that provide them with opportunities to play their sports than it is to focus on distance.

Student-athletes should factor in the price of visiting home into the overall cost of their education, but be aware that the cost of fuel might be just as much as the cost of a flight. Compare the costs of an hour flight to that of a four-hour drive. Flying home several times a year can cost hundreds or even thousands of dollars in plane tickets. Then again, paying to keep a car on campus (including parking fees, maintenance, and insurance) might be cost-prohibitive, depending on the school. What if a student earned a scholarship to a school that is a five-hour flight away from home? The athlete can likely afford to make a few trips if he saves $20,000 in tuition.

COACH'S TIP

When considering location, look at the proximity of a major airport and the frequency and price of direct flights. A school five hundred miles away might be closer via plane than a school three hundred miles away with limited flights and no major airport.

The point is this: Although the costs of visiting their child should be considered when evaluating schools, parents need to be careful about limiting their children's options. The bigger the geographic area that is considered, the bigger the opportunities, some of which might pay more than local opportunities. If athletes fail to look at schools simply because they are too far away, they will miss out on great opportunities. If sports make a student happy and help pay for school, opening doors for the rest of her life, parents might want to weigh the advantages before limiting their child's college search just because they want their child close to home.

That said, student-athletes should consider a few questions that will determine preference for location:

- *Do I want to be in a rural, suburban, or urban setting?*

- *Is there a particular climate I would like?* Switching from a warm southern climate to a weather-bound city like New

York or Chicago can often have a profound affect on a child's spirits.

- *Will I miss seasons, or am I ready to trade shoveling snow for year-round sunshine?*

Athletes need to keep in mind that the more they want to play, the less certain factors will matter. I would have traveled to Alaska to play football on a scholarship. How far students are willing to travel from home is a good indicator of their desire to compete.

Size

The size of a school (the number of students and square miles of campus) can also have a profound effect on an athlete's college experience. Big schools with tens of thousands of students can be like medium-sized cities, and the size of a school does not have anything to do with its division. Case in point: The two schools with the largest enrollment are Pima Community College in Tucson, Arizona (enrollment 75,000), and Miami Dale College (enrollment 49,000).

The advantages of a big school can be formidable. They are usually well-financed with great facilities and hundreds of clubs and organizations to join. They have big numbers of students, big academic departments, and big names. The question is: Does this translate into big value? Not necessarily.

Indeed, upon careful evaluation a student might be more concerned about large class sizes, the impersonal nature of such a large community, and dealing with the bureaucracy of a giant school. Athletes should consider the answers to these questions:

- *Is it important that my classes are small, or am I envisioning a school with giant lecture halls packed with students?*

- *When I raise my hand during class, do I want my teacher to know my name?*

- *Is it important that my social environment is intimate, or do I prefer a largely populated school?*

- *Is it important that the administration be accessible?*

Student-athletes often miss many classes due to games or meets. Often smaller schools will be willing to work with the student and allow tests or labs to be made up. A more intimate school environment might be exactly what a student needs to excel in both athletics and academics.

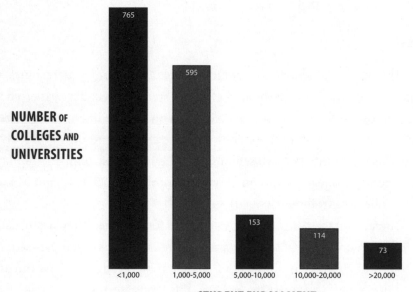

NUMBER OF COLLEGES AND UNIVERSITIES

765
595
153
114
73

<1,000   1,000-5,000   5,000-10,000   10,000-20,000   >20,000

STUDENT ENROLLMENT

Of the eighteen hundred colleges with sports programs, 45 percent have fewer than one thousand students and only 4.3 percent have more than twenty thousand students. A whopping 80 percent have fewer than five thousand students, and only 11.3 percent have more than ten thousand enrolled students. If size matters, the pool of schools is narrowed quickly

Play-Time

Countless stories tell of athletes who could have gone to a bigger, more prestigious school but understood that their play-time would be limited.

Instead, they followed the heart of a true athlete and chose play-time over status.

When considering play-time, student-athletes should consider the following questions:

- *Will I fit in with the team's strategy, or will I be like a passing quarterback in a running offense?*

- *Will I be able to develop my athletic ability as fully as possible in this program?*

- *Has an athletic scholarship ever not been renewed solely because of poor performance or injury?*

- *How does my ability fit in with this school's program? Do I want to be part of a big-time program even if I don't start, or would I rather be a top performer on a lower-level team? (Big fish in a small pond, or small fish in a big one?)*

Coaches

A student-athlete will be under the supervision of a college coaching staff for four or five years. Those coaches—which include strength coaches, position coaches, training staff, academic support coaches, and the head coach—might have more impact on the athlete's life than any professor. A coach can make an experience enjoyable, stimulating, rewarding, or miserable.

Because the coaches can have a huge influence on an athlete's college experience, parents should get to know them from afar. Parents and athletes should work together to find a coach whose values they share, whose personality will benefit the athlete, and who is someone the child respects. Ideally, parents and athletes should look for a coach who cares about the child's continued growth and integrity.

That said, remember, too, that the coach might be gone next year, so parents and athletes should take a look at the assistant, strength, and position coaches as well. A lot of eyes and ears will be directed toward an athlete, and the head coach might not be the strongest role model/disciplinarian when it comes to non-athletic endeavors. Strength or position coaches and training room staff will likely spend more time with the student-athlete than the head coach.

Some coaches are strict disciplinarians, while others are more easygoing. Some coaches cultivate close relationships with their athletes, while others keep their distance. Some will set up a relationship much like a boss and an employee. No one coaching method will work for every athlete. In fact, the best coaches vary their style in their efforts to get the most out of each player. A coach might have to speak sharply to one athlete just to be heard, while another athlete might respond better to a gentler approach.

Here are some questions for both parents and athletes to consider:

- *Will I be comfortable with the coach's approach to practicing or okay with his stance on discipline?*

- *How long has the coach been at the school? Under what circumstances did the coach leave his previous job? Was he fired, or was he recruited away?*

- *What is the coach's win-loss record?*

- *How much turnover is among assistant coaches?*

- *How long is the coach's current contract?*

- *What are the coaches' goals? Where do they see themselves in five years?*

Athletes and their parents should be clear of the expectations and policies for grade-point averages, training, and team rules. Consider the disciplinary actions and what a student must do to keep a scholarship.

Freedom

Student-athletes should ask themselves: *Do I want to go to a college where students are treated like adults, make their own decisions about where to live, what classes to take, and are graded on just midterm and final exams?* Tired of following rules and schedules set by their parents, many college-bound high schoolers would answer with an emphatic "Yes!"

In actuality, this is a tricky question. Sudden immersion into a life with few rules is not always easy. For one thing, if a student has freedom, so does everybody else, including the kids who are carousing outside the athlete's door the night before his chemistry midterm. Parents should ask themselves: *Is my child the kind of person who is easily influenced by friends?* If so, a school with too few rules or a big school where it is easy to get lost in the shuffle may be exactly the wrong place for their child.

Colleges differ widely in regard to how much freedom they grant undergrads. Some schools have detailed rules, like class attendance requirements, designated residential facilities, restrictions on joining fraternities or sororities, and even mandatory breakfast or study halls. Others are very hands-off except in respect to extreme behavior such as plagiarism, cheating, or threats to others. Student-athletes and their parents should consider whether the athlete would blossom or flounder in an unstructured environment. Neglecting to think about this issue might put the athlete wildly out of sync with classmates.

Religion

Many colleges in America consider religion a central element of campus life. If a student has decided to attend a college with a strong Catholic, Jesuit, Mormon, Evangelical Christian, Baptist, or Jewish culture, for example, the choices are easily narrowed to fine institutions like Notre Dame, Loyola, Boston College, Brigham Young, and Brandeis. However, many colleges offer a wide variety of networks and divinity groups within their campuses that encourage kids of all cultures to foster their religious identities and continue with their spiritual growth while integrating with students of other backgrounds.

Medical Treatment

Injuries are part of the life of an athlete, so a student-athlete should expect them when playing at a higher level. The type of medical treatment available to athletes should be a factor in an athlete's decision. Even for non-contact sports (such as swimming or cross country), a certified trainer should be present at practices and games in case an athlete suffers an injury or becomes ill. Pay attention when a child gets injured. Does a medical staff run out or is it just one person? Do any of the coaches get involved?

Also, consider the number of team doctors who work for the school. If a school has five hundred student-athletes and only one team doctor, chances are the doctor's time will be monopolized by major sports (football and basketball), so all the other athletes may not get the same kind of care.

Game/Practice Schedules

If an athlete plays basketball or football, he can pretty much kiss his Thanksgiving and Christmas breaks goodbye. Most winter sports teams have games scheduled during these breaks. If not, the child will be expected to stay on campus for practices. He might get two or three days off between each semester, but parents will not see the child for his three- or four-week vacation. Instead, the student-athlete will spend these vacations practicing.

If a student plays a spring sport like golf or baseball, the same is true of spring vacations. While friends are planning spring break trips, the student-athlete will be on campus practicing with the team or traveling to games. Athletes should consider these questions:

- *How much time and energy am I willing to give to my sport?*

- *How much time and energy is required from each of the schools I am considering?*

If an athlete plays a fall sport, he will have limited fall breaks; winter sports will take precedence over winter breaks; and spring sports will require athletes to spend time on the road competing. The bigger and more competitive the program, the higher the demand and the less vacations a student-athlete will have.

Red Flags

Thanks in part to close media scrutiny and the advent of the academic progress rate (APR), almost all schools are now cognizant of whether athletes are graduating. Academia has stepped into the forefront and schools are being held accountable.

Twenty or thirty years ago, some schools that focused heavily on athletics, and some who wanted to increase their athletic reputations, often encouraged athletes to take easy classes or classes taught by instructors who showed favoritism to athletes. Some programs even made steroids accessible. For some schools, the focus was on winning games and championships at any cost rather than making sure that the athletes were receiving a good education. Fortunately, as time goes on, we hear fewer reports of detrimental and illegal activities.

The schools that have the most invested in sports are the schools that will invest more in the student-athlete's success in sports. This isn't necessarily a concern, so long as academia is also emphasized. When selecting a school, research the percentage of graduating athletes at the school. Pay attention to the reputations of both the athletic department and the coach. Talk to other student-athletes and parents if necessary.

Some issues to be aware of:

- *Do a high percentage of players fail to receive diplomas?*

- *Has the school's athletic department or coach ever received any bad publicity for unscrupulous or abusive behavior? How did the university address this publicity?*

- *Is this school currently (or has it ever) been under investigation for possible violations of NCAA rules?*

- *What if the pressure to win conflicts with educational demands?*

- *If a class conflicts with a child's practice schedule, can the athlete still take the class? Is the school going to honor academics first? Or is the policy that student-athletes put their games first and alter their academic schedule accordingly?*

I had the good fortune of going to a school that placed classes first. While attending Vanderbilt, the only lab available one semester was held at 3:00 p.m. on Mondays. My football practice was also scheduled for 3:00 p.m. every Monday. The school allowed me to attend the weekly lab and arrive late for practice once a week. Unfortunately, not all institutions are that lenient. Athletic departments in schools with a focus on sports have a reputation for encouraging their athletes to spend less time in the classroom and more time on the playing field. But in recent years, the NCAA has created strict guidelines.

Still, there are more than a few students who are pampered by the athletic department.

NARROWING THE LIST

When evaluating colleges, student-athletes want to start by dividing criteria into three categories—*must have* features, *important* features, and *would be nice* features. Refer to the Initial Target List, and remove any college that doesn't have all the student's *must have* features.

Rank the schools according to the highest number of *important* or *would be nice* features clustered at each.

It's likely that students will have to make some compromises, but knowing exactly where they are not willing to bend will save a lot of time up front.

We suggest using the College Ranking Worksheet, which will help student-athletes analyze colleges and universities to determine the best match for their athletic, academic, financial, and social needs. Every student-athlete has a unique set of priorities, which is why this chart is personalized for each child's specific college search. It works like this:

A student-athlete should assign a score—zero (low) through five (high)—for each category on the left side of the chart in the column "Priority Assignment," with zero being "not at all important" and five being "must have." For example, if location is a student's top priority, that priority will be worth five points. If an athlete does not care at all about the gear offered by the school, the athlete can give that category zero points instead.

The athlete should then write the names of his favorite five colleges in the top boxes. At least three should be colleges that are likely to admit the student based on his ability. He should then rate the school on each of the categories, assigning a score of one to five for each category in the column "Rating." A score of one indicates that the school does not fare well in that category, while a five means that the school is excellent in that specific category.

Next, multiply the Priority Assignment and the Rating to find the Total.

Write the number in the appropriate box and tally the scores.

COLLEGE RANKING WORKSHEET

NAME OF COLLEGE/UNIVERSITY

Categories	Priority Assignment (0-5)	1. Rating	1. Total	2. Rating	2. Total	3. Rating	3. Total	4. Rating	4. Total	5. Rating	5. Total
Do they offer my major?											
How are the academics overall?											
How does the graduation rate compare to other programs I'm considering?											
What sort of opportunities will I have to play?											
Does the program fit my playing style?											
How are the school's career planning and career placement programs?											
How do the internship opportunities stack up?											
What is the scholarship potential?											
How do I feel about the size?											
How do I feel about the distance from my home, considering the cost to visit and hours of travel?											
How is the location?											
Does the division level meet my expectations?											

COLLEGE RANKING WORKSHEET (CONT.)

NAME OF COLLEGE/UNIVERSITY

Categories	Priority Assignment (0-5)	1.		2.		3.		4.		5.	
		Rating	Total	Rating	Total	Rating	Total	Rating	Total	Rating	Total
How do I like the social life?											
How well do I like the head coach, and how likely will the head coach be at the school in four or five years?											
What about the position coach?											
What about the strength and conditioning coach?											
How does the school's academic support—such as tutors and study hall—rank?											
What is the training schedule like?											
What is the vacation schedule like?											
What sort of summer job opportunities are available?											
What are the summer school accommodations?											
Does the program cover expenses for summer school, tuition, room, and board?											
Does the program assist in finding summer jobs?											

COLLEGE RANKING WORKSHEET (CONT.)

NAME OF COLLEGE/UNIVERSITY

Categories	Priority Assignment (0-5)	1.		2.		3.		4.		5.	
		Rating	Total	Rating	Total	Rating	Total	Rating	Total	Rating	Total
How is the community support?											
What sort of food options are available on campus?											
What are the facilities like?											
What kind of gear is offered?											
Other: _____											
Other: _____											
Other: _____											
Other: _____											
Other: _____											
Other: _____											
TOTAL											

Additional copies of this worksheet are available a www.athleteswanted.org.

Important to note is that a student might go through this process several times. When starting the recruiting process, an athlete might consider only the schools on the Initial Target List. By the sophomore year, the Correspondence Log (see page 207) might have grown to include another fifty schools, at which point the student might want to reevaluate the choices. And if several schools make offers, the athlete might use the College Ranking Worksheet to determine the top school.

KEY POINTS

<u>1.</u> When helping a child align interests with a potential college choice, parents can encourage their student-athlete to consider whether the child is likely to be accepted to that school.

<u>2.</u> Student-athletes should evaluate the school's overall culture, which might include:

- Academics
- Whether the school is in a rural or urban town
- Location and distance from home
- Size
- Potential playing time
- Coaching philosophy
- Freedom
- Religion
- Medical treatment
- Game and practice schedules
- Red flags that the school might not be a good choice

<u>3.</u> Athletes should narrow the list by using the College Ranking Worksheet.

CHAPTER 5

COMMUNICATING
WITH COACHES

BUILDING RELATIONSHIPS with college coaches is the single most important thing a student-athlete can do to facilitate the recruiting process. But complicating the process is a set of rules that the NCAA created to level the playing field and relieve students of pressure from college coaches eager to secure the best athletes.

COACH'S TIP

Communicating with coaches is the single most important aspect of the recruiting process. It should come directly from the athlete, and it should come early.

The NCAA's rules dictate when and how college coaches can initiate contact, and they extend to include restrictions on:

- The type of mail a student-athlete can receive from a college coach.

- Whether a coach can return a student-athlete's phone call.

- How often a coach can call a student-athlete (if at all).

- Whether the coach can visit the student-athlete off-campus.

The rules change based on the sport, division, and grade of a student-athlete. With certain exceptions, Division I and II coaches cannot call athletes before June 15 following their sophomore year, even though they can receive calls from student-athletes. They cannot send recruiting materials—with the exception of the initial letter and questionnaire, which can be sent at any time.

Daunting? I'd say so! Adding to the confusion, the rules and dates change regularly. Your best bet is to review the *NCAA Guide for the College-Bound Student-Athlete* at least annually.

That said, college coaches from all divisions can send a letter with a recruiting questionnaire to a student-athlete at any time, including the student's freshman year. If the student-athlete knows the rules, this letter can initiate the whole process, as you are about to learn.

INITIATING COMMUNICATION WITH COACHES

These restrictions might at first suggest that the student-athlete is handcuffed until the end of his junior year if wanting to establish a relationship with a Division I or II coach. Fortunately, the rules allow a tremendous amount of recruiting to occur during a student-athlete's freshman and sophomore years. While a Division I or II coach cannot call and initiate communication with underclassmen, they can invite prospects to call with the initial letter and questionnaire. They can include a direct line or cell phone number and encourage a prospect to call them if they have any questions. Moreover, a student-athlete can call, email, or write a college coach at any time. A student-athlete also has unlimited opportunity to visit college campuses and meet with coaches, so long as the student-athlete initiates the communication.

The distinction is important. A coach cannot place a phone call to a student-athlete or return a phone call, nor can a coach send personal letters or emails, or respond to incoming letters and emails from freshmen and sophomores. But a coach can answer the phone, and if a freshman happens to be on the other line, the coach can talk to the student-athlete, answer his questions, express interest, or offer advice. A coach can read correspondence from underclassmen and can agree to meet on-campus with underclassmen.

This loophole in the rules creates a window of opportunity for an educated student-athlete. While other student-athletes are waiting for the restriction periods to expire, the student-athlete can be developing strong relationships, collecting critical information, and preparing for a coveted spot on a college roster.

«« FAST FACT ««

A survey by the National Collegiate Scouting Association of more than one thousand college coaches found that:

- **58 percent of college coaches prefer to be contacted in person rather than by email, phone, or snail mail. Coaches prefer to meet a prospective recruit on campus in the form of an unofficial visit.**

- **The second favored mode of communication was email, and telephone was a close third.**

THE RECRUITING LISTS

Preferably during her freshman year, if not sooner, the student-athlete should introduce herself to as many coaches as possible and show these coaches that she is interested in being recruited. An athlete's first step is to make sure her name is on the recruiting lists of the colleges that may be potential academic and athletic matches. Highly recruited student-athletes will receive questionnaires, brochures, and admissions material from dozens, if not hundreds, of college programs during their freshman and sophomore years. A student-athlete has an opportunity to secure a spot on a recruiting list simply by responding to this material, or by sending a personal letter to a coach who has not sent information to the student. The key to success is that a student-athlete connects with coaches with a realistic likelihood of being interested in that student.

Questionnaires

Questionnaires ask basic information about the student-athlete, her statistics, goals, and athletic ability. College coaches send questionnaires to gather information about students and to determine which students are interested in their programs.

SAMPLE QUESTIONNAIRE

General Information

Graduation Year		Email	
First Name		Home Phone	
Middle Name		Cell Phone	
Last Name		Date Registered with Eligibility Center	
Preferred Name			
Address		Birth Date	
City		Facebook Page (if applicable)	
State			
ZIP		Myspace Page (if applicable)	
Country			

Family Information

Father's Name		Mother's Name	
Father's Occupation		Mother's Occupation	
Father's Employer		Mother's Employer	
Father's Home Phone		Mother's Home Phone	
Father's Work Phone		Mother's Work Phone	
Father's Cell Phone		Mother's Cell Phone	
Father's Email		Mother's Email	
Father's College		Mother's College	
Guardian #1 Name		Guardian #2 Name	
Guardian #1 Occupation		Guardian #2 Occupation	
Guardian #1 Home Phone		Guardian #2 Home Phone	
Guardian #1 Work Phone		Guardian #2 Work Phone	
Guardian #1 Cell Phone		Guardian #2 Cell Phone	
Guardian #1 Email		Guardian #2 Email	
Guardian #1 College		Guardian #2 College	
First and Last Name of Guardian/Guardians/ Parent/Parents You Live With:		Names and Ages of all Siblings:	
Best Way to Reach Me			

SAMPLE QUESTIONNAIRE (CONT.)

Athletic Information

Height		40-Yard Dash	
Weight		200 Meter	
Jersey Number		100 Meter	
Offensive Position 1		400 Meter	
Offensive Position 2		Other Sports	
Defensive Position 1		Academic Interests	
Defensive Position 2		Online Video Link	
Squat Lift		Coach's Name	
Bench		Coach's Office Phone	
Vertical		Coach's Cell Phone	
Clean Lift		Coach's Email	

Scholastic Information

Country		ACT	
School Name		SAT Math	
Address		SAT Verbal	
City		SAT Written	
State		SAT II Subject	
ZIP		SAT II Score	
Class Rank		SAT II Subject	
GPA		SAT II Score	

Club Information

Club Team Name			
Address		Coach's Name	
City		Coach's Office Phone	
State		Coach's Cell Phone	
ZIP		Coach's Email	

SAMPLE QUESTIONNAIRE (CONT.)	
General Information	
My top priorities in college are	My favorite hobbies are
1.	1.
2.	2.
3.	3.
The five schools I plan to visit are	
1.	
2.	
3.	
4.	
5.	

Once a student receives a questionnaire, the ball is in her court. If she does not respond, her name might be removed from that coach's mailing list. Bigger name programs might get a 80 percent response to questionnaires while lesser-known programs may get as little as 10 percent return. Coaches assume that a student-athlete who ignores a request for information is not interested in the program. Because their mailing lists are huge, they embrace this lack of response as an opportunity to narrow the pool of candidates. By responding to all mailings, an athlete will keep her options open. Remember that every coach sends letters to hundreds, if not thousands, of other student-athletes on the recruiting list, and will likely only continue to correspond with those who show interest.

Responding to a questionnaire is fairly simple, but the first rule is this: Student-athletes, not their parents, should fill out the questionnaire. This applies to all correspondence with coaches. A parent's role is to help and assist, not to take the lead and become a helicopter parent.

A student-athlete should:

- Fill out the complete questionnaire, even if the information seems redundant. If the athlete does not have an answer for a question, she should write "N/A" for information that is not applicable or "coming soon" for information that is forthcoming.

- Return the questionnaire promptly. If waiting for ACT test scores, she should send the questionnaire in advance and then update the coach once the scores have been received.

- Write legibly if the questionnaire is in print form.

- Send an email, if the questionnaire is online, that thanks the coach and includes the student-athlete's résumé or profile, additional information, and expression of interest in the program.

- Include a brief and personalized note that thanks the coach for the brochure or questionnaire, provides the coach with a little more information about the student-athlete, and expresses the athlete's interest in the college/athletic program. The student-athlete should also include a copy of her profile or résumé (see Chapter 7 and www.athleteswanted.org). The profile or résumé should include contact information, report card or transcripts, academic achievements, and references.

Dear Coach Smith,

I just received your letter and questionnaire and wanted to thank you for your interest. I am excited about the possibility of playing soccer for your program and receiving an education from Yale University. I aspire to help you bring a third Ivy League Championship banner to New Haven. I am currently researching Yale University, and I just submitted my online soccer questionnaire. Please continue to send me more information about your college and soccer program.

I will send you my tournament schedule, as well as highlights, as they become available. In the meantime, if there is anything you need from me, just let me know!

Thanks again, and I look forward to personally speaking with you in the future.

Sincerely,

Jane Student

What should an athlete do if she has not received a questionnaire from a school she wants to attend? Simple: Questionnaires can often be obtained from the university's website, or the student-athlete can place a call or send an email to the coach and ask for a questionnaire.

Admissions Material and Brochures

Most high school students receive general admissions information and brochures from colleges, and students have a hard time determining what is generated by a college coach and what is generated by an admissions college simply because he is a good student. What about admissions material and brochures? Remember that admissions material is one of the few things Division I and II college coaches can send to freshmen or sophomores. College coaches often give the names of prospective student-athletes to the admissions office, so the prospects will receive general information about the college. The coach waits to see whether the student-athlete responds to the mailing, which indicates the student-athlete's level of interest.

Therefore, if a student is an underclassman, he should research every institution that sends him admissions information. If he has any interest at all in a college, he should:

1. Search the college's website and see if it offers his sport.

2. Look at the roster and evaluate the level of competition to see if he fits in this school.

3. Respond to the admissions officer who sent the information. The student should thank the admissions officer and explain that he is a competitive athlete and would like to receive more information that pertains to his particular sport. If the admissions material was not generated by a coach, this will work to alert the coach of the athlete's interest.

4. Respond directly to the coach. The student-athlete should send a letter or email to the coach explaining that he received general information about the university and that he is very interested in learning more about the specific program. He should ask a few specific questions and include his name, address, email address, and phone number, as well as a copy of his scouting report.

COACH'S TIP

Letters to coaches should include the recruiting coordinator or coach's first and last name, and be sure names are spelled correctly and letters are proofread. "Dear Couch" doesn't leave a good first impression!

Letters and Emails

If an athlete is initiating a first contact with a coach through a letter or email, the initial letter should include an introduction, expression of interest in the university, questions, and a copy of the student's résumé or enhanced video, as well as a link to a highlight, skills, game, or enhanced video (see Chapter 8).

A minor point—but nevertheless an important one—student-athletes need to be sure they are correctly identifying this year's coaches. Coaching staffs have high turnover rates, so athletes should make sure that they are looking at a current roster of coaches. Student-athletes should send personalized letters and be selective about who they are targeting. Nothing should ever be addressed, "To Whom It May Concern." College coaches receive hundred of letters and emails from interested students. If an athlete's letter appears to be a form letter, it may well be overlooked.

SAMPLE FIRST-TIME LETTER TO COACH

Dear Coach Jones,

As a member of the Eclipse soccer club and a freshman varsity starter at Niles North High School, I am beginning my search for a college soccer program where I can make an immediate impact, as well as further develop my skills and strength.

My goal academically is to pursue a degree in medicine, and I am impressed by the pre-med program that Hiram College offers. I also like the small class sizes and professor-to-student ratio. I currently attend a large high school and am looking forward to a more personalized college education.

I know the process is early, but I'm hoping to be considered for your program. Would you be so kind as to send me information about Hiram and a questionnaire?

Enclosed is my profile. I am in the process of putting together a video, and I will send you a link to my video as soon as it is prepared.

As a heads up, I will be at the Disney Showcase and the Las Vegas Shootout, so hopefully you will be able to see me play. In the meantime, please let me know if you have any questions.

I look forward to continuing the recruitment process with Hiram College.

Sincerely,

Jane Student
#3 Eclipse (blue and white jersey)

> ### «« FAST FACT ««
> Athletes need to send emails to coaches one at a time. "CCing" several coaches, or sending a mass email, is not looked upon favorably.

Though including a video might not hurt a student-athlete, it isn't necessary if the student is a freshman first connecting with a coach. Coaches usually do not have time to watch every video sent, so most coaches watch only those that they requested from players on their active recruiting list. If an athlete and parents want to send a video, they should first have it evaluated by a knowledgeable third party to make sure the video meets college standards. Enhanced videos can help a student-athlete put his best foot forward through spot-shadowing and play-sequencing to catch the coach's attention. If the video receives a positive evaluation, the athlete should call the coach to see if he would be interested in taking a look.

> ### «« FAST FACT ««
> A reliable recruiting service with established relationships can expedite the process by sending an enhanced video link with a verified scouting report to college coaches through permission-based email software. Once a coach clicks on the link, the student-athlete is alerted as to which coaches watched the videos, which allows the student-athlete to follow up promptly.

In every correspondence, athletes should request that the coach responds to the letter, especially if they are old enough for the coach to respond per the NCAA rules. If an athlete does not receive a response, he should not be discouraged, especially if he sends the letter before the NCAA communication restrictions expire. Coaches receive hundreds of emails and letters, and they might not have time to respond. Persistence pays off, and a student should feel confident placing a phone call to check on the status of the letter. Remember: Most student-athletes are sitting back waiting to be discovered or letting their parents make the calls. The little things make a big difference, and they are a perfect way for an athlete to stand apart from the competition.

If a student-athlete is late in his junior or early in his senior year and has not received a personal communication from a coach, initiating action is required. If this is the case, see Chapter 15 for information on how a reliable or reputable recruiting service might help the athlete expedite the process and get on the college recruiting radar.

PHONE CALL GUIDELINES

To gain the competitive advantage, a student-athlete should call college coaches as early as his freshman year. Regardless of his age, a child should be in regular communication with coaches, particularly those from programs that top his list of favorite colleges. Following are guidelines for developing and then building on previous conversations with coaches.

Before calling the coach, a student should visit the college's website to learn some facts about the college and the team. Does the college offer the athlete's major? What are the graduation rates? What was the team's record last year? How many senior players are graduating? An athlete should know all this information going into the call. If a student calls to inquire into a program at a school that doesn't offer his major, the athlete will be embarrassed and the coach might be irritated.

Parents should consider role-playing with the child before he makes his first phone call. For adults, the process seems easy: Pick up the phone and call the coach. But parents need to remember that their child is inexperienced and needs to practice calling authority figures. They should have their child record his or her practice calls. Play them back and help their child eliminate "ums" and "ahs." A confident voice mail can pique a coach's interest.

Contacting coaches one at a time is the next step for a student-athlete. He can call those colleges that have sent him questionnaires, as well as those he is interested in attending, but from whom he has not yet received information.

COACH'S TIP

After five or ten calls, a student-athlete will start to get into the rhythm and develop confidence and comfort leaving messages. Practice makes perfect!

So that he gets his sea legs, an athlete should start by calling those colleges who rank at the bottom of his list of favorite colleges. He will probably be nervous, stumble, and mutter when he talks to this coach. By talking to a coach at his least favorite college, he will gain confidence for when he calls the coaches that are higher on his priority list. He can also call during off-hours so he is able to leave messages, allowing him to warm up to the process.

A student-athlete should have a list of questions, as well as a script, to work from when calling the coaches. The script should include the following components:

1. An introduction that includes the child's name, city, and high school.

2. If applicable, acknowledgment that the student received material from the coach.

3. A request to ask the coach a few questions. Remember that the coach is a busy person. If he doesn't have time, the student should ask when he can call the coach back. If an athlete calls a Division I or II coach before July 1 or June 15 of his junior year (depending on sport and excluding football or basketball), the coach is not allowed to return the student's call, so if the coach is unavailable, the student-athlete should ask his assistant when he can reach the coach.

4. A list of questions to ask the coach. Regardless of whether the student is a freshman or junior, or whether this is the first or fifth call with the coach, an athlete should always ask two questions:

    - *What else would I need to do to have a chance to compete for your program and earn a scholarship?*

    - *What is the next step I should take with you?*

    Some students don't feel comfortable being this direct. Rest assured that coaches want to connect with qualified student-athletes as much as student-athletes want to connect with coaches.

SAMPLE SCRIPT

Student-athlete: Hi. My name is Jane Student. I'm a soccer player at Boulder High School in Boulder, Colorado. I received your questionnaire last week. Thanks for sending it. I sent it back a few days ago, and I'm really interested in your program. I'm wondering if you have a few minutes to answer some of my questions.

What GPA and ACT or SAT would I need to have a chance to attend your school and play for your program?

Have you had a chance to see me play? [*If the student-athlete has not sent the coach a highlight or skills video, replace this question with: Would you like me to send you a link to my video?*]

When would be a good time to visit your campus?

How many players are you recruiting from my position?

Thanks so much for your time. I just have two more questions:

What else would I need to do to have a chance to compete for your program and earn a scholarship?

What is the next step I should take with you?

Great! Do you have any questions for me?

[*Pause to allow the coach to ask questions, which the student has prepared for in advance, per page 192 through 196.*]

I really appreciate your time, and I look forward to talking with you in the future.

Questions a student-athlete might want to ask are listed below, organized by a suggested timeline. An athlete should ask a mix of general, academic, and athletic questions, building on previous conversations to continue developing relationships and demonstrating interest in the program.

Questions for a student-athlete to ask during the first communication with the coach:

- *When do I need to take the ACT or SAT, and what scores would I need to be considered by your program? What about my GPA?*

- *What would I need to do to earn a scholarship to your program?* (If Division I or II.)

- *How many players are you recruiting in my position?*

- *When would be a good time to visit your campus?*

- *What would I need to do to be evaluated by your staff?*

- *What camps are members of your coaching staff going to attend this summer? Which camps do you recommend that I try to attend?*

COACH'S TIP

A student-athlete only has one chance to make a first impression, so a parent's role in building a child's confidence in communicating with adults is critical. Parents should start this process early so that a coach does not later mistake an athlete's shyness for lack of interest.

Questions for a student-athlete to ask during the second communication with the coach:

- *Do most student-athletes graduate in four years?*

- *What is your coaching style? What type of game plan do you implement?*

- *What advantages are there for student-athletes as compared to the regular student body?*

- *What would you say are the school's strongest academic components?*

- *Have you had an opportunity to evaluate me? If so, what can I do to compete for your program?*

- *When do you begin to narrow your recruiting list?*

- *What is the housing/lodging situation like?*

- *Do teammates typically live together?*

- *Do many student-athletes stay on campus during the summer months?*

- *What is the graduation rate of student-athletes?*

- *What is the school's average class size?*

- *Does your program have full-time academic advisors?*

- *What goals do you have for your team during the next four or five years?*

- *What is a typical "day in the life" like for a member of your team during the season? What about the off-season?*

- *Can a student-athlete compete in multiple sports?*

- *What type of off-season activities do your players participate in?*

- *Is it realistic to maintain a part-time job, study, and play a sport?*

- *Are student athletes allowed to be a part of the Greek life?*

- *What type of orientation program is offered for incoming freshmen?*

Questions to ask during subsequent communications with the coach:

- *Have I been evaluated by your coaching staff yet?*

- *What would be the best time to visit your campus?*

- *Do you intend to invite me for an official visit?*

- *Are you planning to make an in-home visit to meet me and my family?*

- *Is there an application fee for student-athletes? Do you have an application waiver?*

- *What determines if a scholarship is renewed?*

Discretion in asking these questions should be used depending on where a child is in the process. It might not be prudent for a freshman student-athlete to ask if the coach intends to invite the student for an official visit. (Later, you will learn that coaches offer official visits only to student-athletes to whom they are preparing to offer a scholarship.) And if a freshman student is not a varsity player, a coach is likely not interested in evaluating the student yet or prepared to offer a scholarship.

You will also notice that these questions are not entirely athletic based, nor are they all academically centered. Coaches are interested in well-rounded students who show an interest in the all-around college experience.

Once an athlete has a series of communications with a coach, including official and unofficial visits, it might be appropriate for him to ask the following questions, but only after the athlete and his parents are thoroughly familiar with Chapter 9.

Questions a student-athlete might want to ask coaches who have shown interest and either offered an official visit or paid a visit to the athlete's home:

- *What types of financial assistance do your student-athletes normally receive?*

- *What would I have to do to receive this assistance?*

- *Am I in the running to receive a scholarship or grants-in-aid package?*

- *What types of academic scholarships are available? What about other grants-in-aid?*

- *Do I have to apply before a scholarship can be offered?*

- *What determines scholarship or grants-in-aid renewal?*

- *What happens if I get injured?*

- *Will I be eligible to receive more money next year?*

- *How much money will it cost me to attend college?*

- *Are there other scholarships for which I can apply?*

- *Is summer school required as part of my scholarship?*

- *Will I be redshirted?*

- *Do you see me playing in any other positions?*

- *Do you think I will fit in socially?*

COACH'S TIP

Parents should make a list of questions the student-athlete might ask a coach, and keep the list by the phone so the child is not caught off guard when a coach calls.

In addition to preparing their student-athlete with questions to ask, parents should also help their child prepare for the questions the coach might ask. Parents need to remember that this is a two-way interview process. Just as the child is trying to get a feel for different colleges and programs, college coaches are trying to figure out which prospects are the best matches for them. College coaches are looking for student-athletes who are personable, interesting, and who give more than one-word answers. Coaches want to build teams of players who demonstrate strong character, great work ethic, and teamwork, so they want to get to know a student-athlete as a person, as well as an athlete.

Questions college coaches commonly ask students:

- *Have you visited our campus?*

- *Do you plan to come visit?*

- *What other universities are recruiting you?*

- *What other colleges are you interested in? What other colleges have offered you a scholarship? What other colleges are you visiting?*

- *How are you doing in school? How is your GPA? Have you taken the ACT or SAT, and how did you do?*

- *What is your favorite subject? What is your least favorite subject?*

- *What about my university interests you?*

- *What are you looking for in a college?*

- *What other universities are you looking at?*

COACH'S TIP

If a college asks a student to list his top three universities, the athlete should list that institution first. He should be honest about the others and try to mention colleges that are equal or greater athletically and academically. Coaches need to know that other programs are recruiting the student.

If a rival university wants to recruit a student-athlete, his stock will likely rise.

Instead of saying: *I'm looking at the following colleges*, a student-athlete should say: *I'm talking with the following colleges*, or *I'm in the process of setting up visits with the following colleges.* This will likely trigger a stronger response and sense of urgency for the coach to evaluate or visit the athlete.

- *What do you consider to be your strengths as a player? Weaknesses?*

- *What is your upcoming schedule?*

- *Do you plan on attending our camp?*

RESPONDING TO LETTERS AND EMAILS

If a student-athlete has been promoting himself by contacting coaches and responding to general material, he will likely begin receiving personal written correspondence at the beginning of his junior year, though some coaches will still be hamstrung by the NCAA from calling students until the spring (for football) or summer following their junior year.

Let's take a look at some excerpts from actual recruiting letters, and then discuss how an athlete should respond.

LETTER FROM COACH, SAMPLE #1

Dear Susan:

I am pleased to learn of your interest in our athletic program. Your accomplishments in your sport and in the high school classroom are quite impressive. We look forward to continuing a correspondence this year and evaluating you at various competitions. Please return the enclosed profile sheet as soon as possible and include a copy of your schedule so that we can arrange to see you compete.

Thank you,

Coach Anderson

What this letter means, and how a student-athlete should respond:

A coach who sends a letter like this is responding to a letter from the student-athlete. Something in the letter caught the coach's attention, and effort is being made to evaluate the student. The athlete should complete the profile form, send her schedule, and keep in touch. This represents an opportunity to call the coach, and the athlete might as well take advantage of it, especially if this is a top school.

Notice that the coach did not invite the student-athlete to call with questions. If an athlete receives such a letter, the student-athlete should follow up with the coach upon receiving the letter if she has an interest in the program. If the coach is not receptive to the student's call, the coach is probably not interested in the student-athlete.

LETTER FROM COACH, SAMPLE #2

Dear Julie:

We have watched you compete several times over the last year and are very impressed with your performance. We have spoken to your high school coach, and he has emphasized your skill and dedication. It is obvious to us that you are a player who makes an impact. You are among a small group of select athletes we would like to continue evaluating for a possible athletic scholarship. If you have any questions, please contact me directly at my home, (312) 555-7400; office, (312) 555-1212; or on my cell, (773) 555-1212.

Sincerely,

Coach Anderson

What this letter means, and how a student-athlete should respond:

A coach is seriously interested anytime he mentions "athletic scholarship" in a letter. If an athlete receives a letter like this, the coach has actually seen the student-athlete compete and is pursuing the athlete as a potential recruit. If an athlete receives such a letter, she should contact the coach by phone immediately and assure them of her interest. At this time, she can also ask the coach if there is anything specific she should do to proceed with recruitment at that institution.

LETTER FROM COACH, SAMPLE #3

Dear Will:

Our staff has identified you as one of the top junior recruits this year. We enjoyed watching you compete in San Diego. With the graduation of eleven seniors from this year's team, we are interested in and are in need of bright young athletes to carry on our tradition of excellence. Please fill out the enclosed player profile as completely as possible. We look forward to seeing you compete again soon. If you have any questions, please contact me directly at my home, (312) 555-7400; office, (312) 555-1212; or on my cell, (773) 555-1212.

Sincerely,

Coach Anderson

**What this letter means,
and how a student-athlete should respond:**

If a student receives a similar letter, it means that a member of the coaching staff has recognized him as a possible recruit. Although the letter did not mention a scholarship, this may still be a possibility. The student should fill out the player profile immediately and send it back along with a personalized thank you note and a copy of his profile. The athlete needs to keep the coaching staff updated of progress and to call and ask the coach if he would like a copy of the student-athlete's video.

LETTER FROM COACH, SAMPLE #4

Dear Robert:

You have been identified as an athlete who may have the potential to contribute to our college program. We are interested in the possibility of you becoming a student-athlete at our university. If you are interested in being evaluated by our staff, please complete the enclosed questionnaire and send us your competition schedule so that we can arrange to evaluate you. Feel free to call our office with any questions or to request more information at (312) 555-1212.

Thank you,

Coach Anderson

What this letter means, and how a student-athlete should respond:

Someone the coach trusts has personally recommended the athlete, or the student's athletic accomplishments have been documented, and the coach is willing to give the athlete a serious evaluation. He thinks the student has potential. The athlete needs to be sure to return the profile and keep the coach updated on his schedule. He might also consider calling the coach to personally introduce himself. The potential for scholarship money is unclear, but some type of financial aid cannot be ruled out. A lot depends on future evaluations. If the athlete has video available, he should ask if the coach would like a copy, or if he would like to view video.

LETTER FROM COACH, SAMPLE #5

Dear Lisa:

Thank you for your interest in our college program. Our recruiting is on a national level, and we are looking for talented students who can meet the high-level athletic and academic demands of a challenging program. Please complete the enclosed questionnaire and return it as soon as possible. Include a schedule of events where you will be competing. If you have video available, send it to us at your convenience.

Thank you,

Coach Anderson

What this letter means,
and how a student-athlete should respond:

The coach is responding to the student's letter, but Coach Anderson has not seen her compete. The comment that the program is recruiting on a national level implies that the coach expects to recruit players who are at the very top of their graduating class. While a schedule request and offer to view a video are encouraging, no actual commitment has been made to evaluate the athlete. She should pursue her interest in this school, but keep her options open!

LETTER FROM COACH, SAMPLE #6

Dear Jacob:

At this time, I am confirming our decision to offer you a scholarship to attend Boston College and become a student-athlete in our football program. A full scholarship will cover the cost of room, board, books, tuition, and fees. Our offer is based on the following requirements:

- You must continue to excel in the classroom and obtain the grades and test scores that are required for admission.

- You must complete the requirements set forth by the NCAA Eligibility Center.

We want you and your parents to feel comfortable with your opportunity to succeed as a student-athlete at Boston College. This offer is being made in good faith, with the hope that it will be accepted in the same manner.

Sincerely,

Coach Anderson

What this letter means, and how a student-athlete should respond:

The student-athlete has been offered a scholarship. This constitutes a written offer, and if the student accepts it, he should feel confident that he has secured a scholarship. However, nothing is guaranteed until the student-athlete signs on National Letter of Intent Day (see Chapter 10). The athlete should keep in touch with the coach to make sure that the opportunity does not fall through the cracks. As a measure of respect, the student should immediately alert other coaches that he has made a verbal commitment to sign with another program.

LETTER FROM COACH, SAMPLE #7

Dear Brian:

Thank you for your interest in our program. We feel that the history of our program is truly unique. We have produced thirteen All-Americans and made ten NCAA appearances, including two trips to the Final Four. If you continue to have an interest in our program, please return the enclosed player questionnaire. Again, thank you for your interest, and best of luck in the recruitment process.

Sincerely,

Coach Anderson

What this letter means,
and how a student-athlete should respond:

Brian hasn't made much of an impression on Coach Anderson. Nothing has been said about evaluating him in the future. The student received a response and profile form because admissions departments frown on college coaches who ignore prospective students. The intent of this letter could be to discourage the athlete from continuing to seek recruitment from this school. If he is still interested, he should fill out the form and hope that something he writes will make an impression. He should also call the coach and ask specific questions about how he can increase his likelihood of being recruited. He should also start connecting with other coaches who might make more of an effort to evaluate him.

BUILDING THE RELATIONSHIP

A student-athlete will not be guaranteed a spot on a college roster simply by showing interest in a program. The process continues throughout a student's high school years, and based on how recruited an athlete is and what school she is attending, the process might be frantic, slow, hard, or easy. The key is to keep it going. At a minimum, a student should:

1.   Call each coach on her priority list at least twice a year, and:

     a.   Ask the right questions. Each conversation with a coach should move the student-athlete one step closer to a decision. If a freshman, the athlete should learn about qualifying benchmarks. If a sophomore, the athlete might want to make an unofficial visit. If a junior, the athlete should ask to get evaluated and whether a scholarship offer is under consideration. If a senior, the athlete should schedule an official visit and ask whether the coach plans to offer the student a scholarship.

     b.   Be proactive and direct. An athlete should be asking enough questions to know where she stands and whether the school is a good fit for the athlete.

2.   Send emails to all coaches on her Correspondence Log with updates, which might include:

     a.   A notice that the student-athlete received a high GPA or test score.

     b.   An email about an honor (academic or athletic) the student received.

c. News about camps, clubs, or games that the coach might be able to attend.

d. New benchmark scores or combine stats.

e. An article or story that mentions the athlete, but only if the story features the student-athlete, or is a spread in a major publication. **Be very careful here—coaches do not want to receive hundreds of clippings with box scores and mentions of the student-athlete's name.**

3. Keep the doors open. A student-athlete should have plenty of backups in case her first choices do not come through. By keeping in touch with every coach on her Correspondence Log, she will have an opportunity to secure a scholarship with a second- or third-choice college if no first-choice college spots are available.

CORRESPONDENCE LOG

All recruited athletes receive a ton of mail, and sometimes the volume of envelopes can be overwhelming. Add to this the phone calls—some with coaches who are interested and some with coaches who are not—and emails, requests for videos and student profiles, and a student-athlete could easily get confused about which coaches he has communicated with and which he hasn't.

Student-athletes should create and maintain a Correspondence Log that notes date, school, type of contact, and notes for each contact, whether it be returning a questionnaire or calling a coach.

CORRESPONDENCE LOG

Correspondence Date		Type	
College		Coach	
Phone		Next Step	
Email		Priority Indicator	
Level of Interest		Response Type	

Notes:

Correspondence Date		Type	
College		Coach	
Phone		Next Step	
Email		Priority Indicator	
Level of Interest		Response Type	

Notes:

Correspondence Date		Type	
College		Coach	
Phone		Next Step	
Email		Priority Indicator	
Level of Interest		Response Type	

Notes:

The Correspondence Log should also note the student-athlete's next steps, indicating when and how he will next communicate with a coach, as well as a priority indicator.

The priority indicator aligns a student's interests with those schools that are likely to recruit him (see the College Rankings Worksheet in Chapter 4) to place a priority on future correspondence. A student-athlete will not engage in the same activities with a third-choice school that seems uninterested in her as she would with a first-choice school that seems extremely interested.

From this, the students will track who they receive questionnaires from, who responds favorably to their letters and phone calls, and what their next steps are. I suggest categorizing each school with one of the following priority indicators:

1. **Dream**—These represent the schools the student-athlete would like to attend, though the student might or might not be qualified. She should be sure to ask coaches how she can increase her likelihood of winning a spot on a team. The student-athlete should call these schools anytime her status changes drastically. If, for instance, she has a major increase in her GPA or goes through a growth spurt that would increase the likelihood of admittance, she should call these coaches immediately. She should try to secure official visits with dream schools.

2. **Reach**—These are schools the athlete would like to attend but are not likely to admit the student. The student-athlete should call coaches from these schools at least twice a year and email them with regular updates. She should be sure to ask coaches how she can increase her likelihood of winning a spot on a team. The student-athlete should call these schools anytime her status changes drastically. If, for instance, she

has a major increase in her GPA or goes through a growth spurt that would increase the likelihood of admittance, she should call these coaches immediately. As well, she should go on unofficial visits and try to secure official visits with at least three coaches from reach schools.

3. **Likely**—These are schools to which the student is likely to be accepted and would be satisfied attending, but are not her top choice. The athlete should call coaches from these schools annually and send emails with regular updates. If she has time, she should go on unofficial visits at these schools. If no reach schools offer her official visits, she should request official visits with these schools.

4. **Backups**—These schools represent programs that are sure things, but not in the athlete's first- or second-tier. To some extent, backups should be nurtured as much as reach and dream schools. If the student fails to build relationships with backup schools, the sure things might turn into nothing at all, leaving the athlete in the cold. That said, wasting official visits on backups is not advisable. The student should accept official visits to backups only if the dream, reach, and likely schools do not offer official visits. The student-athlete should call these schools at least twice a year, send regular updates, and take unofficial visits, if she has time.

5. **Not Qualified, Not Interested**—These are schools the student is not interested in attending or not interested and not qualified to attend. If the athlete is absolutely sure she is not interested in attending these schools, she does not need to maintain contact with these coaches, though keeping them updated through emails wouldn't hurt and might help if the student-athlete changes her mind.

Help! Is it too late for a junior or senior athlete who has not been in touch with coaches?

Not at all. Though Division I schools likely have their rosters filled by the time a child is a senior, 80 percent of college programs make their final recruiting decisions after January 1 of the student-athlete's senior year.

If a child is a junior or a senior, he should follow the communication guidelines outlined herein with one crucial difference: He should call as many coaches as possible as quickly as possible. As well, depending on how late in the game he starts, he might want to consider using a recruiting service, as discussed in Chapter 15.

KEY POINTS

1.   Communicating with coaches is the single most important aspect of the recruiting process. It should come directly from the athlete with assistance from the parents, and it should come early.

2.   Though the NCAA places restrictions on when and how a college coach can contact a student-athlete, a high school athlete can and should assist the process by initiating communication with college coaching staff. This can happen at any time.

3.   College coaches send admissions material, brochures, and questionnaires to high school students to see which ones respond. Those who respond will stay on the recruiting list; those who do not respond will be removed. If a student-athlete receives a questionnaire, admissions material or brochure from a college coach, she should respond immediately, regardless of whether she wants to attend the school. If she has not received questionnaires by the end of her freshman year from schools she is interested in attending, she should contact the coaches to ask for questionnaires.

4.   Once the student-athlete has introduced herself to the college coach— either by responding to a questionnaire or by sending an introductory letter—she should begin phoning the coaches to build relationships and ask questions that allow her to determine whether the program is a good match. She should also be prepared to answer specific questions the coach will likely ask.

5.   Throughout a student-athlete's high school years, she should continue building her relationships with college coaches by calling, sending email updates, and sending letters. A Correspondence Log will help a student-athlete track her communication with coaches, indicating the next steps and priority of each future interaction with a coach.

CHAPTER 6

UNOFFICIAL AND OFFICIAL VISITS

EQUATE THE RECRUITMENT PROCESS to marriage—a person does not go on one or two dates and then decide to get hitched. This process is about building trust between the student-athlete and coach, so the relationship should extend beyond phone calls and emails. We suggest that student-athletes begin taking unofficial visits to colleges as freshman, continuing until they have signed on the dotted line.

UNOFFICIAL VISITS

An unofficial visit is any visit to a college or university campus that is not funded by the institution. Unlike official visits, the NCAA does not place restrictions on when or how often an athlete can take an unofficial visit, so a student can start as early as his freshman year. A coach cannot, however, pay for any portion of the athlete's unofficial visit, including lunch, parking, transportation, or accommodations.

During an unofficial visit, a coach will typically talk to the athlete about the university and athletic program, as well as give the student-athlete a brief tour of the athletic facilities. If a coach has seen the child play, he may give the student an indication as to how interested he is in recruiting the athlete. In some cases, highly recruited student-athletes receive verbal scholarship offers during unofficial visits.

COACH'S TIP

Connecting with the coaching staff before an unofficial visit is critical. The purpose of an unofficial visit is to allow the athlete to experience campus life and build a relationship with the staff. But if the coaches are not eager to host a student, they likely are not interested in recruiting that athlete.

Scheduling Unofficial Visits

If an athlete takes the initiative to schedule an unofficial visit and arrives with some knowledge about the university, as well as questions to ask the coach, the athlete is more likely to move up the coach's list.

Before the visit, an athlete should call or email the coach to set up a meeting. Division I and II coaches are restricted from returning phone calls during a student's freshman and sophomore years (and some sports restrict contact during the junior year, as listed in the *NCAA Guide to the College-Bound Student-Athlete*), so a student-athlete might need to make several phone calls before connecting with the coach.

A student who has a highlight or skills video available can send it, along with a résumé, in advance.

SAMPLE EMAIL

Dear Coach Smith,

I am in the process of scheduling my official visits and am wondering if there is anything specific I should do to set up an official visit with your university. In particular, I am wondering if you are available to meet on June 2 or June 3, and whether you recommend that I arrange for an admissions interview.

Please click on the following links to view my highlight video.

The athlete must arrive on time with a copy of his profile, highlight or skills video, and a list of questions. The student should also take notes during the interview. Parents should work with their child before the meeting to identify the specific athletic, student life, and academic question to ask (see Chapter 5 for sample questions). Of course, athletes should always ask these two crucial questions:

1. *What else would I need to do to have a chance to compete for your program and earn a scholarship?*

2. *What is the next step I should take with you?*

These specific questions let the coach know the student-athlete's intentions and that the athlete is serious. Compare these to: *Coach, I am very interested in your program.* This statement does little to establish expectations, and might tell the coach that the student-athlete is interested in walking on.

Parents need to counsel the athlete about which questions are appropriate to ask and which should be postponed until the relationship has been built. If this is the first time the college coach has spoken with the freshman, the student might not want to ask if a scholarship is waiting for him, especially if the coach has not seen his skills video. But if the athlete has spoken with the coach three times, met with the coach once, and has been evaluated by the coach, she should find out exactly where she stands on the coach's priority list.

Athletes should also be prepared to answer questions, such as:

1. *What other colleges/programs are recruiting you?*
    Students should be prepared to list colleges comparable to, rivals with, or better than the institution they are visiting.

2. *What colleges will you visit?*
    Answers should be honest but tactical. If this is the first college visit, the athlete should state that he is in the process

of scheduling the rest of his visits, and then name other institutions that are comparable to, rivals with, or better than the institution he is visiting.

3.   *Has anyone offered you a scholarship?*
     If the student has been offered a scholarship, he should tell the coach about it. If no scholarships have been offered, the athlete should state that he is in the process of taking visits and plans to discuss scholarships with those coaches when he meets with them.

4.   *When can you commit?*
     If this is the student-athlete's number one choice, he can commit, so long as he has completely researched all other choices. If he has other visits pending, he should tell the coach that he wants to visit a few other colleges just to make sure he is making an educated decision. He could say something like this, "I know that this is a decision that will impact not only the next four years of my life, but possibly the next forty years, so I want to make absolutely sure I have made the right choice that is a good fit for both me and the college."

     He should also ask the coach how long the offer stands.

Game Day Visits

Game day visits provide student-athletes with the opportunity to visit a campus with three tickets to watch a game. Game day visits are most common in football recruiting, but they take place in other sports as well. (See www.athleteswanted.org for a sample game day schedule.) Most football programs will offer game day visits to student-athletes on their recruiting list. Remember that the coaching staff will be busy preparing their team, so recruits usually do not get much attention during a game day visit. If this happens, athletes should not get discouraged, but be sure to follow up by calling to thank the coach.

OFFICIAL VISITS

If an institution pays for any part of a visit, the visit is considered an official visit. The NCAA restricts official visits: A student cannot take more than five official visits to Division I and II universities, and a student can only take one visit per university. With a few exceptions, official visits generally cannot begin until opening day of the athlete's senior year in high school.

COACH'S TIP

Student-athletes should make the most of official visits. Athletes should walk around campus and get a feel for the atmosphere. Do the students seem friendly? Is this a place they can imagine living for the next four years? Student-athletes might also want to try to meet the team, sit in a class, or watch a practice. They need to be sure this is a school they would want to attend if athletics were not part of the picture. This might also be time for student-athletes to arrange an interview with a department head or academic advisor.

Generally, coaches offer official visits only to their top recruits. The number of official visits a college offers varies by division, sport, and the school's budget.

If a coach offers an athlete an official visit, the student is most likely very high on the coach's list.

Scheduling Official Visits

By the time he is a senior, a student should be comfortable calling coaches, and he should have established relationships with several coaches. His best bet is to be upfront with a coach and ask if the coach plans to offer an official visit.

«« FAST FACT ««

If a Division I or II coach does not extend an offer for an official visit, the athlete is probably not high on that coach's list and not being considered for a scholarship.

If the coach extends an offer, the athlete should ask what he should bring on the visit. By now, the coach should have the student-athlete's highlight or skills video and profile. The student will also need to send a copy of his transcripts before taking the official visit and be registered with the NCAA Eligibility Center.

Student-athletes should be prepared to answer questions similar to those listed on page 215 and 216. If a coach asks what other colleges the student-athlete is considering, the athlete should always list universities that are comparable to, rivals with, or better than the one he is visiting. If a coach believes his competitors are recruiting the student, it will raise the athlete's stock!

As always, student-athletes should ask questions during the official visit. Refer to Chapter 5 for a sample of questions. Asking questions shows the coach that they are serious and prepared for college.

>> **FAST FACT** <<

With a few exceptions, football programs are limited to offering fifty-six official visits, basketball programs can offer only twelve official visits, and baseball only twenty-five.

A student-athlete should be aware that being offered an official visit, does not necessarily mean he will receive a scholarship or a spot on the team. The coaching staff has identified the athlete as a top prospect, but the official visit gives them the opportunity to judge personality, lifestyle, and character. They often will use "hosts" to help get a real flavor of the student's personality and character.

Though it isn't a guarantee, many offers **are** made during an official visit, and parents might not be with their children when the offer is made. This tends to make both athletes and their parents uncomfortable. To navigate through this situation, athletes can simply tell coaches that they need to let their parents review any financial information before committing. If a university really wants the athlete, the coach will wait a few days or a week.

A student who feels pressure can say, "You are my number-one choice, but I promised my parents I would talk it over with them before making a commitment. For how long will this offer be extended?"

COACH'S TIP
Since the NCAA restricts student-athletes to taking only five official visits, he or she should be sure to use them only at schools that are likely fits.

Usually, coaches will match recruits with team members who host them around campus. These hosts are also evaluating student-athletes. The student should be himself, but remember that coaches want athletes who will be positive assets to their university and team. At some point during or after the visit, the coaches will ask the host about the athlete, so the student-athlete needs to be positive, courteous, and respectful.

Host Evaluation Form

Prospect: *Roger Thomas*
Host: *Alex Cole*

1. How well will he fit in?
   (X) Very well
   ( ) Well
   ( ) Okay
   ( ) May not
   ( ) Will not

2. Would you want to work with him for four years?
   (X) Absolutely
   ( ) Probably
   ( ) Not sure
   ( ) Probably not
   ( ) Absolutely not

3. Is he interested in our university?
   (X) Yes. We're his #1 choice.
   ( ) Yes. We are in the top.

( ) Not sure
( ) I don't think so.

4. The biggest competition we have, in order, and why?
   a. *State College* Why? *Loved the campus.*
   b. *Academic U.*   Why? *Wants to visit*

5. Character Evaluation
   (*X*) Tops
   ( ) Good
   ( ) Not sure, check out further
   ( ) Bad

6. What does he like about our university?
   Has liked us for a long time. Likes the togetherness of the team. Likes the fact that students can go out and have fun or stay on campus if they want it to be quiet.

7. Where do his parents stand?
   Concerned at first about distance, but they seemed to be less concerned by the end of the visit.

8. Any other comments, concerns, or information?
   He doesn't want to stay near home, and I would be surprised if he didn't come.

KEY POINTS

1. Student-athletes should start taking "unofficial visits" as freshmen. Unlike "official visits," unofficial visits can be taken by any student at any time, though the coach does not pay for any portion of these visits. To schedule an unofficial visit, the student-athlete should call the coach. Because Division I and II coaches cannot call underclassmen, freshmen and sophomores might have to make several phone calls before connecting with the coach.

2. Student-athlete who take the initiative to schedule an unofficial visit will likely move up the recruitment list if they:

- Bring a list of questions to ask the coach,

- Express knowledge about the program, and

- Arrive on time with a copy of their résumé and highlight or skills video.

3. Parents should counsel their children about the types of questions they should ask and be prepared to answer.

4. Normally, a student can take five official visits during his senior year, though he can only visit each university once. Official visits are an opportunity for student-athletes to get a feel for the campus and find out exactly where they stand on the coach's recruiting list.

5. Many offers are made during official visits. If a coach does not offer a senior an official visit, that student is likely not high on the coach's list.

THE STUDENT-ATHLETE'S RÉSUMÉ

ANY TIME STUDENT-ATHLETES mail or email letters or packages to coaches, they should send a résumé, also called an athletic profile or, when verified by an objective third-party, a verified scouting report.

The résumé should include the following information about the student-athlete:

1. First and last name

2. Contact details: home address, email, cell phone, website

3. School and graduation year

4. Sport and position, including home and away colors

5. Grade-point average on 4.0 scale

6. Academic honors

7. Community involvement

8. Academic clubs

9. Athletic statistics

10. Athletic accomplishments and honors

11. Club, combine, showcase, or camp involvement

12. Links to online highlight or skills video

13. References from coaches

14. Picture

The basic rules of a résumé apply. Hard copies should be on good-quality paper. Regardless of whether the résumé is being delivered via email or hard copy, the résumé should be easy-to-read, free of typos, and well-formatted.

Résumés should also be an accurate representation of the student's abilities and statistics. Some student-athletes are tempted to over-exaggerate their abilities, height, or weight in an attempt to make them more attractive candidates for a spot on a college team. This is a big mistake. College coaches are already skeptical about résumés because they are self-reported. If one piece of information is incorrect, coaches will assume all of it is false. Coaches will eventually discover the athlete's actual abilities and stats, and they will be quick to eliminate for future consideration any student-athlete who lacks integrity.

COACH'S TIP

"Having the accurate height and weight can be as valuable as having an accurate 40-yard time," said Rob Ianello, recruiting coordinator at the University of Notre Dame.

An alternative to the résumé is called a "verified scouting report." Verified scouting reports are athletic profiles created by objective scouting services (for instance, the NCSA Student-Athlete Clearinghouse). In essence, they contain the same information as résumés, but, because they are controlled by a third party, coaches place more weight on verified scouting reports than they do on self-reported résumés. Sport-specific samples and information about scouting services that provide verified scouting reports can be found at www.athleteswanted.org.

A student-athlete should send each coach on his Correspondence Log an updated résumé anytime something positive changes in his status. If his grade-point average increases, or if he goes through a growth spurt, wins an award, or is promoted to team captain, the student-athlete should send an updated résumé, along with a cover letter indicating the changes in his status.

Résumés or profiles are also sent to coaches when a student introduces himself via email or snail mail. Today's savvy parents and student-athletes create websites to electronically house the student's résumé or profile electronically to alert coaches of updates in status. This eliminates the need to constantly send letters to coaches, and it allows easy access to a highlight or skills video via computer and high-speed Internet connection.

SAMPLE RÉSUMÉ

Justin Sherman

Grad Year	Height/Weight	Age	GPA
2009	5'10"	17	3.53/4.0

Position: Center Field, ShortStop, RHP
Parents: Kelly and Lynn

ADDRESS:

1415 N. Dayton Street, Apt. 4
Chicago, IL 60622
Home Phone: (888) 333-6846
Mobile Phone: (555) 555-0000
Email: mgolf@ncsasports.org

SCHOLASTIC INFORMATION:

Belvidere North High School
Phone: (555) 555-1111
Enrollment: 2200
Overall GPA: 3.6/4.0
SAT[1600]:   1240
Math: 600
Reading: 640
Writing: 590
Honors Classes: Algebra, English
Desired Major: Undecided
Eligibility Center: Yes

ACADEMIC HONORS/AWARDS:

National Honor Society (2007-09)

ATHLETIC INFORMATION:

- Four-time varsity letterman (golf, 2005-08)
- Third in state meet (70, 73) (2008)
- First-Team All-Conference (2008, 2007)
- First-Team All-District (2008)
- District Qualifier, Fifth Place (2008)
- Team Captain (2008)

CLUBS/CAMPS:

- AJGA Tournaments
- Sixth in Myrtle Beach Invitational (72, 71)
- Tenth in Chicago Jr. Invite (70)

STATISTICAL DATA:

Home Course:	Beckett Ridge Country Club
Course Par:	72
Course Slope:	136
Course Rating:	73.3
Course Yardage:	6857

08 AJGA

Handicap:	1.3
Nine-Hole Average:	37
Nine-Hole Low:	34
Eighteen-Hole Average:	73
Eighteen-Hole Low:	70
Average Drive:	295 yards
Driving Accuracy:	85 percent
Greens in Regulation:	14
Putts/18 Holes:	29

08 HIGH SCHOOL

Handicap:	0.1
Nine-Hole Average:	35
Nine-Hole Low:	32
Eighteen-Hole Average:	71
Eighteen-Hole Low:	68
Average Drive:	295 yards
Driving Accuracy:	90 percent
Greens in Regulation:	16
Putts/18 Holes:	26

KEY POINTS

__1.__ An athlete should create a professional student-athlete résumé or pro-file that includes first and last name, contact details, school and grade, sport and position, GPA, academic and athletic honors, community in-volvement, links to streaming highlight or skills video, athletic statistics, and academic or athletic clubs, combines, showcases, or camps.

__2.__ When a student introduces himself to a coach, he should provide a copy of his résumé. If the athlete's status changes for the better, he should up-date his résumé and send a copy, along with a cover letter, to all coaches on his Correspondence Log. In connection with a student-athlete's web-site, this will help coaches keep updated on any progress academically and athletically in real time. It also allows coaches to watch a highlight or skills video via the Internet.

__3.__ Coaches can be skeptical of self-reported information. An upgrade to the résumé is a "verified scouting report" created by an objective third-party. For more information, visit www.athleteswanted.org.

VIDEOS

IF MOST COLLEGE COACHES had their choice, they would always prefer to watch a student-athlete play live. Due to busy schedules and budget restrictions, coaches cannot travel to evaluate every player they are recruiting. When a personal evaluation is not possible, video allows a coaching staff to evaluate the mechanics and specific talents of a prospect, providing the coaches with the necessary tools to draw legitimate interest in a student-athlete. Coaches across the country welcome the opportunity to evaluate a prospect from their office chair.

Videos (which have been referred to as "tapes" or "video tapes") come in three forms: skills, highlight, or game. Some sports require only one; others request two, and in some cases, a student might send a game, highlight, and skills video. The requirements will vary by sport and program. See www.athleteswanted.org for sport-specific information about skills, highlight, and game videos.

- **Skills videos** showcase a student's fundamental abilities. Skills videos are not necessarily composed only of game footage. In fact, some skills videos show only drills during practice, showcases, and the like, demonstrating the student-athlete's abilities.

- **Highlight videos** consist only of game footage and, as the name implies, should consist of a student-athlete's on-field highlights.

- **Game videos** are exactly what they seem like: recorded footage of an entire game. Coaches usually will not request a game video until they have viewed a student's highlight or skills video.

COACH'S TIP

An athlete should send videos only to college coaches who have requested the videos. An athlete's video might not be looked at if a coach is not expecting it, especially if the coach is from a big program that receives forty or fifty videos a week. If students want to mail a video or email a link to a coach who has not requested their highlight or skills video, the athletes should call and make sure the coach is expecting the video. One father of an elite athlete reports that he spent $2,250 and two hundred hours sending unsolicited packages to college coaches. Not a single coach called him based on these packages.

Regardless, a student-athlete should send his video only if a coach has requested it or is expecting it. Once a coach calls, emails, or sends a letter requesting a video, the student should send the video promptly and let the coach know that the video is on the way or has been sent via email.

Though most freshmen do not have enough footage to create highlight videos, skills videos can be created as soon as a student-athlete begins playing a sport. The student-athlete should start putting together the video as soon as possible. Remember that the student-athlete's video is a significant part of the recruiting process and the earlier the video is prepared, the earlier the athlete can respond to all coach requests.

Contents of a video will vary widely from sport to sport. Highlights do not apply in all sports, so in some instances, game and skills footage may become more important. For example, a softball coach may request a skills video of the student-athlete swinging, fielding, and throwing to evaluate mechanics. Baseball coaches want to know pop times, home-to-first times, sixty-yard dash times, the athlete's throwing velocity, and the like. It is more important for them to see the athlete's fundamentals and ability level rather than actual game film. A volleyball coach can watch a skills video; on the other hand, a basketball coach needs to see actual game footage.

In general, the student-athlete should follow certain basic guidelines no matter what the sport.

1. Start with a short introduction that states name, school, and contact information.

2. Start the video with the most impressive plays. Athletes only have one chance to make a first impression.

3. Do not produce video that is shot at either a tight or far angle. Find a happy medium. Coaches want to see the whole play develop to see how the player reacts to each situation.

4. Use video that is clear and easily identifies each player. If coaches cannot identify the player, they will move on to the next video. Use spot-shadowing or an arrow to identify the student-athlete.

5. Keep things short and sweet. The student-athlete's video should not be any longer than three to five minutes. Coaches receive hundreds of videos; if the athlete's video drags, the coach will be bored, not an association the student should form with the coach.

6. Include a wide variety of plays that show all of their talents. Versatility is important.

7. Consider eliminating music and background noise. Some coaches will watch the video with the volume off, but if music is included in the video, choose songs that are acceptable to a wide range of personality types!

8. Remember that college coaches don't look at footage the same way parents do. Colleges are looking for athletic ability, speed, explosiveness, technique, drive, and fundamental skill sets of the sport and position. If possible, a coach, former collegiate athlete, or scouting or recruiting service should help pick the child's best plays and sequence them properly.

In addition to the résumé, profile, or scouting report, most coaches use highlight and skills videos as the initial layer of evaluating an athlete's likelihood of receiving an athletic scholarship. After reviewing a student scouting report, the coach will use a highlight or skills video to assess the student's in-action abilities.

Once the video is created, consider how it will be delivered to coaches. Postal mail can be expensive, and most coaches prefer to watch videos electronically. College coaches overwhelmingly favor personal websites updated with transcripts and links to highlight or skills video and game footage. The athlete can then send hyperlinks and update coaches when new information is available or accomplishments are made. Advanced sites like these can track viewership by college coaches, making it easy to know who is watching. Visit www.athleteswanted.org for sample websites.

COACH'S TIP

Today's technology makes it easy to create an online package that includes the scouting report and a streaming video highlight or skills footage so that the coach can look at an athlete's stats and watch his performance easily and quickly. Imagine how impressed a coach will be if an athlete sends a well-composed, reader-friendly email containing a link to a high-quality video within moments of a phone call!

NEW TECHNOLOGIES: VIDEO VS. ENHANCED VIDEO

New technologies and professional video-enhancing services help the student-athlete create a high-quality video that uses spot-shadowing to highlight the athlete, high frame-rate filming and high definition flash technology that allows the greatest detail in slow-motion viewing, and professional editing to sequence the video appropriately. Some even post the videos online, which allows coaches to watch the videos easily from their laptop. Some services provide a list of those college coaches who have watched the videos, which allows the student-athletes to follow up promptly after the coach has viewed their videos.

Enhanced video can be a great way to make a student-athlete stand out from the crowd and gain the attention of the college coach. Visit www. athleteswanted.org for more information about these services.

«« **FAST FACT** ««

Coaches who are impressed with an athlete's highlight or skills video will likely request a full game video. When sending a DVD, students can include the game footage after the highlight or skills footage.

KEY POINTS

_1._   When a personal evaluation is not possible, coaches rely on highlight and skills videos to evaluate the mechanics and specific talents of a prospect.

_2._   Depending on the sport, a student-athlete should create either a skills or a highlight video. A skills video showcases the student's fundamental skills and does not necessarily include game footage. A highlight video, on the other hand, is comprised solely of the best game footage the student-athlete has.

_3._   Before sending a video, the student-athlete should call the coach to make sure he is expecting it.

_4._   Consider hiring a service that makes use of the newest technologies to create an enhanced streaming video that can spot-shadow and stream videos, which are easily distributed to college coaches for evaluation. Some services even deliver a verified list back to the student-athlete detailing the college coaches who viewed the video, which allows the student-athlete to follow up quickly.

_5._   Contents of video vary from sport to sport. See www.athleteswanted. org for sport-specific information about highlight and skills videos.

SCHOLARSHIPS, FINANCIAL AID, AND ADMISSIONS

WHEN ALL IS SAID AND DONE, how does it work? At what point does a student-athlete receive and accept a scholarship offer? The truth is that there is no etched-in-stone formula. If a student has been communicating with coaches and is a top prospect in his sport, the athlete should know whether he is going to receive a scholarship by the end of his junior year or the beginning of his senior year. An athlete who does not have a verbal or written offer should immediately realize that he has some work to do.

Scholarships are available only for student-athletes who meet the NCAA or NAIA's minimum standards for academic achievement and, in many cases, more rigid standards established by individual schools. Scholarships are awarded one year at a time, for a maximum of five years (though the NCAA can grant sixth-year exceptions for students who are injured or have other extenuating circumstances), and are renewed each year.

Division III schools, as well as Division I non-scholarship programs (Ivy and Patriot League schools), are not allowed to provide athletic scholarships, but this rule is a technicality. As discussed later in this chapter, a Division III school hungry for a talented student-athlete can assemble a grants-in-aid package, whether it be academic, need-based, or non-need-based. A non-need-based grant serves the same purpose as an athletic scholarship: It pays for the student's education, usually with fewer strings attached.

ATHLETIC SCHOLARSHIPS: HEAD COUNT VERSUS EQUIVALENCY

The most commonly known scholarship, also referred to as a "grant-in-aid," is the full scholarship, or "full ride."

The term "grant" is literal. This is not a loan, and students do not have to pay the money back. A full ride normally covers tuition, books, room, board, and associated fees. Bottom line: It's a free education, which with today's higher-education costs, is an extraordinary package. The average debt for typical students after college is about $25,000; imagine the foundation established by a student-athlete who plays sports for four or five years and emerges from college without owing a single penny!

Full-ride athletic scholarships are generally reserved for high-level athletes. Approximately 70 percent of the decision to award an athlete with a full-ride scholarship is based on the athlete's ability and projectability (the athlete's potential and expected future abilities) while about 30 percent of the decision is based on academics, character, work ethic, and intangibles.

But full-ride scholarships are only one of the two types of athletic scholarships a school might offer. The NCAA breaks sports into two categories—head count sports and equivalency sports. Students who are offered a scholarship to play a head count sport are being offered a full scholarship, while students who play equivalency sports might receive only a partial scholarship.

«« FAST FACT ««

An athlete who receives a scholarship to play a "head count" sport is always given a full-ride scholarship. An athlete who receives a scholarship to play an "equivalency sport" might receive only a partial scholarship.

Head count sports are those sports that generally bring revenues to the school. For men, revenue sports include basketball and Division IA football. For women, head count sports include basketball, tennis, volleyball, and gymnastics.

HEAD COUNT SPORTS	EQUIVALENCY SPORTS
Men's Basketball	Baseball
Women's Basketball	Cross Country/Track
Football (Division IA)	Field Hockey
Women's Gymnastics	Football (except Division IA)
Women's Tennis	Golf
Women's Volleyball	Men's Gymnastics
	Ice Hockey
	Lacrosse
	Soccer
	Softball
	Men's Swimming
	Men's Tennis
	Men's Volleyball
	Wrestling

Any other sport is considered a "non-revenue" or "Olympic" sport, meaning the sport does not produce revenue for the school. Indeed, most non-revenue sports are at least partially funded by football and basketball revenues. In non-revenue sports, coaches typically divvy up their allotment of scholarships using the equivalency method. While head count sports have a set number of scholarships that must be awarded in full to one student, equivalency sports have a set number of scholarships that can be divided among athletes. A head count sport with five available scholarships will award five full rides to five students, while an equivalency sport with five available scholarships might offer one student a full scholarship, divide the second scholarship among two students, the third among three students, the fourth among four students, and the fifth among five students. In other words, fifteen students might share the equivalency of five full-ride scholarships.

Equivalency scholarships are generally split so that the more important players receive a higher percentage of the scholarships. For instance, the top-flight softball pitcher might receive 95 percent of one scholarship while the backup outfielder receives only enough scholarship money to cover books. Students from out of town also fare better with equivalency sports than local students. Because in-state tuition is not as costly, most coaches in these sports prefer in-state students to pony up for tuition so they can save their resources for high-level out-of-state students.

"NEED-BASED" SCHOLARSHIPS

The term "need-based" is most often applied to a student's financial need, with the financial aid, grant, or scholarship being awarded based on the economic profile of the student-athlete's family.

But parents and their student-athletes should consider that other "need-based" scholarships exist. These scholarships are awarded to a student-athlete based on the **school's** need for the student. A student-athlete attending a Division III school, for instance, cannot technically be awarded an athletic scholarship as the NCAA prohibits scholarships based solely on athletic ability at this level. Colleges give out scholarships based on leadership, academics, or merit, as well as their desire to create a competitive grants-in-aid package to attract a student they need for their team and campus.

COACH'S TIP

The pot of scholarship money is limited, so the recruitment process should be started early. The earlier it is started, the more money will be available for the student-athlete.

NEGOTIATING SCHOLARSHIPS

One way or another, the key to negotiating a scholarship is to leverage the resources the athlete brings to the table. This means that:

- The better a student's grades, the more money he can receive.

- The more extracurricular activities an athlete brings to the table, the more attractive he will be. If he is the editor of the newspaper or a member of 4H, more scholarship money can be available, particularly for Division III and Division I non-scholarship programs, which do not technically offer athletic scholarships. Instead, these schools look for academic, need-based, or non-need-based scholarships to offer to students they want on that campus. Most happen to be athletes as well. If a student plays the trumpet, even poorly, he might earn a scholarship that will facilitate his ability to play sports.

> **«« FAST FACT ««**
> Many of the bigger scholarship packages come from Division III and Division I non-scholarship programs.

- The more choices an athlete has, the more leverage he has. If a coach knows that other schools are also recruiting a top athlete, especially if these schools are rivals, he might offer the student more in scholarship money. This simply creates interest in the athlete. If a student's first choice knows that its rival is trying to scoop up the athlete, the school will be even more eager to offer a better scholarship package.

The most important thing to remember is that nothing is guaranteed until a student signs on the dotted line. Carmen Bucci, who went on to become a professional baseball player, learned this the hard way. The Chicago Catholic League player of the year, Bucci had a 4.0 grade-point average in high school; later, he was drafted by the Padres, but Bucci's college story is less than ideal.

Bucci was a sought-after high school athlete who was recruited by quite a few schools, including his-top choice college. The school's coach promised Bucci that the school would make him an offer and sign him on National Letter of Intent Day.

While waiting for his offer to come through, Bucci received several other offers. He did not understand the process of negotiating for a scholarship, so he simply turned down the scholarship offers. Had Bucci called his first-choice school to let the coach know other schools were making him offers, Bucci likely would have seen scholarship dollars. Instead, he simply waited.

Four months later, Bucci received a phone call from the coach of his top school.

"We're excited to have you," said the coach, "but unfortunately we do not have any scholarship money left." Bucci was asked to walk on.

Later, Bucci received a baseball scholarship to another school, and he went on to have a fine career with the Padres. But Bucci could have avoided the initial rocky start if he had asked two critical questions:

1. *Can I have the offer in writing?*

2. *How long does the offer stand?*

COACH'S TIP

If a coach makes an offer prior to Signing Day, the athlete should ask for the offer in writing. If the student is unable to commit verbally, he should also ask how long the offer stands.

The college recruiting process is based entirely on relationships and the ability of the student and parent to ask the right questions. The student-athlete should know exactly where she stands with each coach, and she should use every tool available, including offers from other schools, to help a college make a decision.

Some families and athletes are afraid that the process is subtle. They try to read between the lines, wondering whether an athlete will be offered a scholarship. Instead, the student can ask questions that will shed light on the reality of the situation.

If a school is truly interested in an athlete, its coaches will let the student know, but a little probing from the student-athlete can clear up any misconceptions and move a school to act faster.

Student-athletes should ask the following questions:

- During the first unofficial visit or phone call with a coach (freshman year), an athlete should ask this question:

  "Can you give me some idea what to expect? Given my grades and athletic ability and compared to the other kids on your team, what would I need to do to compete for your program on an athletic scholarship?"

  During this conversation, the student is simply asking a hypothetical question, not pressuring the coach. Unless the student is an elite athlete, the coach will not be able or willing to make a verbal commitment, and the athlete should not expect one. Instead, the athlete can explain that he is setting goals for himself and would like the coach's help understanding how the process might work should he achieve his goals.

- During sophomore year, a student should be sure to find out how interested a school is in recruiting him. A good question to ask might be:

  "Coach, if I continue to work hard and build my skills, do you think I'll be considered for a spot on your team? If so, do you think I would be eligible for a scholarship? If not, what would I need to do to compete for your program on an athletic scholarship?"

- During junior year, assuming the athlete has continued making regular contact with the same coaches, he should come right out and ask:

  "Do you plan on offering me an official visit? What kind of package do you think I might qualify for?"

- If a coach offers a scholarship, the athlete should ask:

  "Can I have the offer in writing and how long does the offer stand?"

  "How many others at my position have you offered or will you be offering?"

- If an athlete is awaiting other offers, or wants to negotiate for a better package by leveraging other offers, the student-athlete should ask:

  "How long does the offer stand?"

- And if a student is waiting for a school that hasn't made an offer, he should simply ask something like the following, which lets the coach know which schools he has offers from:

  "Right now I have an offer from Michigan and Ohio State. Do you feel I might be getting an offer from your program?"

  This is an important question to ask a coach from the athlete's first-choice school, especially if a coach from another program has made an offer. Before accepting an offer, a student needs to know where he stands with his first-choice schools.

FINANCIAL AID

Because few athletes will receive full scholarships, understanding the financial aid process is vital so that a family can supplement partial scholarships with grants and financial aid. Simply knowing four steps of the financial aid process can save a family thousands of dollars. Families should:

1. Calculate their expected EFC during the athlete's sophomore year.

2. Adjust their assets and prepare for the FAFSA while their student-athlete is a junior.

3. Submit the FAFSA on January 1 of the student's senior year.

4. Follow up after receiving the official EFC.

COA=Cost of Attendance

EFC = Expected Family Contribution

FAFSA = Free Application for Federal Student Aid

SAR = Student Aid Report

Calculating EFC

The expected family contribution (EFC) is the amount a family can be expected to contribute toward a student's college costs. Financial aid administrators determine need for federal student aid by subtracting the EFC from the student's cost of attendance (COA). The EFC formula is used to determine the extent to which a student needs federal student financial assistance in the form of Federal Pell Grants, subsidized Stafford Loans and assistance from the "campus-based" programs—Federal Supplemental Educational Opportunity Grants, Federal Perkins Loans, and Federal Work-Study. The lower a family's EFC, the greater the student's need.

COA-EFC=Need

Obviously, an athlete is best positioned to receive grants and financial aid by showing a low EFC and a high need.

John Letts, CEO of Collegiate Financial Advisors, said that most parents make a huge mistake in not calculating their expected family contribution early. Waiting is a big mistake. Ideally, parents should calculate their EFC early in their children's college search so that they will have some idea of what the government will expect them to contribute toward their son or daughter's college education. In fact, counsels Letts, if a parents knows the process and estimates his EFC, he might find tricks to reallocate assets and lower the EFC, which in turn increases the student's need.

Visit www.athleteswanted.org for information about calculating a family's EFC.

Preparing for the FAFSA

The Free Application for Federal Student Aid, or the FAFSA, is a form required by the government for application to any federal education aid program. The FAFSA is the form used to determine the expected family contribution and, in turn, the specific aid programs that will be contributed to a student's total financial aid proportions. While filling out the FAFSA, a family will disclose certain financial information.

At the beginning of their child's junior year, parents should be sure that they review the FAFSA and meet with their accountant to discuss the adjustments they can make that might decrease their EFC and increase their grants-in-aid potential. For instance, the FAFSA will consider the amount of money in a student-athlete's name. If a student has money in excess of a certain amount ($1,500 in 2007), the FAFSA will expect the student to apply 100 percent of this money to the first year of college tuition. If the money is held in the parent's name, the FAFSA will expect a smaller percentage to be earmarked for the college fund. By transferring the money out of the student's name and into the parent's name, the expected family contribution will be lower and the family need will be higher.

COACH'S TIP

This might be the most confusing part of the entire recruiting process. At a minimum, parents should meet with their accountant to discuss adjustments they can make to increase need and lower their EFC.

Said Letts, "Sure, you could do it on your own, but only if you have a few kids you can use as guinea pigs."

By figuring out how to best position their student-athletes for financial aid, families can then create a financial plan that works within their budgets to determine how they will cover any expenses that fall above and beyond financial aid and scholarships.

Submitting the FAFSA

During an athlete's junior or senior year, the athlete's family can submit a FAFSA using last year's tax return figures so long as the family does not expect a significant change in income from the following year. One way or another, the family should submit its FAFSA as soon as possible. Applications can be submitted as early as 12:01 a.m. on January 1 of a student-athlete's senior year, and funds are distributed on a first-come, first-serve basis.

Letts counsels 100 percent of parents to fill out the FAFSA, though statistics say about half of families do not submit the form, a big mistake. Families should never assume they will not qualify for grants, said Letts.

"Colleges will not make the effort to lower the bottom line cost of college unless you make the effort," he said, adding that no costs are associated with submitting the FAFSA, and every child is entitled to a government loan if his family submits the form.

Following Up

Upon completing the FAFSA, which determines an athlete's official EFC, the student-athlete will receive a SAR, which is the Student Aid Report. The SAR is the official documentation from FAFSA indicating a student's EFC.

A student should turn a copy of the SAR into the Financial Aid Office of the universities the athlete is interested in attending. The SAR gets the ball rolling. Upon receiving the SAR, the college will offer the athlete a financial aid package. This package will outline in detail the type of award (financial aid or scholarship) the college is offering. It might include athletic scholarships, academic scholarships, merit scholarships, state awards, grants, loans, work study, or other need-based aid.

Remember that a family can appeal its financial aid package. Simply by appealing, many families are given an extra $3,000 to $5,000 in aid money. Often, a well-written explanation of why a family needs more financial help, coupled with a statement noting rival schools offering more financial help, can help land a student-athlete a more competitive package.

To appeal, a student-athlete can simply call the coach or admissions office and ask, "How do I appeal the SAR?"

ADMISSIONS

Based on how accommodating the coaches are, a student-athlete will have a feeling for the level of interest the coach has, but at this point, the athlete should know exactly where he stands. Some colleges can waive the application fees for those candidates in which they have serious interest. A student-athlete should apply to two or three backup choices just in case the top choice falls through. Student-athletes usually find the admissions process relatively hassle-free, so long as they have help from an accommodating coaching staff.

The admissions process for a student-athlete is generally the same as it is for the student at large, the only differences being that:

- A college coach can expedite a student's application; and

- The colleges can often, but not always, waive a student's application fee. Applying to a college can be a costly expense. The cost of submitting a single application can range from $25 to $250. But a student who is being recruited can ask the coach to waive the application fee. In fact, NCSA reports that it has worked with student-athletes who have applied to more than fifteen colleges for free due to athletic waivers.

«« FAST FACT ««

A student-athlete will most likely be accepted to any college or university as long as the coach wants the athlete and the athlete has a 3.5 GPA and either: 1) a 1200 SAT score out of 1600; 2) an 1800 SAT score out of 2400; or 3) a 28 or above ACT score.

Assuming that a student has kept in contact with the coaches in his queue, the application process should be smooth. If a student-athlete is interested in attending a university, the student should simply use the normal admissions process as a guide. By now, a student-athlete should know whether he meets the academic requirements for admissions. If an athlete has been in touch with college coaches, he has discussed his eligibility with coaches.

COACH'S TIP

When applying to a college that is recruiting a student-athlete, the student should always ask for an application waiver. The normal cost to apply for admission ranges from $25 to $250, which can be costly, especially if an athlete is applying for multiple universities. Asking a coach for an application waiver lets the coach know that the student knows how to play the game. In turn, it lets the student-athlete know how interested the coach is. If the coach is willing to help a student-athlete with the admissions process, this is a good indication the coach is interested in the athlete.

Prior to applying, a student-athlete should also ask the coach if there is an athletic application or athletic waiver. The coach might send an application directly to the student; others will direct the athlete to apply online. Student-athletes can also ask about application costs. Sometimes, but not always, coaches can waive application fees.

Low-income students can also request a Fee Waiver Request Form/ Financial Hardship Waiver from their guidance counselor or online at www.nacac.com/feewaiver.html.

During the admissions process, athletes should be negotiating the best package available by leveraging other offers. In exchange for their talent, the school will educate student-athletes. This means that the student should put it all on the table, especially if the athlete is an average or below-average student. If a student has a 2.2 cumulative grade-point average and is applying for admission to a university with a 3.0 average, the athlete should highlight not only his athletic abilities, but also his community service and extracurricular activities. This gives the coach an opportunity to go to bat for an athlete if the admissions office is considering turning down the student's admissions request.

Remember that it is never too late to become a good student. The last report card is the most important. A college coach will look for trends. If a student-athlete's grades have steadily improved, recent report cards might be weighted more heavily than older report cards.

»« FAST FACT »«
Some out-of-state athletes can negotiate for in-state tuition.

KEY POINTS

1. To be eligible for a scholarship, a student-athlete must meet NCAA or NAIA minimum standards for academic achievement. Some schools have more rigid standards.

2. Athletic scholarships are awarded either on a "head count" or an "equivalency" basis. Full-ride scholarships are given to students who play "head count" sports (basketball, Division IA football, women's tennis, women's volleyball, and women's gymnastics) while partial scholarships may be given to students who play "equivalency" sports.

3. Division III and Division I non-scholarship programs are not technically permitted by the NCAA to provide athletic scholarships. However, if a Division III or Division I non-scholarship school wants an athlete enough, the school will find a need-based or academic scholarship to provide to the student.

4. Students with better grades, extracurricular activities, and multiple offers to leverage will negotiate the best packages.

5. If offered a scholarship, a student should always ask for it in writing. Remember that nothing is guaranteed until the athlete signs on the dotted line on Signing Day, but a written offer will provide a student with some level of assurance.

6. The scholarship process is not subtle. Throughout the high school years, a student-athlete should be direct with a coach, asking questions that provide the student with information about what to next expect.

7. Because few athletes will receive full athletic scholarships, a parent can supplement partial scholarships with grants and financial aid. Parents should know the four-step financial aid process:

- Calculate their expected EFC.
- Adjust their assets accordingly to prepare for the FAFSA.
- Submit the FAFSA on January 1 of their student's senior year.
- Follow up and appeal decisions, if necessary.

8. The student-athlete should work with the coach to facilitate the admissions process, which is generally the same for student-athletes as for non-athletes, with two exceptions. First, if the coach is interested in recruiting the student, the coach can expedite the process. Second, the coach can waive the application fee.

9. Asking the coach for an athletic application waiver can save a family hundreds or thousands of dollars!

SIGNING DAY

AFTER COMMUNICATING WITH the admissions office, colleges will offer a student a scholarship only if the athlete is assured acceptance to that school. If a student-athlete receives a scholarship, the athlete will likely be asked to sign a National Letter of Intent on "Signing Day," a specific date designated by the Collegiate Commissioners Association and the NCAA Eligibility Center. The student-athlete, parents or guardians, and the athletic directors must all sign the NLI certifying that the student intends to enroll during the coming fall academic year.

The NLI confirms that a student-athlete is committed to attend a specific college or university for one academic year, and some schools may ask non-scholarship athletes to sign the NLI. By attaching a scholarship offer to the NLI, the college or university commits to provide the student-athlete with athletic financial aid for one academic year, provided that the student is admitted to the institution and eligible for financial aid.

Once a student-athlete signs a National Letter of Intent, other colleges must stop recruiting the student. One of the Collegiate Commissioners Association's primary goals with the NLI is to reduce and limit the recruiting pressure on a student-athlete.

A student who signs the letter of intent should also sign the grants-in-aid letter that outlines the school's financial commitment to the student. The NLI binds the student to the school; the grants-in-aid letter binds the school's commitment to the student-athlete.

An NLI can become null and void if the student-athlete fails to graduate or fails to pass required core course requirements to meet the NCAA eligibility requirements. An NLI can also become null and void if a student-athlete gets arrested.

«« FAST FACTS ««

Signing Day has two components: 1) the NLI binds the student-athlete to the school and spells out the details of the scholarship and grants-in-aid offered to the student for the upcoming year; and 2) the NLI binds the student-athlete to the school, detailing the terms the student must meet to receive the scholarship offer. Remember that the NLI is for one year only. The student-athlete should find out what he needs to do to be offered the same terms the following year.

SAMPLE LETTER OF INTENT AND SCHOLARSHIP OFFER

ATHLETIC LETTER OF INTENT/ SCHOLARSHIP OFFER

The following terms and conditions define an offer of an athletic scholarship for participation in the sport of baseball by Smith University and the acceptance of that scholarship by Todd Forte for the 2008-09 academic year.

I. AMOUNT OF OFFER:

This offer is a scholarship in the amount of $ 8,736.00 which is equivalent to 70% of the tuition cost for the 2008-09 academic year only; $ 4,368.00 will be applied to the Fall 2008 semester and $ 4,368.00 will be applied to the Spring 2009 semester.

II. QUALIFICATION FOR ATHLETIC SCHOLARSHIP

1. The student-athlete must be eligible to participate in intercollegiate athletics upon enrollment at Smith University according to the Constitution and By-Laws of the National Association of Intercollegiate Athletics. Signing of this letter indicates intent only and does not guarantee admission to the College and/or eligibility to participate. If either condition is not met, both parties agree to void the agreement.

2. The student-athlete agrees to follow all rules and regulations established by the college for students as detailed in the Student Handbook and shall sign a supplementary agreement as required by the Dean of Enrollment Services.

3. The student-athlete further agrees to follow all rules for participation in the scholarship sport as determined by the head coach. These rules include, but are not limited to:

   A. The student-athlete will not use drugs, alcohol or tobacco, at any time, while under contract.

   B. The student-athlete will not use expletive, offensive or derogatory language at any time.

C.   Physical or verbal acts of intimidation or violence by the student-athlete will not be tolerated.

D.   All team members are required to attend team meetings, functions, practices, games and road trips—arriving on time for each. Student-athletes are excused from class **only** to participate in regularly scheduled games. Every effort will be made to schedule practices and team functions so that they do not interfere with class meetings.

E.   All team members will be expected to participate in team community service projects and to work on team fund-raising events.

4.   The student shall obey all federal, state and local laws and ordinances.

5.   Participation in a sport other than the scholarship sport is at the discretion of the head coach of the scholarship sport.

III. CONTINUANCE AND/OR DISCONTINUANCE OF SCHOLARSHIP

1.   The student-athlete shall not have his/her scholarship discontinued prior to the end of the academic year for poor athletic performance.

2.   The student-athlete shall not have his/her scholarship discontinued prior to the end of the academic year if the student is prevented from participating in the scholarship sport because of illness, injury or other genuine emergency.

3.   The student-athlete may have his/her scholarship discontinued immediately if he/she becomes academically ineligible to participate in athletics or the scholarship sport according to the NAIA. The student should familiarize him/herself with these regulations.

4.   The student-athlete may have his/her scholarship discontinued immediately if he/she voluntarily withdraws from the team or is dismissed from the team for just cause. To emphasize: Being removed from the team for lack of playing ability does not constitute just cause.

5. The student-athlete <u>may</u> have his/her scholarship discontinued immediately if he/she breaks any of the terms of this agreement; is convicted of violating federal, state or local law other than a minor traffic offense; is found to have violated the rules established for the conduct of students at large at Smith University as detailed in the Student Handbook or breaks any of the rules established by the head coach of the scholarship sport.

6. The student-athlete <u>may</u> have his/her scholarship discontinued immediately if he/she is discovered to have fraudulently misrepresented prior academic records or any other information requested during the admissions and/or financial aid process.

7. Discontinuance of the scholarship would mean the student-athlete would immediately be responsible for paying prorated balances which may result.

8. This scholarship is granted for the <u>2008-09</u> academic year <u>only.</u> The student-athlete must agree to attend both the Fall and Spring semester regardless of what semester the sport is played. Continuance beyond the Spring <u>2009</u> semester is at the discretion of the college and/or head coach.

9. This offer does not guarantee a roster spot on the Patten University baseball team. The student-athlete <u>shall not</u> have his/her scholarship discontinued in the event the student-athlete does not make the final active roster.

This document represents an offer regarding only an athletic scholarship between Smith University and the student-athlete. The scholarship must be confirmed by an official award letter from the Financial Aid Office after completion of all documents required by the college. All Smith University Scholarships require a semester and cumulative grade-point average (GPA) of 2.0. Student-athletes who fail to maintain these grading standards will have their scholarships terminated at the end of the term in which they fell below the standards.

IV. APPEAL OF DISCONTINUANCE

1. Discontinuance of scholarship for cause prior to the end of the <u>2008-09</u> academic year may be appealed by the student. A committee consisting of the Faculty

Athletic Representative, the Director of Athletics, Director of Financial Aid and the Dean of Enrollment Services shall consider the appeal. If any member of this committee is unavailable or disqualifies him/herself from hearing an appeal, the Dean of Enrollment Services shall appoint a replacement to the committee. If the Dean of Enrollment Services is not able to head the appeal, the President of the College shall appoint his/her replacement.

V. DECLARATION OF INTENT:

By signing below, I agree to attend Smith University during the 2008-09 academic year and to participate on the college's intercollegiate team in the scholarship sport specified on page 1 of this agreement. I have read each of the forgoing conditions and understand each. I agree to abide by the conditions and to represent the college in a positive manner. I understand that if this letter is not signed and returned to the Head Baseball Coach by June 5, 2008 Smith University may elect to withdraw its offer:

_____ _____ _____ _____,

2008
Name   Signature   SSN#   Date

As representatives of Smith University, the undersigned agree to offer the Athletic Scholarship described to the above named student for the 2008-09 academic year under the agreed-upon conditions.

_____   _____

Head Coach   Date

_____   _____

Director of Athletics   Date

_____   _____

Dean of Enrollment Services   Date

Refer to athleteswanted.org for the NLI signing date for each sport. Be aware that not all colleges use the National Letter of Intent. Visit www. national-letter.org for a list of participating colleges and universities.

EARLY DECISION ENROLLMENT

A student-athlete might be asked this question by college coaches: "Do you plan to apply early?"

Primarily selective colleges and universities use early admissions programs as a way to help applicants secure an admissions decision ahead of schedule. Early admissions policies vary from school to school, so it is important that students understand the process before marking the "early" box on the application.

Some programs offer "Early Decision Enrollment." As its name suggests, this allows a student-athlete to sign before Signing Day. Early Decision Enrollment is binding, meaning a student must attend the college (with exceptions for certain students who face financial burdens). An athlete should avoid applying Early Decision to a college unless 100 percent sure this is the athlete's first-choice school. If an athlete is accepted as an Early Decision student, the acceptance will close the doors for other opportunities. At a minimum, a student who accepts an Early Decision lowers future negotiating potential.

Early Action Acceptance, on the other hand, is not binding. A student who receives Early Action Acceptance is admitted but not required to attend the university.

RECRUITED WALK-ONS

On the other hand, if Signing Day comes and goes without a scholarship offer, the student-athlete might be invited to walk on. An athlete who has evaluated all other options and decided to walk on to a team should know where he stands.

First, he should be sure he is a preferred walk-on and not just another random freshman trying out for a team. Preferred walk-ons have been in communication with the coaching staff and generally have been promised a roster spot.

Walk-ons should also let the coach know that they will work to earn a scholarship in the future. If an athlete falls into this category, he should ask the coach what he must do to earn a scholarship. He should also find out if he will have access to the academic support systems available for scholarship athletes like tutors, preferential course registration, training tables, housing, and athletic gear.

Walking on should be used as a last resort, and some students might choose to attend a less desired school where they are offered some sort of financial aid package instead of attending a preferred school as a walk-on, but others are more interested in attending a specific university and might need to resort to walk-on status.

KEY POINTS

_1._ Many colleges have an official Signing Day, which is also called National Letter of Intent (NLI) Day. On this day, which differs based on sport, the student-athlete, his parents or guardian, and the athletic director must sign a letter certifying that the student intends to enroll during the coming fall academic year. The NLI ties the student-athlete to the college program.

_2._ Nothing is official until the student-athlete signs the NLI, which is a legal, binding agreement.

_3._ Once a student signs an NLI, other colleges must stop recruiting him.

_4._ The student-athlete should sign the grants-in-aid letter that outlines the school's financial commitment to the student. The NLI binds the student to the school; the grants-in-aid letter binds the school and its financial commitment to the student-athlete.

_5._ Some students can apply for "Early Decision Enrollment," which allows them to sign on the dotted line before the official Signing Day. Be aware that Early Decision Enrollment closes the door to other opportunities, so students should agree to this only if they are 100 percent sure that they are attending their top-choice school.

_6._ Refer to www.athleteswanted.org for the NLI signing dates for each sport. Be aware that not all colleges use the National Letter of Intent. Visit www.national-letter.org for a list of participating colleges and universities.

THE NCAA, NAIA, AND THE STUDENT-ATHLETE

FOR SHEER COMPLEXITY, there's nothing quite like the NCAA rulebook. It's as fat as the *Manhattan Yellow Pages*, as complicated as the U.S. Tax Code, and as daunting as *War and Peace*. These rules are summarized in the annual *NCAA Guide for the College-Bound Student-Athlete*. This book is important for three reasons:

1. It explains the core course and test requirements for eligibility to over one thousand colleges and universities.

2. It explains the process of registering with the NCAA Eligibility Center.

3. It explains the rules of when and how college coaches can recruit students.

Fortunately, parents and athletes are only required to know and understand a portion of the rules, though it is critical to understand the recruiting regulations. College coaches must memorize every rule in the book, from early recruiting contacts to whether they can give players money to fly home to see parents during holidays (they cannot).

In the following pages, we will focus on the key rules regarding recruiting. We will also show how to avoid the pitfalls that have gotten so many athletic programs, especially football and basketball, in hot water with the NCAA.

THE NAIA AND THE NJCAA

A significant number of smaller schools belong to the National Association of Intercollegiate Athletics, or NAIA. The NAIA's rules regarding athletic scholarships are designed to level the playing field among its divisions. That is not to say that attending an NAIA school and playing sports is a lesser experience; indeed, many NAIA programs are highly competitive with NCAA teams and are excellent academically. These schools have simply chosen to compete in a less-restrictive and generally less-expensive environment.

Another organization unaffiliated with the NCAA is the National Junior College Athletic Association (NJCAA), which is comprised solely of two-year schools. Junior colleges are generally for students and athletes whose grades are not NCAA-caliber or who simply need a comfortable stepping stone to bridge the wide gap between high school and a four-year college. Most athletes spend the full two years at a junior college—often referred to as a "JC" or "juco"—but many play just one year, make the necessary grades, and move up. Juco schools are often less competitive, which means student-athletes can improve their skills in preparation for a position on a team at a four-year college or university.

The NCAA overseas more than 400,000 athletes at one thousand member schools from coast to coast as well as Alaska and Hawaii. Over the years, the organization, once based in Kansas but now in Indianapolis, has grown to consist of three distinct divisions: Division I, Division II, and Division III, commonly known in athletic jargon as D-I, D-II and D-III.

NCAA DIVISION I

To be a Division I program, schools are required to meet minimum stadium-capacity and attendance (fifteen thousand at least once every two years) standards. Approximately 350 schools are categorized as NCAA Division I.

In football only, Division I is split into two categories. Known as Division IA and Division IAA, these divisions have technically been distinguished as the Football Bowl Subdivision (FBS) and Football Championship Subdivision (FCS), respectively.

«« FAST FACT ««

Division I teams are segregated into two categories in football only. Commonly called Division IA schools, schools in the Football Bowl Subdivision are larger schools while schools in the Football Championship Subdivision (Division IAA) are smaller.

The FBS schools (approximately 120) are larger and familiar to those who watch ESPN: Southern California, Louisiana State, Michigan, Ohio State, Tennessee, Texas, Oklahoma, and the like. They are allowed to have up to eighty-five student-athletes on scholarship in a given season. These teams vie to play in Bowl games such as the Rose, Orange, Sugar, and Fiesta Bowls. The biggest Bowls, which dish out the most money and are more publicized, are set aside for the so-called BCS (Bowl Championship Series), with one Bowl each year determining a national champion. In 2009, the Florida Gators defeated the Oklahoma Sooners for the BCS title.

The smaller Football Championship Subdivision, formerly Division I-AA, is comprised of schools that are allowed to tender sixty-three scholarships. This division, and all other levels in college football, determine a national champion via a playoff system involving sixteen teams. In 2007, the FCS's Appalachian State made national headlines by upsetting traditional FBS powerhouse Michigan. Appalachian State went on to win the national title over Delaware in the playoffs.

Exceptions in FCS, which include Ivy and Pioneer League schools, do not participate in postseason playoffs and use a Division III-philosophy toward scholarships. Ivy League grants-in-aid are given based purely on need, and such institutions do not offer athletic or academic scholarships. In fact, these "non-scholarship" schools are excluded from post-season play in the FCS.

Division I schools are segregated only in football. In all other sports, including basketball, all Division I schools compete against each other and determine a national champion through a playoff system. The bigger schools whose football teams compete in Bowl games are called "major" programs and the teams from smaller Division I schools are labeled "mid-major." On the playing field, though, they are considered equals. Better-known examples of "mid-major" programs in basketball are Gonzaga, Davidson, and Nevada.

«« FAST FACT ««

Except in football, all Division I teams compete against each other. Though bigger schools are considered "major" programs and smaller Division I schools are considered "mid-major" programs, on the field they are considered equals, with "major" teams playing "mid-major" teams. Some Division IA programs will play Division IAA programs (for example, Appalachian State beat Michigan).

NCAA DIVISION II

Currently, the NCAA Division II has about 290 members, primarily smaller public universities and private institutions. Athletic scholarships offered at Division II schools tend to be more stringent in terms of the numbers offered. In Division II football, for instance, schools can give up to thirty-six scholarships while Division I FBS schools can give eighty-five.

Occasionally a Division II program will be competitive in a scheduled contest with a Division I or NAIA program, but generally, Division II schools play other Division II schools and Division I schools play other Division I schools.

While Division I programs tend to travel nationally, Division II schools tend to focus on regional competition.

NCAA DIVISION III

NCAA Division III schools are those who choose not to offer athletic scholarships and instead focus primarily on academics. Approximately 450 colleges and universities comprise Division III, making it the largest of the three NCAA divisions.

THE NCAA'S GUIDE TO THE COLLEGE-BOUND STUDENT-ATHLETE

Important to realize is that a school's designated division level, as well as whether the school is affiliated with the NAIA, NCAA, or NJCAA, has nothing to do with the size, enrollment, or quality of education. Duke, Notre Dame, Northwestern, and Vanderbilt all have fewer than eight thousand undergraduate students, while the two largest enrolled colleges are junior colleges.

Regardless of which school or division an athlete chooses, parents and their student-athlete must know the rules. *The Guide for the College Bound*

Student-Athlete lists dates when phone contacts, official visits, unofficial visits, and other correspondence are allowed. Elite or highly recruited student-athletes **will** receive phone calls from coaches on these days. Be aware that the dates for each of the NCAA's three divisions—I, II, and III—are different. Parents, students, and high school coaches should take the time to read the guide thoroughly and more than once.

Most coaches do play by the rules, especially in the so-called non-revenue arena. In fact, these are the programs where more attention is paid to the student-athlete as a whole, with academic and social progress considered just as important as championships and individual accolades. Generally, only in the elite reaches of Division I football and men's basketball are the pressures to win so strong that coaches are moved to go around the rules. Breaking these rules can be painful for the student-athlete, who might lose eligibility not only with the program in question, but also in all member schools.

Athletes and their families can do their part by understanding the rules and toeing the line. They should be especially aware of the time restrictions, number of allowed visits, times when phone calls are allowed, and dates they can meet with recruiters. This can be a pleasant shared experience that benefits all of the involved. The more a family knows, the better prepared they are to compete for those hard-to-attain dollars. And the better the chances for a successful fit for all.

Even unknowingly breaking a rule can cause a student to lose eligibility. An athlete who fails to pay attention to the NCAA or NAIA rules might lose a free college education. The rules change annually, so visit www.athleteswanted.org for more information about the latest rules, as well as other helpful advice regarding recruiting practices.

THE NCAA ELIGIBILITY CENTER

A student-athlete must register with the NCAA Eligibility Center and complete the NCAA Amateurism Certification questionnaire to be eligible to compete at the Division I or II level. A student should register after the junior year, even if the athlete is not considering Division I or II athletics.

Once an athlete registers with the Eligibility Center, NCAA will begin tracking the student's progress through graduation. If a student-athlete has met the eligibility criteria upon graduation, the NCAA will declare that the athlete is certified to play Division I or II sports.

The purpose of the NCAA Eligibility Center is twofold: 1) to ensure that an athlete meets the minimum academic eligibility requirements set forth by the NCAA; and 2) to determine whether a student has taken the required core courses set forth by the NCAA.

A third party is forbidden from completing the registration paperwork, so students and their parents will need to work together to complete the student release form, which athletes must sign. The cost is $60 for domestic students and $85 for international students, but a fee waiver is available for those who qualify for an ACT/SAT fee waiver.

EARLY CERTIFICATION

Note the option for "early certification." Student-athletes who meet the following criteria can be certified after their junior year:

- Minimum SAT (in math and critical reading) of 1000 or minimum sum score of 85 on the ACT.

- For Division I, a core course grade-point average of at least 3.0 with at least thirteen core courses, including three in English, two in math, two in science, and six in additional core courses.

- For Division II, a core course grade-point average of at least 3.0 with at least twelve core courses, including three in English, two in math, two in science, and five in additional core courses.

Early certification accomplishes two things: 1) it allows coaches to feel early peace of mind that the student-athlete is qualified to play; and 2) it alerts coaches that the student-athlete is accomplished academically.

Remember that an athlete must register with the NCAA Eligibility Center after the junior year, even if the athlete does not qualify for early certification. For more information about the NCAA Eligibility Center, visit www.athleteswanted.org.

KEY POINTS

__1.__ To win the recruiting game, an athlete must know the rules of each regulatory committee—the NCAA, the NAIA, or the NJCAA. The *NCAA Guide for the College-Bound Student-Athlete* is a great place to start.

__2.__ The NCAA breaks schools into three divisions. Each division has its own regulations regarding time restrictions, official visits, phone calls and other communications, and the like.

__3.__ Not knowing or failing to comply with the rules can cause a student-athlete to lose eligibility.

__4.__ Early Certification through the NCAA Eligibility Center alerts college coaches that a student-athlete is on schedule to meet NCAA qualifications to be eligible.

CAMPS, CLUBS, COMBINES, AND SHOWCASES

WHEN USED APPROPRIATELY and with forethought, sports camps, clubs, combines, and showcases can be useful in promoting a student-athlete and developing ability. Be aware, though that camps and clubs come in different shapes and sizes. Some are simply for-profit organizations that invite students of any level to attend, and most student-athletes are not likely to find themselves recruited solely by attending a sports camp.

But don't let this fact discourage you. Good reasons do exist for a student to attend camps, clubs, combines, and showcases. These represent opportunities for the student-athlete to play a sport year-round, develop skills, and experience campus life. From time to time, camps, clubs, combines, and showcases provide opportunities for exposure and evaluations.

SPORTS CAMPS

First, let's talk about sports camps, normally three-day sleepover camps with intense training programs in a specific sport. Keep in mind that sports camps are also full-fledged businesses. They cost the athlete roughly $300 to $750 per camp, so their sponsors want as many athletes to attend as possible.

« « FAST FACT « «

In his twenty-eight years coaching Division I football, Bob Chmiel discovered only two students from camps, one of whom was Tim Biakabatuka, who was born in Zaire and went on to play five years in the NFL.

The camps are generally held on college campuses and are run by college coaches, though in recent years, athletic sports-apparel companies, such as Nike and Reebok, have begun offering select sports camps of their own.

If considering attending a specific college, an athlete should know that this represents an excellent opportunity for the student-athlete to learn more about techniques and training practices, which can help the athlete leap to the next level, particularly when attending a position camp (such as a camp specifically for quarterbacks).

Sports camps held on college campuses also allow the child to experience campus life, tour the campus, meet and interact with the coaching staff, and see the athletic facilities.

Sports camps provide a student with an opportunity to learn from other skilled coaches than their high school or club coach, and to test their skills against those of other potential college players. For skill-building alone, sports camps can make the difference between a student who plays at a high school level and a student who plays at a college level.

Attending multiple camps can be costly, but it does add to a student's athletic résumé and shows potential coaches that an athlete is serious about improving skills.

In addition, most high school associations have rules against organized practice and/or competition during the summer, so camps may be the only way to keep an athlete's competitive edge in the off-season.

Student-athletes should always be on the lookout for opportunities for exposure, but if the student-athlete is attending camps simply to showcase talent, the athlete is barking up the wrong tree, unless invited by the coach. Student-athletes should only attend camps where the coaches know who they are and will have the opportunity to evaluate them in person. If interested in a particular program, and if meeting a particular coach in person, the athlete should ask if the camp offers a one-day camp at a prorated or discounted cost.

Sports camps can be expensive, and they are offered at all different levels. And many are open to anyone, so college coaches are unlikely to travel to another campus to evaluate or recruit talent. However, summer camps and clinics place virtually no restrictions on the type of contact a student-athlete may have with the coaches and/or staff running the camp. If an athlete is interested in attending a specific college, attending a sports camp at that college might be a good idea, particularly if the student-athlete calls ahead of time to let the coach know the athlete will be attending the camp and would like to set up a time to talk.

If athletes from that college are working the camp, the student-athlete might also learn a little more about the program and campus by asking the athletes to share their open and honest assessment of the school, coach, and opportunities.

Choosing the right summer camp can be difficult early in the recruiting process as the student-athlete likely does not know which coaches are actively recruiting the athlete and which are looking only to increase the size of their camp roster (and the revenues brought in by the camp).

A student-athlete might be enticed to attend a large Division I camp, but keep in mind that many smaller Division II and III colleges/universities might provide camps with a better coach-to-player ratio, which increases the student-athlete's probability of receiving one-on-one help and improving. Being discovered at a Division I college camp is rare. Athletes cannot afford to waste opportunities, so attending smaller camps where they have a more realistic chance of being recruited can potentially be the better option. An athlete attending a camp in the hopes of boosting chances of playing for that particular school should be sure the coach is actively recruiting the athlete, which is difficult in the early stages.

COACH'S TIP

Adrienne Treado, former Division I soccer player at Michigan State, said students should consider the answer to these two questions when considering specific camps:

1. *Has a coach from the school called me and specifically invited me to the camp?*

2. *Have I had any face-to-face contact with any of the coaches holding the camp?*

If the answer to both of these questions is a no, the only reason to attend the camp is to build skills or gain experience.

Unless an athlete has actively developed relationships as a freshman or sophomore with coaches, his best course of action should be to ask the high school or club coach, as well as any college coaches with which the athlete has contact, to recommend the best skill-development sports camps. Once the student has identified the camps, the student can ask a coach for a one-day prorate to attend the camp and be evaluated. And if the student-athlete has developed relationships with coaches all along, the student can plan in advance to attend many one-day prorated camps, giving coaches an opportunity to evaluate skills.

More than a few camps promise exposure but deliver very little. Find a camp that has a good reputation, and one that exceeds at getting college coaches to attend. If college coaches are not going to be present, the athlete might overpay for a camp that will produce very little. If a student-athlete plans to attend a summer camp with the hopes of being evaluated by college coaches, the athlete should be sure to get his hands on the list of those coaches who will be attending the camp this year. He might want to start by looking at the coaches who attended the camp last year. Many camps say they invite hoards of college coaches, but this does not mean all the coaches come.

Also, a student should see how many top prospects are attending and whether attendance is by invitation only. If a large group of top prospects are attending an invite-only camp, the athlete can safely assume that the event will attract a higher number of coaches. If the camp is considered an "exposure" camp, be sure that the camp publishes the participating student-athletes' résumés and disseminates them to college coaches so that the athlete's name is promoted to local and regional coaches. These camps often publish books with all participants' statistics and contact information, which college coaches can purchase.

> ## «« FAST FACT ««
> If a coach is willing to offer a one-day prorate for a student-athlete to attend a summer sports camp, the student-athlete is probably high on that coach's recruiting priority list. (Note that some sports do not offer one-day prorates.)

If the athlete happens to find a camp that offers the exposure needed, the student-athlete should make the most of it. Opportunities to play in front of college coaches don't come along too often, so when they do, the student-athlete should be ready for the challenge. One great performance can often open a college coach's eyes to a student-athlete's potential and a possible scholarship down the road. But remember that very few students are discovered at a camp. College coaches might attend a camp to evaluate a student-athlete they are already evaluating, but they are unlikely to attend camps if they do not already know the student-athlete. A student-athlete should develop relationships with coaches before attending camps.

SHOWCASES

As with camps, showcases are not a place for most athletes to be discovered. Coaches attend showcases with a list of identified players they want to evaluate. If a student-athlete is not on that list, the coach will probably not watch him.

Though fifty coaches might attend a showcase, all fifty are at the showcase to watch and evaluate the same five or ten players, which makes showcases a disappointing event for student-athletes who hope to be discovered. As with camps, the best way to determine whether a showcase is worth the athlete's time and money (usually about $150) is for the athlete to ask coaches for an evaluation at a showcase.

College recruiting may change and alter slightly from year to year, but the student-athletes who create a connection with college coaches will always be a step ahead of those who sit back and wait to hear from a coach first.

CLUBS

Check the by-laws of any ball club, traveling club, or select club, and you will find the same mission statement: to promote the *advanced* players. In the late 1970s, the idea of creating teams—select teams with more advanced players—gained popularity as parents and coaches attempted to provide more challenging matches among better, advanced athletes, specifically swimmers and volleyball, soccer, and softball players. These teams played against the better teams from the communities, cities, and even states for title matches. Thus, the term *traveling team* was borne.

»« FAST FACTS »«

Clubs have the most influence in volleyball, soccer, hockey, softball, and swimming.

Select or traveling teams do offer more challenging games to young athletes. But another driving force behind the club movement is prestige. Both kids and parents feel a great deal of pride in being associated with a "select" group of athletes.

The process typically works like this: An athlete is invited by a coach who has seen the student play. The athlete might also try out for a team after hearing about it from other parents or through an ad. If the student-athlete makes the cut, the athlete is asked to sign a one-year contract. This is a binding contract whereby the athlete or the athlete's family is obligated to pay a flat-out fee or make monthly payments to the club—fees that can cost hundreds or thousands of dollars. The contract may also forbid the athlete from playing with any other teams during the off-season. After signing that contract, the athlete must adhere to the club's practice and to game times and places.

Athletes who play select or club ball often have a higher level of commitment. Because these athletes have paid a higher price (literally), and are willing to travel and train more intensely than recreational athletes, the competition will be fiercer, but so will the rewards.

Prior to signing on the dotted line, parents and athletes should be sure to talk to other parents and athletes to determine costs they may not have thought of, such as uniforms and equipment, lodging and food, transportation, tournament fees, and tournament t-shirts or other souvenirs. They should also consider the travel schedule to determine the hours or days involved in individual games and weekend tournaments.

And, by all means, a student-athlete's club involvement should be listed on his scouting report!

«« FAST FACT ««

The highest-level clubs for soccer, softball, and swimming can cost about $9,000 a year, including travel, training, membership, and tournaments.

COMBINES

Modeled after the NFL Scouting Combine in which the best college players are evaluated by NFL coaches, combines are an emerging opportunity for the best high school football players to showcase their abilities before national scouts and media. Because combines are most often by invitation only, they offer a better opportunity than camps for a student-athlete to demonstrate his skills before national scouts and media. These combines include the U.S. Army National Combine, the Nike Combine, and Shuman's National Underclassmen Combine. Combines for underclassmen are becoming very popular as well, such as the Ultimate 100 National Underclassmen Combine hosted by Dave Shuman. Other exclusive invite-only combines—such as the U.S. Army and Nike SPARQ—feature the best juniors and have been the leaders in the combine world.

The NCAA no longer allows college coaches to attend combines. However, coaches use statistics from the combine to cross reference data on a prospect to confirm his size, speed, and strength.

Combines can be a useful measuring stick to compare a student-athlete's statistics (height, speed, strength) with others competing for scholarship opportunities. A student who performs well at a combine often has the benefit of attracting attention from a scouting service, which can lead to national exposure.

Combines are often sponsored by apparel or shoe companies. If a cost is associated with attending the combine, the cost is nominal: about $150.

For recommendations to camps, clubs, showcases, and combines, visit www.athleteswanted.org.

KEY POINTS

1. Sports camps are an excellent opportunity for an athlete to build skills, experience campus life, or connect with a coach. However, students are usually not discovered at sports camps. Sports camps are businesses that most often accept as many students as will pay to attend the camp, which means coaches do not often recruit from camps because the level of play is so diverse. If a coach is already recruiting a student-athlete and will meet with the student during the camp, a sports camp might be a good opportunity for the student-athlete to develop a relationship with a college coach, particularly if the student is interested in winning a scholarship from that coach's program.

2. The same rule applies to showcases. Unless a student-athlete can meet with a coach from a school the athlete wants to attend, a student-athlete should not attend a showcase if the only goal is to be discovered.

3. Clubs are offered for advanced players. Clubs provide student-athletes with an opportunity to play at a more competitive level and to play year-round. As such, a certain amount of prestige is associated with clubs.

4. Football combines are an emerging opportunity for the best high school football players to showcase their abilities for scouts and scouting services. Some combines are by invitation only. Those combines usually attract higher levels of talent and are an important source for authenticating a student-athlete's physical attributes (height and weight), strength (for example, bench press), and athleticism (for example, 40-yard-dash time). They offer a better opportunity than camps for the student to validate his skills before scouting organizations.

THE MULTI-SPORT ATHLETE

IMAGINE THAT YOU WERE looking to purchase a car stereo for around $100, and these were your options:

- am/fm with CD player

- am/fm with CD player and detachable face

- am/fm with CD player, detachable face, and mini-stereo input for iPod or other MP3 player

If every stereo cost the same amount ($100), of course you would want to purchase the one with the most features!

College coaches also want to get the most bang for their buck. An athlete who brings skills, techniques, and that extra edge of playing two or more sports is always going to win out over a single-sport athlete costing the same amount of scholarship dollars but with less diverse skills.

Within limits, students should try to participate in as many sports as possible while in high school. College coaches love to find student-athletes who love to compete!

"Any person who is good at multiple things has a marketing edge," said Ty Garland, former multi-sport star in the Big Ten at Michigan State. "The more a student can show a coach, the better."

Yet parents and students should keep some considerations in mind. First and foremost, a high school child's academics must be considered first. Involvement in several sports should not cause overload, especially when two sports overlap.

"A coach will not even consider a student's athletic ability if his grades are not up to par," said Augie Maurelli of Georgetown University.

"Be careful to balance academics with love of sport. If a student loves football but is three times better at wrestling and can earn a full scholarship to a great academic school, the student might prefer to focus on wrestling instead of football, especially if football is getting in the way of his academic performance," agreed Garland.

For a high school athlete that plays two sports, one sport is generally the primary sport, while the other is secondary. An athlete is rarely gifted with the skills to excel in two sports equally, although it is possible. Garland suggested that an athlete should begin considering not only which sport is more marketable, but also which sport the athlete excels at, by the junior or senior year.

Often, one sport will have far greater opportunities than the other due to popularity or an abundance of programs. Football, baseball, and basketball players today are always going to have the most options, because the number of programs is greater. However, that also means that competition in those sports is very fierce.

If a student is gifted in a sport that has fewer programs around the nation, it could be that the athlete's chances of getting noticed and of finding a good match are much higher, simply because both the student and the coaches have fewer options and less legwork. The student is less likely to get "lost in the shuffle" of a more niche sport.

An athlete should consider whether participation in a second sport will increase the chance of injury so much that participation in the primary sport is endangered. For example, a gymnast who specializes in vault might also be a hurdler, which can cause severe ankle injuries and set a gymnastic career back months and months. A missed competition could mean missing out on an offer to join a college team.

COACH'S TIP

A student forced to choose between two sports should choose the sport the athlete loves most which may or may not be the stronger sport. During college, playing a sport can be a full-time job, so being passionate about the sport is critical to success and longevity.

Some sport combinations work synergistically—track and football, for example. For running positions on a football team, the sprints of the short distance runner and the conditioning of the long-distance runner are icing on the cake. While other players might be doing half-hearted jogs to keep in shape during the off-season, the student-athlete is following a rigorous, systematic training program to keep his body in peak physical condition while improving his speed. Competition (in heats or races) also serves to sharpen his competitive edge.

Though competing in multiple sports is encouraged at the high school level, most Division I revenue sports frown on a student-athlete competing in more than one sport because they do not believe there is enough time to excel in both. It takes a rare student-athlete to compete at the high Division I level in one sport, let alone two. The best option for the multi-sport athlete who wants to continue playing both sports in college is usually at Division II, Division III, or NAIA levels.

KEY POINTS

1. The athlete who participated in multiple sports in high school often brings more skills and techniques and better conditioning than a single-sport athlete.

2. An athlete whose GPA is hurt by participating in two sports might also have a lesser chance of being recruited. The athlete must balance sports with academics, being sure that academics are given a higher priority than being a multi-sport athlete.

3. The second sport should not significantly increase an athlete's likelihood of injury.

4. When deciding which sport is the primary sport, an athlete should consider not only level of ability and passion, but also which is more marketable.

5. Though competing in multiple sports is encouraged at the high school level, most Division I revenue sports frown on a student-athlete competing in more than one sport because they do not believe there is enough time to excel in both. It takes a rare student-athlete to compete at the high Division I level in one sport, let alone two. The best option for the multi-sport athlete who wants to continue playing both sports in college is usually at Division II, III, or NAIA levels.

MARKETING THE STUDENT-ATHLETE:
The **five** things you must do

IF THIS ALL SEEMS like a tremendous amount of work and effort, remember the game of college recruiting has five layers:

1. The objective, third-party evaluation.

2. The student-athlete's résumé posted online.

3. A winning highlight, game, or skills video.

4. Contact with coaches from one hundred to two hundred college programs.

5. Education, maintenance, and tracking.

THE OBJECTIVE, THIRD-PARTY EVALUATION

The first critical step is to assess the most likely level of competition for which an athlete is best suited both academically and athletically. With over eighteen hundred colleges offering opportunities in sports, narrowing the focus to realistic options makes sense. The goal-setting process can be aided if the parent and student-athlete solicit an objective third-party evaluation early in the game.

If the student and parents are aware of the critical measurables (GPA, ACT, SAT, as well as height, weight, speed, and statistical benchmarks) for an athlete's individual sport, they can begin the search with some level of confidence. The parent's time, the student's time, or the coach's time will not be wasted if the search is limited to those schools the athlete has a realistic likelihood of attending.

To obtain an honest evaluation, a student-athlete can schedule time to talk to his high school coach, a former college coach, or established scouting service with a demonstrated history of results. Depending on the service, the charge for this kind of evaluation generally ranges from $50 to $200.

RÉSUMÉ POSTED ONLINE

Years ago, the one-page paper résumé or profile was used. Today, the use of technology has simplified the process. The personal website has become the best way for an athlete to showcase abilities because it is easy to update and keep current. A live website can also house academic statistics like report cards and transcripts along with a verified ACT or SAT score. Another key feature of the student-athlete website is its ability to help the student-athlete keep college coaches updated with progress on and off the field. The coach can easily access information and conduct its own assessment of a student-athlete's likelihood of playing for his program.

The cost of this usually includes the software, hosting fee, and web administrator's time creating the site. A standard website can cost as little as $300 or as much as $1,500, depending on how many videos are hosted and how many features the site offers.

A WINNING HIGHLIGHT, GAME, OR SKILLS VIDEO

The highlight, game, or skills video is the third layer of recruiting, as discussed in Chapter 8. The highlight, game, and skills videos (which are generally DVDs or streaming videos as opposed to VHS tapes) make it simple for coaches to verify what is on the student-athlete's website and determine if the student-athlete has the athletic ability and skill-set to compete for that college coach. Depending on an athlete's sport, the highlight, game, or skills video can make the difference between a student-athlete's ability to stay on the coach's recruiting list or not. A highlight, game, or skills video can be enhanced, digitalized, sequenced, and spot-shadowed, and then downloaded and hosted online. It can even be integrated onto a student-athlete's website as streaming video.

A quality highlight, game, or skills video can cost anywhere from $400 to $4,000 to put together, depending on the athlete's resources. The cost of digital cameras, editing equipment, computer programs, hosting fees, and time are some of the items that will determine the overall price tag for a student-athlete's video.

COMMUNICATION WITH ONE HUNDRED TO TWO HUNDRED PROGRAMS

Distribution and marketing is the most critical step of the recruiting process. Connecting with coaches (Chapter 5) drastically helps a student increase his chances of winning a college spot. An athlete should not limit his efforts to just one coach if the staff at a specific school consists of ten coaches. Who knows which coach the student-athlete might impress, or which one is responsible for the student's region? The athlete should load his gun with as many bullets as possible.

Following is a sample contact list for initiating communications with college coaches. This list represents just one set of coaches from one college (the University of Southern California's 2008-2009 coaching staff).

USC'S FOOTBALL COACHING STAFF, 2008-2009

Title	Name	Extension	Email
Head Coach	Pete Carroll	x4190	fraser@usc.edu
Tight Ends/Recruit. Coord.	Brennan Carroll	x4185	bpcarrol@usc.edu
Defensive Coordinator/Defensive Line	Nick Holt	x4182	holtv@usc.edu
Running Backs	Todd McNair	x4189	tmcnair@usc.edu
Wide Receivers/Passing Game Coord.	John Morton	x8131	johnmort@usc.edu
Linebackers	Ken Norton Jr.	x4180	
Offensive Line	Pat Ruel	x4183	ruel@usc.edu
Asst. Head Coach/Off. Coord./QBs	Steve Sarkisian	x4192	ssarkisi@usc.edu
Secondary	Rocky Seto	x8790	seto@usc.edu
Defensive Line	David Watson	x4188	dwatson@usc.edu
Secondary Graduate Assistant	Kris Richard	821-3026	
Quarterbacks Graduate Assistant	Yogi Roth	x1310	yroth@usc.edu
Director of Football Operations	Dennis Slutak	x4198	slutak@usc.edu
Assistant Director of Football Operations	Jared Blank	x7780	jblank@usc.edu
Recruiting and Operations Assistant	Justin Mesa	821-6596	wmesa@usc.edu
Video Assistant	Sam Anno	x4181	anno@usc.edu
Administrative Advisor	Terrel Ray	x1982	tray@usc.edu
Offensive Administrative Assistant	Albert Dorsey	821-3020	albert.dorsey@gmail.com
Defensive Graduate Assistant	Pete Dalis	x4204	dalis@usc.edu
Director of Online Media	Ben Malcolmson	x4204	malcolms@usc.edu
Executive Assistant to Head Coach	Morgon Fraser	x4191	fraser@usc.edu
Admin. Asst. to Football Coaches	Joyce Hirayama	x4176	jhirayam@usc.edu
Receptionist	Irene Puentes	x4204	igarza@usc.edu

Just one program might require twenty-five individual letters, emails, or phone calls because a student-athlete might not know which coach or assistant holds the key to getting the athlete on the recruiting list. Note that some colleges do not post their coaching directories on the Internet. An athlete might have to call some schools to request contact information.

A student-athlete can purchase email addresses or do the homework. Either way, count on about fifteen to thirty minutes per college program for the initial research and letter campaign.

COACH'S TIP

Before sending emails to twenty-five coaches and administrators, an athlete might want to call, make an introduction, and ask for the name of the person to whom the athlete should forward information in order to be evaluated to compete for the program.

If eight hundred colleges offer a student-athlete's sport, and the athlete is good enough to compete for any of these schools, the student must contact at least two hundred (25 percent) to receive the responses necessary to move forward. Our studies show that using this method should yield a 10 percent return, which will give a student twenty programs to consider. An athlete who receives fewer responses should contact more college coaches.

EDUCATION, MAINTENANCE, AND TRACKING

The final critical step in the plan is that the student-athlete follows up with coaches, builds relationships, continues learning about the recruiting process, and tracks progress.

SAMPLE CORRESPONDENCE LOG

Correspondence Date	1/28/2008	Type	Email
College	Daniel Webster	Coach	Paul LaBarre, Mgr
Phone		Next Step	Send video
Email	labarre@dwc.edu	Priority Indicator	Likely
Level of Interest	Interested	Response Type	Email

Notes: Sent him an email introducing myself and referring him to my scouting report. He wants to view game day tape as soon as available.

Correspondence Date	1/28/2008	Type	Email
College	Finlandia	Coach	Joe Burcar
Phone		Next Step	Send video
Email	joe.burcar@ finlandia.edu	Priority Indicator	Backup
Level of Interest	Interested	Response Type	Email

Notes: Sent him an email introducing myself and referring him to my scouting report. He wants to view game day tape as soon as available. Said it is very likely I would be offered a scholarship.

Correspondence Date	1/28/2008	Type	Email
College	Hamilton College	Coach	Phil Grady
Phone		Next Step	Call
Email	pgrady@hmailton.edu	Priority Indicator	Likely
Level of Interest	Interested	Response Type	None

Notes: Emailed to introduce myself. Did not hear back.

Correspondence Date	1/28/2008	Type	Questionnaire
College	University of Nebraska	Coach	
Phone		Next Step	Call to introduce myself
Email		Priority Indicator	Reach
Level of Interest	Very high	Response Type	None

Notes: Filled out online recruiting form. Call next week to introduce myself and make sure they received.

While researching colleges and connecting with coaches, students should log their efforts and follow up with coaches to update them on information, ask questions, and build relationships. An athlete's initial goal should be that the coach knows and remembers the student's name. The more an athlete can communicate with the coach, the more opportunities for building a relationship.

A student-athlete should spend on average fifteen to thirty minutes following up with each program. The faster the athlete can find those programs willing to look at a highlight or skills video, the faster the athlete will move through the recruiting process. In total, this step will cost one hundred to two hundred hours in addition to the cost of mailing DVDs. This is why some families find a reliable recruiting service, which can save them time and offer a huge return on investment.

Remember that a student-athlete will delete colleges from the Initial Target List just like colleges delete athletes who do not meet their needs. An athlete must cast a wide enough net to end up with five offers.

Don't skimp and be forced to play catch up in the fourth quarter! This is not a four-year decision but a forty-year decision!

KEY POINTS

The game of college recruiting can generally be broken into five steps:

1. Every student-athlete needs an objective third-party evaluation to determine "best fit" qualifications for various college programs. A knowledgeable third party helps set realistic expectations about programs, competition levels, and academic fit, helping the athlete target one hundred to two hundred realistic prospects.

2. Every student-athlete needs a résumé posted online. The days of delivering paper résumés are over. Coaches now view websites that contain all the athletic and academic information needed to recruit a prospect. This allows coaches the ability to see more athletes, more efficiently.

3. Every student-athlete needs a winning highlight, game, or skills video that best conveys athletic ability. Videos are typically streamed online and sent through email. A student-athlete should not send dozens of unsolicited DVDs to college coaches. Unless the video has been requested or is sent from a credible third party, coaches will likely never receive it, much less watch it!

4. Every student-athlete must contact college coaches from at least one hundred to two hundred college programs. Receiving a few emails or letters from college coaches does not constitute serious recruitment. College coaches contact thousands of student-athletes so that they have enough options to fill their needs. Student-athletes should play the same game, contacting one hundred to two hundred college coaches. About 10 percent will show serious interest, giving the athlete about ten to twenty programs to actively consider.

5. Every student-athlete needs a step-by-step plan to successfully navigate through the recruiting process. Doing it right takes hard work, perseverance, and a consolidated team effort among the student-athlete, parents, coaches, guidance counselors, and credible inside recruiting experts.

The last step alone will take one hundred to two hundred hours, which is why many families turn to reliable recruiting services to handle the bulk of the work.

RECRUITING SERVICES

GIVEN THE RESTRICTIONS placed by the NCAA, the limited recruiting calendar, the competition to land top talent, and budgetary constraints, college programs have increasingly become dependant on trusted and reliable services to help them save valuable time and money to help streamline the recruiting process.

Emerging technology has been a critical tool for expediting the entire process. With more programs, more teams, and more student-athletes, programs need to find ways to distill the nation's 7.3 million high school athletes into a manageable pool, and scouting and recruiting services can help accomplish this. Most Division I and II football and basketball programs, and an increasing number of non-revenue sports, subscribe and use dozens of services, and spend thousands of dollars to save much more in time and money. These services allow coaching staffs to identify talented athletes easier and earlier than ever.

SCOUTING SERVICES

What is the difference between a scouting service and a recruiting service? The lingo can be confusing, but the general differences stem from where they are funded and for whom they work. In most cases, scouting services work for the college coaches in the revenue sports of men's basketball and men's football. These services sell lists to coaches of the top athletes by state, region, and country. Other sports, like women's basketball, volleyball, baseball, and softball, use scouting services to a lesser degree.

These lists often begin the process for college prospects. After being identified by a national or regional scouting service, students' names are added to a list, which is then purchased by a coach, who disseminates marketing material to the entire mailing list in hopes of accumulating information from interested students. These services start creating prospect lists from students as young as seventh or eighth grade. Some scouting services include:

- Collegiate Sports Data (football)

- Randy Taylor Recruiting (football)

- The Forbes Report (football)

- NCSA (all sports)

- Bob Gibbons All Star Report (basketball)

- Tom Lemming's *Prep Football Report*

- Rich Kern Recruiting Registry (volleyball)

- Sunshine Preps (Florida football players)

- Chicago Hoops (Chicago basketball players)

- Texas Video (Texas football)

RECRUITING SERVICES

Recruiting services, on the other hand, generally work on the family's behalf to promote a student-athlete. The athlete or the athlete's family pays the recruiting services to promote the athlete. Started over twenty years ago, many of the services have served as helpful resources for parents and coaches at all levels. They have proven to be extremely helpful at Division I, II, III, NAIA, and non-revenue levels, especially when coaches have small recruiting budgets and would otherwise be unable to expand their searches beyond local areas.

Recruiting services range from free services whereby a student-athlete simply lists his name on a web-based database to customized services that individually promote the student-athlete. Some charge $20 for a student-athlete to search a database of coaches and be listed on a website; others charge for state-of-the-art technology that matches talent with coaching staffs through permission-based email databases. Others produce enhanced recruiting videos that spot-shadow and professionally sequence performances. Others simply send thousands of coaches information about thousands of students, hoping to get the students on recruiting lists.

Then come the services that provide one-on-one coaching of student-athletes and recruitment education. These services, albeit more expensive, systematically match student-athletes with programs. Such services generally have stronger relationships with coaches because they do not accept student-athletes who do not meet minimum standards. Some of the best services have a greater than 90 percent success rate.

When considering a recruiting service, athletes should ask nine critical questions:

1. *Does the organization recruit only legitimate prospects, or will it accept any student-athlete, regardless of his qualifications?*
    Put yourself in a college coach's shoes—would you rather work with a recruiting service with a proven track record of sending only verified scouting reports, or a recruiting service that wasted your time by sending you unrealistic, unsolicited prospects?

If the organization sends only legitimate prospects, continue with Question #2. If the latter, find another recruiting service.

2. *What type of delivery and confirmation method does the organization use to let student-athletes know what college coaches actually looked at them?* Look for a service that uses permission-based email addresses and has a system to confirm whether colleges look at a student-athlete's scouting report or video. In this way, athletes can quickly focus on those colleges that have looked at them.

3. *Does the service use recruiting guidelines and power rankings to best determine realistic levels of play for each specific athlete?* By evaluating a school's recruiting guidelines and an athlete's profile, a recruiting service can systematically determine the most realistic fit—both academically and athletically—for both the program and the student.

4. *Does the service use an actual scout to evaluate the prospect?* College coaches rely on services with a history of providing informed evaluations, transcripts, and videos. Scouts who take a personal approach to a student-athlete's success will provide a coach with references from the high school coach, as well as club and combine coaches. This takes the burden off the college coach.

5. *What is the service's success rate, and how many students has the service helped receive scholarships?*

6. *Does the service edit highlight, game, or skills video with the help of scouts or coaches?* If the service uses scouts and coaches to edit the videos, the student will be shed in the best possible light. And a service that takes advantage of spot

shadow for early identification and stream capabilities will allow the student-athlete to "pop" while being evaluated.

7. *Does the service have a staff large enough to handle personal requests and updates throughout the process?* The best services will have recruiting coaches and member service departments that offer coaching and mentoring throughout the entire process.

8. *Does the service teach the student-athlete how exactly to follow up with the college coaches and develop a plan of action for the student to follow step-by-step until successfully committed and enrolled at the best-fit college?*

9. *Is it worth using a service?* If all of the above questions can be answered with a *yes*, the recruiting service is probably well worth the cost. After all, a family or athlete who goes through this process alone will likely spend:

    - $400 to $4,000 on creating a quality highlight or skills video.

    - $300 to $1,500 on a personal website for the athlete.

    - $2.50/mailing to college coach, if you are including a highlight or skills video ($250 for just one hundred schools).

    - At least $1,500 and over two hundred hours of work!

Recruiting services are becoming more and more critical as families understand that they must be proactive in the recruiting process, and they must begin early. Recruiting services can assist in many, if not all, of the five phases of the recruiting process.

1. **Evaluating the athlete.** By obtaining an objective third-party evaluation from a reputable recruiting service, a student-athlete can build from an honest evaluation and realistically assess potential.

2. **Résumé, profile, and website.** A service can help organize and verify an athlete's information into a presentable and organized profile or website to be used to promote efficiently and easily. A scouting or recruiting service can also add reliability to a student by verifying his information.

3. **Highlight, game, or skills video.** Services often make use of former coaches to enhance a student-athlete's video through spot-shadowing and play-sequencing. Highlight and skills videos are then turned into streaming video. Some services can even report back to the student-athlete when a coach watches the video!

4. **Contact with college coaches.** Since student-athletes who send personal letters are most successful, some recruiting services have started helping athletes expedite this process to make sure the athletes are connecting with the right coaches. Recruiting services that use "permission-based email" can be invaluable if multiple updates need to be sent to the coaching community. Reputable recruiting services have databases that contain the entire nation's list of coaching staff for each individual sport and coach. Rather than finding a general athletic department email online, student-athletes who use reputable recruiting services can be sure that their information is sent directly to the relevant coaches. Because the emails are permission-based, spam filters will not file them in the "junk" folder, and the service can give

valuable feedback to the student-athletes, letting them know which coaches watched the videos and when. This can eliminate hundreds of hours of follow-up time, allowing the student-athlete instead to follow up at the appropriate time, confidently calling on coaches they know have accessed their information and video.

5. **Guidance, coaching, and tracking.** A reputable recruiting service usually charges a one-time fee and offers ongoing guidance, education, maintenance, tracking, and coaching. When started early enough, the cost of a full-service recruiting organization can be as low as $200 per year, which can yield more than one hundred times the return on investment!

WHAT IS YOUR TIME WORTH?

Assume that Mom and Dad are helping their son find a football program where he can play collegiate athletics. Consider the amount of time this will take if the athlete wants to connect with just 25 percent of the college programs that offer football.

First, a family would spend time looking at college websites to research the coaching staff, find email addresses, and create personal letters to coaches and recruiting staff. Then consider the amount of time necessary to fill out online questionnaires and send DVDs. If they spent just fifteen to thirty minutes per school and wanted information on just one-quarter of the eight hundred available programs, a family would spend fifty to one hundred hours on these activities alone.

**If their time is worth just
$7.25 per hour (minimum wage),
the cost is $362 to $725.**

Now consider how much time parents will spend helping their child update schools about his progress. At ten minutes per school, they would spend thirty-three hours updating two hundred schools, or $240.

If Mom and Dad helped update the schools three times, this would cost $720 in time (again, calculated as though their time is worth minimum wage).

Then consider the cost of sending the DVD to interested programs. If replicating the DVD, stuffing packages, and driving to the post office takes just ten minutes per school, and the DVD is sent to just one-eighth of the schools, Mom and Dad will spend another seventeen hours.

This adds approximately $120 to the bill.

Ignoring all other costs (such as postage, developing a video, toll telephone calls, and creating and maintaining a website), the total cost is between $1,480 and $1,845! This doesn't even consider the time spent following up, creating plans, and maintaining records!

On the other hand, a recruiting service costs between $500 and $5,000, and top recruiting services will handle all of the above for the athlete, not to mention save the time and effort in creating a marketing strategy. If the service also provides education, an athlete will learn about the process, as well as how to talk to coaches. The savings families receive from knowing how to negotiate their child's scholarship and appeal the financial aid package is worth five times the cost of any service!

Remember that a student-athlete has only a small window of opportunity to be recruited. A student cannot start too early or have too many opportunities to become branded a collegiate student-athlete for life!

«« **FAST FACT** ««

The National Collegiate Scouting Association (NCSA)—which places more than 90 percent of its member student-athletes with college programs—reports that its high school student-athletes win on average $15,500 a year in scholarships, grants, and financial aid to play sports. Its student-athletes who attend public schools win on average $12,850 in scholarships, grants, and aid, while those who attend private colleges receive on average $21,266.

KEY POINTS

1. Scouting services work for college coaches, most often in basketball and football. These services sell lists to coaches of the top athletes by state, region, and country. Depending on how prestigious the scouting list, membership is dictated by the student's level of ability. A student cannot buy his way onto a list.

2. Recruiting services work on the student-athlete's behalf to promote the student to a college coach. Recruiting services range in level of sophistication and prestige. Some will accept any student, which means coaches will most likely ignore their attempts to promote a student. Others offer systematic matches and promote a student to a coach only if the student is qualified. These recruiting services generally have more success and better relationships with coaches.

3. Athletes and their families should ask nine critical questions when considering a recruiting service:

   - *Does the organization recruit only legitimate prospects, or will it accept any student-athlete, regardless of qualifications?*
   - *What type of delivery and confirmation method does the organization use to let student-athletes know what college coaches actually looked at them?*
   - *Does the service use recruiting guidelines and power rankings to best determine realistic levels of play for each specific athlete?*
   - *Does the service use an actual scout to evaluate the prospect?*
   - *What is the service's success rate, and how many students has the service helped receive scholarships?*
   - *Does the service edit highlight, game, and skills video with the help of scouts or coaches?*
   - *Does the service have a staff large enough to handle personal requests and updates throughout the process?*

- *Does the service teach the student-athlete how exactly to follow up with the college coaches and develop a plan of action for the student to follow step-by-step until successfully committed and enrolled at the best-fit college?*
- *Is it worth using a service?*

4. A reputable recruiting service can help with all five layers of marketing a student-athlete:

- Evaluating the athlete
- Résumé, profile, and website
- Highlight or skills video
- Contacts with college coaches
- Guidance, coaching, and tracking

THE *HOW TO* GUIDE DURING COLLEGE

THIS SECTION WILL COVER the major issue that student-athletes often face while in college: maintaining their scholarship.

While getting into a good college with good scholarships and making the team may have seemed like the hard part, it is no less a concern to capitalize on all that effort. Keep in mind, scholarships are for one year at a time only, and they do not transfer should an athlete wish to go to a different school.

Three criteria dictate whether a student-athlete will keep a scholarship:

1. Perform well for the team

2. Adhere to all rules and regulations

3. Maintain the required GPA

PERFORMING WELL

Once a student has entered college, the student must maintain the habits he formed prior to college that enabled him to succeed.

RULES AND REGULATIONS

Numerous rules and regulations govern scholarships. Some of them are unique to a student's school and sport; others are defined by the NCAA or NAIA. Below are some standard rules governing student-athletes.

In general, to keep their scholarships, student-athletes must:

- Remain amateur athletes the entire duration of the scholarship (including refusing to make agreements to play professional sports).

- Refuse payment or the promise of future payments for playing their sport.

- Never participate on other teams, including exhibition teams or for tournament games.

- Refuse to promote or have their name or likeness used to promote a commercial product.

- Refuse gifts from interest groups or individuals involved in the athletic program at their school.

- Decline representation by agents. The student-athlete must also refuse to promise to be represented by an agent in the future.

- Never receive benefits not open to other students at their university.

- Refrain from knowingly taking banned substances.

- Refrain from sports gambling.

- Refuse professional services, such as legal advice, for less than a normal fee.

MAINTAINING THE REQUIRED GPA

Few college athletes will go on to play sports professionally, and even for those who do, the primary purpose of college is receiving a valuable education. Indeed, one of the factors reliable recruiting services look for when dealing with athletes is their commitment to learning. Stereotypes aside, success off the field is a great predictor of success on the field.

Moreover, given college rules, an athlete can no longer get by with low grades, nor can he retain his scholarship. Bad grades can be expensive. College is not easy, even for students who are able to devote the bulk of their time to classes and studying. For a student who is also spending a great deal of his time playing sports, good study habits and a committed work ethic are non-negotiable.

So how can a student-athlete make sure he is able to excel in the classroom?

Broadly, he should continue doing what made him successful in high school: attend class, study hard, prepare diligently. But those basics and a bright mind are not always enough. Most students are never taught how to study.

Student-athletes should pay attention to a few tips that will help them improve their study habits so that they can achieve more in less time.

The most important study habit is to set aside the time to do it and then do it! While poor study skills are widespread, more widespread is the tendency to procrastinate and try to recover by all-night cram sessions. The results are usually reflected in poor grades that could have easily been prevented through pacing. Students who get help early, meet the tutors, and get in touch with the academic support systems are positioned for success.

Likewise, students are wise to schedule classes favorably to coincide with the training schedule. If chemistry is a required course, but not a student's strong subject, the athlete should consider scheduling it during the off-season.

That said, assuming an athlete is setting aside time to study, what else can a student do to improve efficacy? Let's look briefly at each of the core skills of studying: reading, remembering, note-taking, and preparing for and taking exams.

Reading

Glancing over the words on a page is not enough. Active reading requires identifying the essentials of what is being said, and identifying what ideas and concepts are important, and then working to assimilate them. This means underlying key passages, making relevant notes in the margins of one's textbook, noting any overlap between the reading and the student's class notes, memorizing key definitions, and condensing important points into a few retainable notes.

Remembering

Numerous books are available on improving one's memory. But the basics still hold true. Students should:

- Tell themselves: "I need to remember this."

- Review the material several times.

- Use mnemonic (memory aids or techniques) devices where applicable.

- Review classes online using a podcast, if available.

In many cases, students have trouble retaining an idea because they don't actually understand it. This is why active reading and focused attention in class are crucial. Memorizing a baffling list of archaic terms and bizarre formulas is much more challenging than if the words and concepts are clearly understood.

Note-taking

Thankfully laptops have made it easier than ever to take good notes and organize them. The days of having to learn shorthand or take a magnifying glass to one's own scrawls are disappearing. Nevertheless, proper note-taking is still something of an art.

Students make two basic errors with notes: their notes are either too detailed or not detailed enough. If notes are not detailed enough, then the student will miss out on important ideas that will be necessary to review later. But if notes are too detailed, the student will have a hard time keeping up with the teacher and focusing on important ideas later on.

Notes should include:

- All definitions and key concepts.

- Any points the professor repeats.

- Any idea that was also covered in the reading.

- Any idea the professor says will be on the test.

Eventually, students will learn what works best for them, but a good rule of thumb is: When in doubt, don't leave it out.

Preparing for and taking exams

The primary issue here is to put to work all of one's reading, remembering, and note-taking. Prior to a test, students should review their reading, review their notes, and work to remember any items which they know or have reason to suspect will be on the test.

During the actual test, the key is to be well-rested, to read all the directions, and to work through the test at a regular pace, keeping track of how much time is permitted to finish it.

This of course is only a brief sketch to point students in the right direction. If a student has difficulty studying, many resources are available, including professional tutors, classmates, and books on the subject.

TRANSFERRING SCHOOLS

Deciding which college to attend is a difficult task, and often students discover that the decision they made during high school was not the best decision for them. In the rare case, a transfer might make sense. But transferring colleges is not a decision to make lightly. For starters, student-athletes' scholarships do not transfer with them. Moreover, depending on the relevant rules and regulations, students who transfer schools may be prevented from playing, at least temporarily. The first principle of transferring schools is: Students should not transfer unless they cannot meet their academic or athletic goals at the current school.

Let me say at the outset that this is a complex topic. Depending on which sport a child plays in which conference at which school, the rules and regulations that apply can be different. Any student who is considering transferring schools should contact a recruiter who can help guide the athlete through the process while avoiding the many landmines. For more information, visit www.athleteswanted.org.

Here are the most essential guidelines to keep in mind:

- The student-athlete should start by talking with the coach, athletic director, and counselor to discuss options and penalties of transferring.

- Consider both the educational and athletic qualities of the new school.

- The student must obtain written permission to contact the coach in another athletic department at a different school.

- The student-athlete will have to relinquish any current scholarships to transfer.

- Some conferences require a student-athlete who transfers to sit out for a year or more.

- For more help about transferring, visit www.athleteswanted.org.

KEY POINTS

__1.__ Once awarded a scholarship, a student-athlete must maintain the scholarship. Three criteria dictate whether the student-athlete will maintain the scholarship:

- Performing well for the team.
- Adhering to the NCAA or NAIA rules and regulations.
- Maintaining the required GPA.

__2.__ If athletes are unable to meet their academic or athletic goals, they might need to transfer schools. However, depending on the relevant rules and regulations, students who transfer may be prevented from playing immediately. And a student's scholarship does not transfer with the athlete.

__3.__ Because of the complications and risks of transferring, an athlete should meet with a recruiting specialist and visit www.athleteswanted.org before transferring.

THE *HOW TO* GUIDE
AFTER COLLEGE

THIS IS THE STORY OF the Eason brothers, Bo and Tony.

Bo and Tony attended Delta High School, population three hundred, in Walnut Grove, a rural farming community in northern California. The school's football team, which recruited all able-bodied males to fill its roster, shocked everyone by winning every game of the season. Four of its players were later drafted by the NFL. Four or five others, said Bo, were better than those recruited, but they did not know the rules of the game.

Bo and Tony didn't even receive recruitment letters from colleges. When their father took them to visit a coach at a state college, the coach laughed and pointed to the door.

"You're not big enough," he told the boys.

Tony attended junior college. After completing junior college, he was offered only one scholarship from the University of Illinois, where he became "Champaign Tony" Eason. You might have heard of "Champaign Tony" Eason. Tony would go on to play for the New England Patriots and New York Jets, and he was part of the famous 1983 NFL Draft that saw the likes of John Elway, Dan Marino, Jim Kelly, and Ken O'Brien.

Younger brother Bo was also not recruited out of high school. Instead, he was a walk-on at the University of California at Davis.

To be totally accurate, Bo was not technically a walk-on. He was a joke.

At 5'10" and weighing in at 150 pounds, Bo was turned away when he tried to attend the first day of practice as an uninvited walk-on.

"But I plan on being the best safety in the world within four years," Bo told the equipment manager, who had refused to allow Bo to suit up. Bo explained that when he was nine years old, he wrote a twenty-year plan that had two missions: 1) to be the best safety in the world by the time he graduated college; and 2) to be on a Super Bowl team.

The equipment manager laughed and gave Bo a practice uniform. The jersey was old—the design had since been replaced—and it did not match the rest of the team. His helmet was too big and bobbed up and down while practicing.

At the end of practice, the coach sent Bo home.

"You tried hard," said the coach, "but you aren't big enough to play for this team. Maybe you can come back when school starts and play in freshman practice."

With no dorm to sleep in, Bo slept in his truck that night. The next day, he went back to the equipment window.

"My parents think I'm part of the team," he told the equipment manager. "You have to give me a uniform."

For three weeks, the team let Bo practice with them. Bo would later learn that the head coach was watching from afar. Despite repeated requests from the team and assistant coaches to the contrary, the head coach wanted to keep Bo around.

"We need this kid," the coach told the rest of the team. "He shows up every day in 100-degree weather to play for a team telling him that he will never see the field. He is sleeping in his pickup truck and practicing as hard as he can."

"When you play that hard, someone will eventually take notice," said Bo.

When the time came for the first game, Bo convinced the team to allow him to suit up and stand on the sidelines. After all, his parents were coming to the game, and they thought he was on the team.

The UC Davis Aggies were squashing their competitors, so Bo decided to ask the team captain if he could run down during kickoff.

Remember that Bo was tiny—a joke who would never belong on the football field. So when the team captain granted his request, it was only because the captain thought it would be funny. The Aggies were so far ahead that Bo couldn't hurt their chances of winning.

In fact, Bo helped them. He was the first down the field, and the tackle he made was enough to earn a brand new varsity jersey and a spot on the team. Four years later, he would be one of the first two safeties to be drafted by the NFL. Mission one of Bo's two-part twenty-year plan was accomplished: He was indeed the best in the country.

And five years later, after playing for the Oilers, he was traded to San Francisco, who played in the Super Bowl that year.

It is an amazing story, one that Bo has turned into an off-Broadway play and will be adapting as a screenplay. He is also writing a second screenplay about Heisman Trophy winner John Cappelletti.

"Most people ask me how I make a living as a writer, performer, and speaker. I didn't have training. I don't have a background in the entertainment industry, but what I do know how to do is work," said Eason. "Even though everyone else is younger, smarter, and more talented than I am, I know I can outwork them. I know how to put in the miles. I know how to wake up at 5:00 a.m. so I can surpass the competition."

This is the DNA of the athlete. It will stay with the athlete forever. The athlete will always know what it tastes like to be a part of a winning team. The athlete will always know about discipline. The athlete will always know that the team that works the hardest will win.

Upon graduating, student-athletes might feel as though they have few marketable skills, but this couldn't be further from the truth. Student-athletes are experts in:

- Teamwork
- Time management
- Goal-setting

- Discipline

- Commitment

- Organization

- Communication

- Sportsmanship

- Conflict management

- Personal responsibility

- Leadership

- Hard work

And employers desperately want these students. When the National Collegiate Scouting Association conducted a survey of one hundred CEOs, they learned that 100 percent of these employers would be more likely to hire a student-athlete than a non-student-athlete if all other factors were equal. A whopping 60 percent would hire a student-athlete with a lower grade-point average before a non-student-athlete with an A average.

Remember that the goal of college athletics is to position the athlete for a successful life. Sports are a parable for life. They are not the goal, but a vehicle to reach the goal. By becoming a collegiate student-athlete, a student will be branded for life and can leverage these acquired skills for future opportunities. In fact, most companies do not care nearly as much what a student's major is; they want to know that the student-athlete is passionate about hard work and success. A major indicator of this is an athlete's dedication to achieving both academic and athletic success while graduating with a meaningful degree.

Student-athletes should leverage their relevant experience during job interviews and in their résumés and cover letters. The following pages provide examples of how students can highlight their background as athletes.

COACH'S TIP

Student-athletes should start to develop their own personal network for future opportunities by collecting business cards of successful alumni and influential people they meet during their college careers. You never know who might hold the key to a career or an opportunity of a lifetime. The student-athletes could keep these people informed on their achievements. Remember, it is not just who you know but, more importantly, who knows you.

October 27, 2008

Jane Smith
Sports Organization
231 Any Street
Chicago, IL 60622

Dear Ms. Smith:

Coach John Greer[1] suggested I contact you to apply for the position of account manager. As one of Coach Greer's former swimmers, I suspect you are well-aware of the time demands associated with being team captain of Northwestern University's women's swim team.[2] This position has developed my skills in time management, goal-setting, and leadership.

As well, I excelled in the classroom, earning a 3.4 grade-point average; as an athlete, winning the All-Big Ten honors for the 2006-2007 season; and as a manager, leading the *Zephyrus* advertising team to sell the most advertising space in the history of the student newspaper and earning the nomination for the Emerging Leaders program for Pi Beta Phi Fraternity for Women.

My enclosed résumé provides more details.

Sincerely,

Sharon Sembrook

---

1 Employers will always pay more attention to candidates who are referred by trusted sources. Student-athletes likely have large networks of coaches and fellow athletes who can introduce them to employers.
2 Student-athletes will have instant commonalities with other former athletes. They should leverage this shared history when applying for jobs.

SHARON SEMBROOK[3]
1415 N Dayton Street
Chicago, IL 60622
(888) 333-6848

Education:	Northwestern University: School of Communication, Evanston, IL Bachelor of Arts Degree, June 2007
Major:	Communication Studies
Specializations:	Relational Communication, Organizational Communication
GPA:	3.4
Relevant Courses:	Professional Linkage Program: *Sports Marketing in the 21ˢᵗ Century*; Professional Linkage Program: *Contemporary Issues in PR*; Special Topics: *Organizational Change & Problem Solving, Introduction to Macroeconomics, Introduction to Microeconomics, Marketing Management, Editing & Writing the News*
Accomplishments:	Business Institutions 394-0: Professional Linkage Program – *Sports Marketing in the 21ˢᵗ Century*

Final Project: Sponsorship

- Worked with four classmates to design mock sponsor-property negotiation

- Analyzed sponsor's (Gatorade) objectives and strategies to ensure fit with property (Michael Phelps)

---

3 Notice that the student-athlete's experience shows achievement both in and out of the classroom, along with evidence that the student-athlete is able to set goals, manage time, and work as a team member. Highlighting the blueprint of a collegiate student-athlete makes the résumé attractive to a potential employer.

- Produced sponsorship details, including entitlements, benefits and activation and leveraging plan

- Consummated imitation sponsorship agreement between sponsor and property

Work Experience: Northwestern University Athletic Media Services   04/05-04/07
Intern

- Assisted in day-to-day operation of office by researching records, writing weekly reports and editing images

- Updated and maintained portion of official website, NUsports.com

- Worked home spring sporting events, performing duties such as scoreboard operation and statistics compilation

Leadership Experience: Pi Beta Phi Fraternity for Women   01/03-Present
Vice President of Fraternity Development

- Nominated by chapter members to the Leadership Program due to interest in improving leadership within chapter

- Built unity between leadership and membership in chapter by resolving conflicts related to conduct, participation, poor scholarship and financial responsibility

- Provided on-going education activities to raise an awareness of and appreciation for the history and values of the chapter

- Restored admiration for chapter traditions to improve chapter loyalty and pride

Northwestern University Varsity Women's Swimming[4]   09/03-03/07
Recruitment Chair; Team Captain

---

4 Student-athletes should be sure to include their participation in collegiate sports on the résumé. This information can be included in one of a variety of sections, including experience, accomplishments, or leadership.

- Executed new team recruitment techniques to help increase team membership by 63 percent between 2004 and 2007

- Participated in workshops focused on: leadership, time-management, and organization

- Organized team activities and projects to promote team unity and sportsmanship

- Demonstrated time management, perseverance and passion by balancing various responsibilities and schedules

Zephyrus   09/02-06/04
Advertising Manager; Entertainment Page Editor

- Recruited, designed and maintained advertising department

- Composed and produced entertainment page layout

Personal:
- Earned Academic All-Big Ten honors for 2006-2007 swimming season

- Competitive swimmer for 14 years

- 2005 and 2006 NCAA Championship competitor

- 2004 and 2008 U.S. Olympic Trials qualifier in women's 100-meter butterfly

June 1, 2005

John Jones
Medical Organization
231 Any Street
Los Angeles, CA 90048

Dear Mr. Jones:

I am applying for the pharmaceutical sales position within your organization.[5] As the enclosed résumé will testify, competition runs through my genes. During my tenure as pitcher for the University of Wisconsin-Milwaukee's baseball team, I pushed myself to break records and earn the nomination of assistant team captain. In academics, I maintained a 3.7 grade-point average while devoting thirty hours each week to athletics.

As a pharmaceutical sales representative for your organization, I would apply my competitive nature to my career. As well, my team-building skills and experience with customer service would allow me to excel in meeting client needs and driving your organization to the top.

Enclosed, please find my résumé. I look forward to hearing from you.

Sincerely,

Shaun Gensler

---

5 A three-part formula can be applied when writing cover letters: First, athletes should state the position for which they are applying, followed by a synopsis of why the student-athletes are qualified. If possible, student-athletes should use the same language as the want ad. For instance, if the want ad requests candidates who are competitive, students should be sure to highlight evidence of competitiveness. Finally, mention that the résumé is enclosed.

SHAUN GENSLER
1415 N Dayton Street
Chicago, IL 60622
(888) 333-6848

Summary of Qualifications: As a student-athlete who excelled at Division I athletics. I will apply the same degree of diligence and dedication to my career that allowed me to maintain a 3.7 grade-point average while devoting an average of thirty hours per week to baseball.

Education: Bachelor's Degree in Physical Therapy   May 2007
University of Wisconsin-Milwaukee

Lawrence University   2003-2005

GPA: 3.7/4.0

Experience: Events Inc.   Chicago, Illinois
Team Member   June 2007-Present

- Work collectively to assemble large festival tents

- Consult with customers to establish their expectations

- Position tents to leverage best opportunities

University of Wisconsin-Milwaukee Panthers
Baseball Pitcher   2005-2007

- Maintained the team's best earned run average (2004 and 2005)

- Earned a spot in the University of Wisconsin-Milwaukee record-book for pitching strikeouts (2005)

- Nominated to assistant team captain (2005)

Logan Community Fitness Center   Chicago, Illinois
Customer Service   January 2005- July 2007

- Answered questions about exercise machines and helped members complete workouts successfully

- Encouraged and persuaded potential candidates to open memberships by explaining options offered

- Assisted each member personally and enthusiastically during his or her time at the fitness center

Lawrence University Sports
Information Department   Milwaukee, Wisconsin
Sports Information Assistant   October 2003-2005

- Tracked game statistics and engaged in research for Lawrence University media guides

- Organized post-game press conferences and supplied statistics to the media

- Utilized telecommunications to relay statistics to the media

- Logan Yacht Club Milwaukee, Wisconsin

- Dock Attendant May 2003-Summer

- Issued dock permits to guests

- Interacted, greeted, and helped the members with their yachts

- Available and alert at all times to assist the members when docking

Athletic Achievments:[6]   All-Conference Selection

- Newcomer of the Year by the Horizon League in 2002

- Four-time Player of Week in the Horizon League

- Featured Article in Inside Illinois Sports magazine June 2005

---

6 An attractive résumé highlights awards and achievements that show the student-athlete stands above the rest of the crowd. If student-athletes are involved in internships, have won awards, or have volunteered their time, they should include this information on the résumé.

December 12, 2007

Amanda Rufus
School Organization
231 Any Street
Boulder, CO 80304

Dear Ms. Rufus:

I am writing in response to your newspaper ad for an athletic department office assistant manager. My professional, athletic, and academic experiences qualify me to juggle administrative responsibilities while responding to student-athletes' needs. As the enclosed résumé shows, I have an ongoing commitment to volunteering for educational outreach programs. As well, I graduated with honors while serving as a member of the varsity basketball team, an extracurricular activity that added thirty hours to my schedule.[7]

I look forward to hearing from you.

Sincerely,

Kerry Simpson

---

7 A cover letter should be short and sweet, directing the recipient to review the résumé for more information.

KERRY SIMPSON
1415 N Dayton Street
Chicago, IL 60622
(888) 333-6848

Education:	The University of Chicago, Chicago IL
	Bachelor of Arts, June 2008
Major:	Human Development
GPA:	3.14/4.0
MGPA:	3.4/4.0

Experience: National Collegiate Scouting Association   Chicago, Illinois
                Intern   3/31/08 – Present

- Aids in helping high school athletes with the recruitment process.

- Responsible for sending out mailings to new clients.

- Performs data entry for new coach requests to be put on the website.

Peck Elementary School,
Gear Up Program, Depaul   Chicago, Illinois
Tutor/Teaching Assistant   Summer 2007

- Successfully tutored eighth-grade summer school students.

- Assisted students with problems in math and reading.

- Helped prepare students with the skills to pass the ISAT test.

Ratner Athletic Center,
University of Chicago   Chicago, Illinois
Office Assistant   Summer of 2005 and 2006 and 2007

- Performed data entry accurately entering information into the database.

- Responsible for initial written correspondence to new recruits.

Activities: Member, Varsity Basketball Team,
University of Chicago,   2004-Present

- Manage time required for 30-hours/week of basketball and rigorous academic coursework.

Volunteer, Athletes Against Drugs Golf Outing, AAD,   2007[8]

- Assisted with set up for the banquet and managed the silent auction.

- Helped set up for the golf outing and worked registration.

Volunteer, Blue Gargoyle Tutoring, University of Chicago,   2007

- Tutored elementary and high school students.

Volunteer, Special Olympics, University of Chicago,   2006

- Helped set up for the sporting events.

- Efficiently kept score for the soccer games.

Volunteer, Tutoring Program, University of Chicago,   2005

- Tutored children of various ages from elementary school to high school.

Volunteer, Community Program,
University of Chicago,   2005- Present

- Coach the game of basketball to children of various ages from elementary school to high school.

---

8   A student-athlete who juggles academic and athletic requirements with other extracurricular and volunteer activities will appeal to prospective employers.

Honors and Awards:	• University of Chicago Dean's List	2006-2007
	• National Honor Society Member	2002-2004
	• 2003 Athletes Against Drugs Student Honoree	
	• Graduated within the top 8% of Lane Technical High School's class of 2004	
Skills:	• Proficient in Microsoft Word, Excel, Power Point, Works, Microsoft Internet Explorer and Netscape Navigator	

NCAA RULES AND REQUIREMENTS

GENERAL INFORMATION

This information is summarized from the *NCAA Guide to the College-Bound Student-Athlete*. Visit www.ncaa.org for complete and up-to-date information as the rules and regulations change regularly.

Division I Academic Eligibility Requirements

Students who enroll in a Division I college who want to participate in athletics or receive an athletic scholarship during their freshman year must:

1. Graduate from high school on schedule (in eight semesters) with the student's incoming ninth-grade class, though the student-athlete can complete one—and only one—core course in the summer or academic year following graduation.

2. Complete sixteen core courses, including: four years of English; three years of math (algebra or higher); two years of natural or physical science (including one year of lab science

if offered by the high school); one extra year of English, math, or natural or physical science; two years of social science; and four years of extra core courses from any of the aforementioned categories, a foreign language, nondoctrinal religion, or philosophy.

3. Earn a minimum-required GPA in the core courses.

4. Earn a combined SAT or ACT sum score that matches the core-course grade-point average on the NCAA's test-score sliding scale. The higher the grade-point average, the lower the SAT or ACT score necessary for eligibility. For instance, a 3.55 GPA requires a 400 SAT or 37 ACT score, whereas a 2.00 GPA requires a 1010 SAT or 86 ACT.

If the student does not meet these requirements, he:

• Cannot practice or compete for his college or university during his first year of college.

• Cannot receive an athletic scholarship during his first year of college, though he can receive need-based financial aid.

• Can play only three seasons if he maintains his eligibility from year to year. To earn a fourth season, he must complete at least 80 percent of his degree requirements before beginning his fifth year of college.

If the student does meet these requirements, he:

• Is eligible to practice or compete for his college or university during his first year of college, if an offer is extended.

• Can receive an athletics scholarship during his first year of college, if an offer is so extended.

- Can play four seasons if he maintains his eligibility form year to year, if an offer is extended.

Division II Academic Eligibility Requirements

Students who enroll in a Division II college who want to participate in athletics or receive an athletic scholarship during their freshman year must:

1. Graduate from high school

2. Complete fourteen core courses, including: three years of English, two years of math (algebra or higher); two years of natural or physical science, including one year of lab science if offered by the student's high school; two extra years of English, math, or natural or physical science; two years of social science; three years of extra core courses from any of the aforementioned categories or foreign language, nondoctrinal religion, or philosophy.

    Students who enroll in college on or after the year 2013 will need sixteen core courses.

3. Earn a 2.00 grade-point average or better in core courses.

4. Earn a combined SAT score of 820 or an ACT sum score of 68.

If the student does not meet any of these requirements, he:

- Cannot practice or compete for his college or university during his first year of college.

- Cannot receive an athletic scholarship during his first year of college, though he can receive need-based financial aid.

- Can play four seasons if he maintains his eligibility from year to year.

If the student graduates from high school and either meets either the SAT/ACT minimum or completes fourteen core courses with a 2.00 grade-point-average, but not both, the student:

- Can practice with his team at its home facility during his first year of college.

- Can receive an athletics scholarship during his first year of college.

- Cannot compete during his first year of college.

- Can play four seasons in his sport if he maintains his eligibility from year to year.

If the student does meet these requirements, he:

- Is eligible to practice or compete for his college or university during his first year of college, if an offer is extended.

- Can receive an athletics scholarship during his first year of college, if an offer is so extended.

- Can play four seasons if he maintains his eligibility form year to year, if an offer is extended.

Division III Academic Eligibility Requirements

Division III schools have opted against being regulated by the NCAA Eligibility Center. For information about policies on admissions, financial aid, practice, and competition, contact the specific Division III college.

FRESHMAN AND SOPHOMORE RECRUITING RULES

FRESHMAN AND SOPHOMORE RECRUITING RULES[1]			
Recruiting Method	Division I	Division II	Division III
Recruiting materials	Student can receive questionnaires, general college admissions information, and brochures for camps.	None allowed.	Students can receive printed material at any time.
	Men's basketball coaches can begin sending recruiting materials June 15 the sophomore year.		
Telephone calls	College coaches cannot call a high school freshman or sophomore, nor can they return phone calls. However, a student-athlete can call a coach at his or her expense as often as he or she wants.	College coaches cannot call a high school freshman or sophomore, nor can they return phone calls. However, a student-athlete can call a coach at his or her expense as often as he or she wants.	No limit on the number of calls or when the college coach can initiate them.
	At the end of a male basketball player's sophomore year, a basketball coach can accept a collect call from a student-athlete.		
	If a student is an international prospect for women's ice hockey, a college coach can call her once in July after her sophomore year.		
Off-campus contact	None allowed.	None allowed.	None allowed.
Official visits	None allowed.	None allowed.	None allowed.
Unofficial visits	Allowed without restrictions.	Allowed without restrictions.	Allowed without restrictions.
Instant and Text Messages	Forbidden.	Forbidden.	Forbidden.

1 Remember that the rules change annually. Visit www.ncaa.org for an updated list of NCAA rules and regulations.

JUNIOR RECRUITING RULES

JUNIOR RECRUITING RULES			
Recruiting Method	Division I	Division II	Division III
Recruiting materials	Beginning September 1 of junior year, a student-athlete can receive recruiting material from coaches.	A coach can begin sending printed recruiting materials September 1 of the junior year.	The student-athlete can receive printed material at any time.
	Men's basketball and ice hockey coaches can start sending recruiting materials June 15 of the summer before junior year.		
Telephone calls	A student-athlete can make unlimited calls to the coach at his or her expense. Starting July 1 after the athlete's junior year, coaches (exceptions noted below) can call once per week.	A college coach can call a student-athlete once per week beginning June 15 of junior year. An athlete can make unlimited calls to the coach at his or her expense at any time.	No limit on the number of calls or when the college coach can initiate them.
	A men's basketball coach can call once per month beginning June 15 before junior year through July 31 after the junior year.		
	A women's basketball coach can call once per month in April, May, and June 1-June 20; once between June 21 and June 30; and three times in July after the junior year with a maximum of one call per week.		
	A football coach can call once from April 15 to May 31 of junior year.		
	A men's ice hockey coach can call once per month beginning June 15 before junior year and through July 31 after junior year.		

JUNIOR RECRUITING RULES (CONT.)			
Recruiting Method	Division I	Division II	Division III
Off-campus contact	None allowed until July 1 after the junior year. For gymnastics, none are allowed until July 15 after the junior year.	A college coach can have contact beginning June 15 after junior year. A coach is limited to three in-person contacts off campus.	A college coach can begin to have contact with a student off campus beginning the summer after the junior year.
Official visits	None allowed.	None allowed.	None allowed.
Unofficial visits	Allowed without restrictions.	Allowed without restrictions.	Allowed without restrictions.
Instant and Text Messages	Forbidden.	Forbidden.	Forbidden.

SENIOR RECRUITING RULES

SENIOR RECRUITING RULES			
Recruiting Method	Division I	Division II	Division III
Recruiting materials	Allowed without restrictions.	Allowed without restrictions.	Allowed without restrictions.
Telephone calls	A student-athlete can make unlimited calls to the coach at his or her expense. Starting July 1 after your child's junior year, some coaches can call once per week. (See exceptions.)	A college coach can call a student-athlete once per week beginning June 15 of junior year. An athlete can make unlimited calls to the coach at his or her expense at any time.	No limit on the number of calls or when the college coach can initiate them.
	A men's basketball coach can call twice per week beginning August 1 before the senior year.		
	A women's basketball coach can call once per week beginning August 1.		
	A men's ice hockey coach can call once per week beginning August 1.		
	A football coach can call once per week beginning September 1.		
Off-campus contact	Allowed. A college coach can contact an athlete or parents off campus not more than three times during the senior year.	A college coach can have contact beginning June 15 after junior year. A coach is limited to three in-person contacts off campus.	A college coach can begin to have contact with a student off campus beginning the summer after the junior year.
	Men's basketball coaches can meet with the athlete beginning September 9.		
	Women's basketball coaches can meet with the athlete beginning September 16.		

SENIOR RECRUITING RULES (CONT.)			
Recruiting Method	Division I	Division II	Division III
Off-campus contact (cont.)	Football coaches can meet beginning November 30. A football coach can contact the athlete or parent not more than six times, including one evaluation during September, October, and November.		
Official visits	Allowed beginning opening day of classes senior year. A student is limited to one official visit per college up to a maximum of five official visits.	Allowed beginning opening day of classes senior year. A student is limited to one official visit per college up to a maximum of five official visits.	Allowed beginning opening day of classes senior year. A student is limited to one official visit per college.
Unofficial visits	Allowed without restrictions.	Allowed without restrictions.	Allowed without restrictions.
Instant and Text Messages	Forbidden.	Forbidden.	Forbidden.

NUMBERS BY SPORT

SPORTS PER DIVISION

Listed on the following page is the number of colleges and universities that offer a particular sport, separated by division.

SPORTS PER DIVISION

SPORT	Division I	Division IAA	Division II	Division III	NAIA	Junior College	TOTAL
Baseball Programs	291	N/A	242	373	213	394	1,512
Women's Basketball Programs	331	N/A	289	436	263	390	1,709
Men's Basketball Programs	333	N/A	288	412	265	435	1,733
Women's Cross Country Programs	327	N/A	270	393	211	122	1,323
Men's Cross Country Programs	301	N/A	241	372	204	113	1,261
Field Hockey Programs	77	N/A	26	158	0	0	261
Football Programs	120	119	154	239	92	71	795
Women's Golf Programs	243	N/A	134	164	139	88	768
Men's Golf Programs	291	N/A	210	284	181	215	1,181
Women's Ice Hockey Programs	35	N/A	2	46	0	0	83
Men's Ice Hockey Programs	58	N/A	7	73	0	11	149
Women's Lacrosse Programs	85	N/A	48	180	0	18	331
Men's Lacrosse Programs	57	N/A	35	151	0	27	270
Women's Soccer Programs	310	N/A	225	424	222	180	1,361
Men's Soccer Programs	198	N/A	179	401	218	216	1,212
Softball Programs	276	N/A	268	408	210	358	1,520
Women's Swimming Programs	139	N/A	72	242	28	18	499
Men's Swimming Programs	193	N/A	56	197	21	17	484
Women's Tennis Programs	311	N/A	220	371	123	92	1,117
Men's Tennis Programs	258	N/A	168	325	107	80	938
Women's Track & Field Programs	307	N/A	174	274	135	82	972
Men's Track & Field Programs	269	N/A	162	267	133	78	909
Women's Volleyball Programs	317	N/A	276	423	251	297	1,564
Men's Volleyball Programs	22	N/A	13	47	17	0	99
Wrestling Programs	86	N/A	45	92	35	44	302
TOTAL	5,354		3,804	6,752	3,068	3,346	22,324

OPPORTUNITIES PER DIVISION

OPPORTUNITIES PER DIVISION	
Division IA Schools with Athletic Programs	333
Division IAA Schools with Athletic Programs	120
Division II Schools with Athletic Programs	291
Division III Schools with Athletic Programs	445
NAIA Schools with Athletic Programs	284
NCJAA Schools with Athletic Programs	516
TOTAL	1,877

MYTH: NCAA Division IA is the only option for collegiate athletic opportunities.

REALITY: Over eighteen hundred U.S. colleges and universities sponsor collegiate athletics and are able to offer financial packages. Most of these opportunities fall outside Division IA schools.

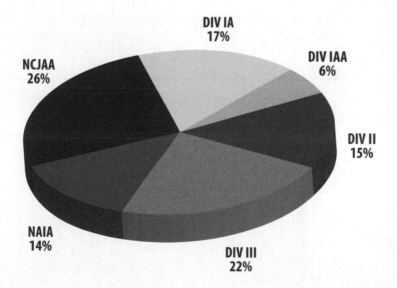

ATHLETES PER SPORT

ATHLETES PER SPORT									
	High School Athletes	Division I	Division IAA	Division II	Division III	NAIA	NJCAA	Total College Athletes
Baseball Players	478,029	10,195		8,603	11,588	6,390	11,820	48,596
Women's Basketball Players	449,540	4,765		4,291	6,251	3,945	5,850	25,102
Men's Basketball Players	552,935	5,119		4,768	7,194	3,975	6,525	27,581
Women's Cross Country Runners	190,349	5,311		3,054	5,126	2,532	1,464	17,487
Men's Cross Country Runners	221,109	4,453		2,901	5,124	2,448	1,356	16,282
Field Hockey Players	62,557	1,791		564	3,278	0	0	5,633
Football Players	1,108,286	13,758	11,900	15,764	22,813	9,200	7,100	80,535
Women's Golfers	69,243	2,047		973	1,076	973	616	5,685
Men's Golfers	159,958	2,960		2,280	1,267	1,482	1,505	9,494
Women's Ice Hockey Players	8,621	837		52	1,007	0	0	1,896
Men's Ice Hockey Players	36,667	1,632		218	2,156	0	250	4,256
Women's Lacrosse Players	61,086	2,317		919	3,594	0	360	7,190
Men's Lacrosse Players	82,860	2,507		1,258	5,135	0	540	9,440
Women's Soccer Players	346,545	7,955		5,344	9,383	5,106	4,140	31,928
Men's Soccer Players	383,561	5,556		4,801	10,674	5,104	4,968	31,103
Softball Players	371,293	5,285		4,905	6,964	4,200	7,160	28,514
Female Swimmers	147,197	5,155		1,392	4,691	560	360	12,158
Male Swimmers	111,896	3,670		1,080	3,632	420	340	9,142

ATHLETES PER SPORT (CONT.)

	High School Athletes	Division I	Division IAA	Division II	Division III	NAIA	NJCAA	Total College Athletes
Women's Tennis Players	172,455	2,891		2,004	3,826	1,230	920	10,871
Men's Tennis Players	156,285	2,680		1,619	3,551	1,070	820	9,740
Women's Track & Field Participants	447,520	11,230		4,451	6,682	4,050	2,460	28,873
Men's Track & Field Participants	548,821	10,266		5,052	8,161	3,990	2,340	29,809
Women's Volleyball Participants	397,968	4,650		4,020	6,045	3,312	297	18,324
Men's Volleyball Participants	46,780	456		238	604	255	0	1,553
Wrestlers	259,688	2,648		1,318	2,344	910	1,144	8,364
TOTAL	6,871,249	132,034	11,900	81,869	142,166	61,152	62,335	479,556

NCAA, NAIA, AND NJCAA SCHOLARSHIP LIMITS

SCHOLARSHIP OPPORTUNITIES

Listed on the following page is the number of athletic scholarships any one NCAA, NAIA, or NJCAA university can award in a given year. Remember that an athlete who receives a scholarship to play a head count sport (basketball, football, women's gymnastics, women's tennis, or women's volleyball) will always be given a full-ride scholarship, whereas an athlete who receives a scholarship to play an equivalency sport might receive only a partial scholarship. Therefore, the 4.5 scholarships offered by a Division I men's golf program might go to five students (four full scholarships and one partial scholarship), nine students (nine partial scholarships), or any other variation that amounts to 4.5 full scholarships.

ATHLETIC SCHOLARSHIP OPPORTUNITIES

Maximum Number of Scholarships Offered By Any One:	Division IA	Division IAA	Division II	NAIA	NJCAA	Total
Baseball Program	11.7	N/A	9	12	24	56.7
Women's Basketball Program	13	N/A	10	18	15	56
Men's Basketball Program	13	N/A	10	18	15	56
Women's Cross Country Program	18	N/A	12.6	12	30	72.6
Men's Cross Country Program	12.6	N/A	12.6	12	30	67.2
Field Hockey Program	12	N/A	6.3	0	0	18.3
Football Program	85	63	36	24	85	293
Women's Golf Program	6	N/A	5.4	5	8	24.4
Men's Golf Program	4.5	N/A	3.6	5	8	21.1
Women's Ice Hockey Program	18	N/A	18	0	0	36
Men's Ice Hockey Program	18	N/A	18	0	0	36
Women's Lacrosse Program	12	N/A	9.9	0	20	41.9
Men's Lacrosse Program	12.6	N/A	10.8	0	20	43.4
Women's Soccer Program	14	N/A	3.9	12	18	47.9
Men's Soccer Program	9.9	N/A	9	12	18	48.9
Softball Program	12	N/A	7.2	10	24	53.2
Women's Swimming Program	14	N/A	8.1	8	15	45.1
Men's Swimming Program	9.9	N/A	8.1	8	15	41
Women's Tennis Program	8	N/A	6	5	9	28
Men's Tennis Program	4.5	N/A	4.5	5	9	23
Women's Track & Field Program	18	N/A	12.6	12	20	62.6
Men's Track & Field Program	12.6	N/A	12.6	12	20	57.2
Women's Volleyball Program	12	N/A	8	12	14	46
Men's Volleyball Program	4.5	N/A	4.5	4	0	13
Women's Volleyball Program	9.9	N/A	9	12	16	46.9
TOTAL	429	N/A	256	218	433	1,335

GLOSSARY

ACT/SAT: Standardized tests used by colleges for admissions purposes. Students must meet minimum requirements of these tests for the NCAA Eligibility Center and to meet individual college requirements.

Admissions Contact: Postcard, letter, email, package, and/or phone call directly from a college admissions department.

AP: Advanced placement classes offered by a high school. College-level classes. Placement of a college freshman in an advanced class based on work completed in high school. Most often colleges and universities use the College Board's Advanced Placement Tests for advanced placement. Advanced placement may be given with or without credit hours.

Application Waiver: A coach's waiver of the fee for applying to an institution.

COA: See "Cost of Attendance."

Club Teams: Select teams of advanced high school, middle school, or elementary school players. Club teams are by invitation only and represent the top swimmers, volleyball, soccer, and softball players.

Coach Contact: Questionnaire, camp brochure, letter, email, phone coil, or text message directly from a member of the coaching staff.

Combine: High-intensity showcases where student-athletes perform a series of grueling tests before coaches, recruiters, and scouts. Combines provide a venue for student-athletes to be evaluated individually and in great detail. Attendance is by invitation only, and combines generally consist only of the nation's top players.

Contact: An exchange of information between a coaching staff or admissions department and a prospective student-athlete. Contacts include camp brochures, letters, questionnaires, emails, phone calls, and tape requests.

Contact Period: The period when a coach may have in person contact with a student or his/her parents on or off college campus. The coach may watch the student compete or visit the high school.

Core Courses: High school classes required by the NCAA Initial Eligibility Clearinghouse. These include English, Math, Natural/Physical Science, Social Science, Foreign Language, Religion or Philosophy. Refer to the NCAA Eligibility Center regulations.

Cost of Attendance: The total cost of attending a school, the Cost of Attendance (COA) is an important factor in determining a student's financial aid needs.

Dead Period: Periods of time during which it is not permissible for a coach to make in-person recruiting contacts or evaluating on-or off-campus or permit official or unofficial visits.

EFC: See "Expected Family Contribution."

Early Action: Nonbinding plan that requires an athlete to submit his or her application in early fall (usually by November 1 or 15). The college lets the student know whether he or she is accepted by early January, but the student has the right to wait until May 1 before responding. This gives a student-athlete time to compare colleges, including financial aid offers, before making a decision.

Early Decision: A binding agreement whereby a student-athlete accepts an offer prior to National Letter of Intent Day. A student can apply Early Decision to only one college.

Equivalency Sports: Programs that fall into this category—all sports other than men's basketball, women's basketball, football, women's gymnastics, women's tennis, and women's volleyball—can offer full or partial scholarships.

Expected Family Contribution: The Expected Family Contribution (EFC) is the amount a family can be expected to contribute toward a student's college costs. Financial aid administrators determine need for federal student aid by subtracting the EPC from the student's cost of attendance (COA). The EFC formula is used to determine the EFC and ultimately determine the need for aid from the following types of federal student financial assistance: Federal Pell Grants, subsidized Stafford Loans and assistance from the "campus-based" programs-Federal Supplemental Educational Opportunity Grants (FSEOG), Federal Perkins Loans, and Federal Work-Study (FWS).

Evaluation: A coach's review of a student's athletic or academic ability. A coach typically evaluates a student either at his or her high school or during a showcase, practice, competition, club practice, or camp.

Evaluation Period: The period of time during which a college coach may watch students compete or visit the high school. There is no in-person contact away from the college campus allowed during this time. The coach may call and write during this time.

FAFSA: See "Free Application for Financial Student Aid."

Free Application for Financial Student Aid: The Free Application for Financial Student Aid (FAFSA) is a form required by the government for application to any federal education aid program. The FAFSA is used to determine the expected family contribution (EFC) based on family financial information. A FAFSA is used to determine the specific Federal Student Aid programs that can contribute to a student's total financial aid package and in what proportions. The Web site is www.fafsa.org.

Federal Perkins Loan Program: Low-interest (5 percent) loans that must be repaid. The maximum annual loan amount is $4,000 for undergraduate students and $6,000 for graduate students.

Federal PLUS Loans: Unsubsidized loans made to parents. If you are independent or your parents cannot get a PLUS loan, you are eligible to borrow additional Stafford Loan funds. The interest rate is variable, but never exceeds 9 percent.

Federal Stafford Loans: Student loans that must be repaid and are available to both undergraduate and graduate students.

Federal Supplemental Educational Opportunity Grants: Grants available for undergraduates only and awards range from $100-$4,000.

Fee Waiver Request Form/Financial Hardship Waiver: Used to request a waiver for the NCAA Eligibility Center fee. Visit www.nacoc.com/feewaiver.html.

Financial Aid/Scholarship: Money received from a college or another source, such as outside loans or grants. This may be athletic, academic, merit or need-based aid.

FWS/Work Study: Provides jobs to undergraduate and graduate students, allowing them to earn money to pay education expenses.

Game Day Visit: An opportunity for a student to visit a campus to watch a college team play a game.

Game Tape: Footage of actual competition, usually unedited.

GATE: Guaranteed Access to Education (GATE) is a nonprofit private loan program offered through participating institutions in conjunction with Bank of America, Bank of Boston and the National Collegiate Trust (NCT). There is a minimal credit check and colleges can recommend whatever loan amount they'd like the student to receive. The interest rate is also rather low. Students and parents should call 1-617-639-2000 for more information about the program (in New York, 1-212-551-3650). See also their entry in the lenders area of the Financial Aid Information Page.

GPA: Grade-point average. The NCAA Eligibility Center only uses core courses to calculate this number. This should be cumulative over the entire high school academic career.

Gray Shirt: Student is recruited out of high school but delays full-time enrollment.

Head Count Sports: Programs that fall into this category—men's basketball, women's basketball, football, women's gymnastics, women's tennis, and women's volleyball—offer full scholarships only.

Highlight Video: Three to five minutes of footage taken from game tape or skills tape.

Name Game: Term used to describe a student-athlete or his/her family choosing colleges based on the name rather than actual facts.

National Association of Intercollegiate Athletics: The National Association of Intercollegiate Athletics (NAIA) is a separate association of colleges who compete in intercollegiate athletics. The NAIA launched the Champions of Character program in 2000 which is an educational outreach initiative which emphasizes the tenets of character and integrity, not only for NAIA college students, but for younger students, coaches and parents in our communities.

National Collegiate Athletic Association: National Collegiate Athletic Association is the athletics governing body for more than 1,280 colleges, universities, conferences and organizations. Their goal is to govern competition in a fair, safe, inclusive and sportsmanlike manner. The official Web site is www.ncaa.org.

NCAA Eligibility Center: The organization responsible for certifying the academic eligibility for practice, competition, and financial aid of all prospective student-athletes for Division I and Division II.

NCAA Guide for the College-Bound Student-Athlete: An important reference book created by the NCAA for student-athletes interested in competing on college sports. This guide leads the student-athlete through eligibility, amateurism, registration with the NCAA Eligibility Center, financial aid, and recruiting rules. It is available at the NCAA Web site www.ncaa.org.

NCSA Collegiate Power Rankings: NCSA's Collegiate Power Rankings are calculated for each college at the NCAA Division I, II, and III levels by averaging the *U.S. News & World Report* ranking, the U.S. Sports Academy Directors' Cup ranking and the NCAA student-athlete graduation rate of each institution. The NCSA Collegiate Power Rankings provide data that allows prospective student-athletes and parents to evaluate the particular strengths of universities based on academic and athletic factors, as well as student-athlete graduation rates.

National Letter of Intent (NLI): A legal, binding contract in which a student agrees to attend a college for one academic year. In return, a college agrees to provide the student with athletics related financial aid for one year.

Non-Revenue Sports: College sports that do not bring revenue to the school. These sports are often funded, at least in part, by revenue sports such as football or basketball.

Official Visit: Visit to a college campus by a student and/or parents paid for by the college.

Quiet Period: A period of time during which a coach cannot have in-person contact with a student or his/her parents off of the college campus. The coach may cannot evaluate a student during this time, but can write or telephone during quiet periods.

Recruit Match: Collegiate coach database that matches qualified student-athletes with college athletic programs. The Recruit Match system houses more than 35,000 registered head coaches, assistant coaches and college administrative at more than 1,700 colleges, Recruit Match delivers student-athlete data through permission-based email. Profiles or student-athletes are distributed based on coaches wants and needs discovered through phone conversations, surveys and emails with college coaches at every level.

Recruiting Contact: Face to face interaction between a coach and a student-athlete or his/her parents away from the college campus, including high school competitions.

Recruiting Guidelines: Restrictions set by the NCAA and NAIA about when and how a college coach can communicate with a student-athlete.

Recruiting List: Athletes the coaches at an institution are actively recruiting. Typically, a student-athlete is not added to this list until the athlete has been evaluated.

Recruiting Materials: Information sent by a member of a coaching staff to a student-athlete. These include camp brochures, questionnaires and letters.

Red Shirt: A student who does not compete in any competition during a full academic year.

Regular Admissions: The process in which a student applies to a college by a midwinter deadline, receives word from the college in early April, and makes a decision and notifies colleges by May 1.

Revenue Sports: College sports that bring revenue to the school. These most often include men's football and basketball, and women's basketball, tennis, gymnastics, and volleyball.

Rolling Admissions: The process in which a student applies and receives an admission decision within two to six weeks. Applications are accepted until the incoming freshman class is filled. Most public universities and many private colleges use this timeline.

SAR: See "Student Aid Report."

SAT II: Standardized subject test required by some of the most selective colleges.

Scout: An individual who is certified to evaluate, educate and empower student-athletes on the collegiate recruiting process.

Skills Tape: A fifteen to twenty minute tape of staged footage.

Student Aid Report (SAR): The document received after the FAFSA is processed listing all of the answers to the FAFSA. A parent should review these answers carefully to make sure they are correct.

Student-athlete: A high school student who is recruited to attend a particular college to play on one of its athletic teams or a student who reports for practice at a college. Your child becomes a college bound student-athlete the day he or she enters high school, if not sooner. Men's basketball recruiting begins a student's seventh-grade year.

Title IX: Title IX of the Education Amendments of 1972 specifying that, "No person in the United States shall, on the basis of sex, be excluded from participation in, be denied the benefits of, or be subjected to discrimination under any education program or activity receiving Federal financial assistance."

Unofficial Visit: Any visit to a college campus paid for by a student and/or parents. The only expense a student may receive is three complimentary admissions to a home contest.

Verbal Commitment: A student verbally indicating that he/she plans to attend a college or university and play college sports. A verbal commitment is not binding, although it is a generally accepted form of commitment.

Video Guidelines: Specific outlines for video footage to each sport.

Walk-on: A student who does not receive on athletic scholarship, but who is a member of the team.